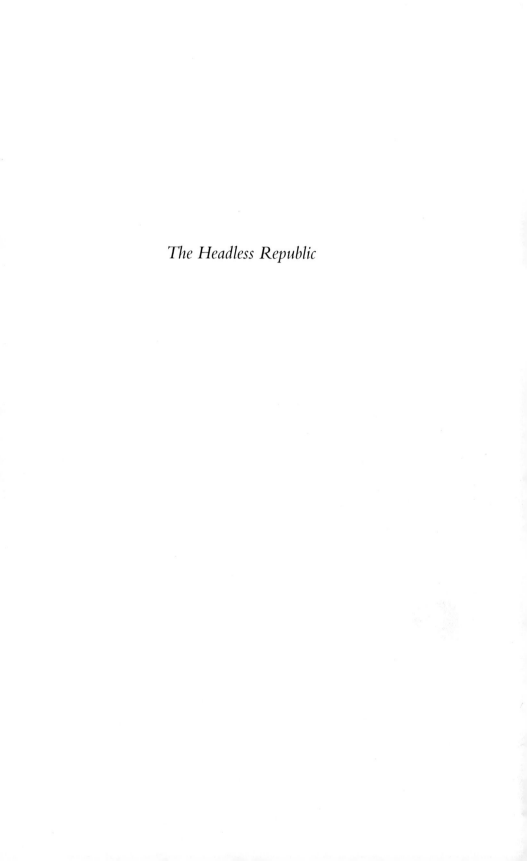

The Headless Republic

THE HEADLESS REPUBLIC

Sacrificial Violence in Modern French Thought

JESSE GOLDHAMMER

CORNELL UNIVERSITY PRESS

ITHACA AND LONDON

First published 2005 by Cornell University Press

Printed in the United States of America

Library of Congress Cataloging-in-Publication Data

Goldhammer, Jesse, 1967–
    The headless republic : sacrificial violence in modern French thought / Jesse Goldhammer.
        p. cm.
    Includes bibliographical references and index.
    ISBN 0-8014-4150-1 (cloth : alk. paper)
    1. Revolutions—Philosophy.   2. Political violence.   3. Legitimacy of governments.   4. Sacrifice—Political aspects.   5. France—History—Revolution, 1789–1799—Influence.   6. Maistre, Joseph Marie, comte de, 1753–1821.   7. Bataille, Georges, 1897–1962.   8. Sorel, Georges, 1847–1922.   I. Title.
    JC491.G57 2005
    321.09′4—dc22

                                                                                    2004023504

Cornell University Press strives to use environmentally responsible suppliers and materials to the fullest extent possible in the publishing of its books. Such materials include vegetable-based, low-VOC inks and acid-free papers that are recycled, totally chlorine-free, or partly composed of nonwood fibers. For further information, visit our website at www.cornellpress.cornell.edu.

Cloth printing   10 9 8 7 6 5 4 3 2 1

For Ariel

Le sacrifice n'est autre, au sense étymologique du mot,
que la production de choses *sacrées.*

—Georges Bataille, *La Notion de dépense*

Contents

Acknowledgments

I wrote this book to elucidate the modern French tradition of thought concerned with sacrificial violence. My interest in this project originated with a desire to understand why violence so often accompanies the task of political foundation. Niccolò Machiavelli guided me to this topic with his reflections on this classic political problem: How do political founders get people to obey the new laws of a new regime? Reading Georges Bataille introduced me to the French discourse on sacrifice that responds directly to Machiavelli's treatment of the problem. Bataille's comprehensive, fascinating discourse presents a novel evaluation of the risks and rewards of using sacrificial violence for political creation. Many scholars dismiss the intellectuals engaged in this discourse because they embrace nasty politics, advocate ritual violence, and condemn the modern world. Yet, after a decade of studying the French discourse on sacrifice, I have found them to offer more enlightenment on political violence than most contemporary scholarship. As is so often the case, sometimes the greatest achievements are entangled with the vilest.

I might never have completed this project were it not for the intellectual and emotional support of several remarkable individuals at the University of California at Berkeley. Foremost among them is Michael Rogin, who untimely passed away in 2001. Mike was an extraordinary intellectual and mentor. I am grateful to him for being so generous with his time as well as for his insights and theoretical counsel, which are in evidence throughout this book. I originally came to Berkeley to study political theory with Mike, and that decision remains one of the best of my life.

I am also deeply thankful to Paul Thomas and Martin Jay for their gracious remarks and pointed criticisms. Paul's outstanding theoretical and historical critiques of the text and Marty's careful readings of my drafts contributed significantly to the clarity of my theoretical arguments. I also owe a great debt to Marty for helping me to understand the unforgiving thought of Georges Bataille.

Several of my Berkeley colleagues deserve mention for their critical insights and their willingness to read and reread my work. Roger Berkowitz's and Ellen Rigsby's excellent critiques of my first chapter helped me to frame my general understanding of French sacrificial violence. I also appreciate the time spent by Nils Gilman reading and discussing several of my chapters. His commentary and those conversations proved extremely useful for elucidating a number of theoretical points. Finally, I cannot overstate the importance of my intellectual connections to Gaston Alonso-Donate, Matt Dallek, and Keally McBride, three invaluable friends from whom I have learned a great deal.

I obtained institutional support for the research and writing of this book from two sources. The Government Department at the University of Texas at Austin—especially Jim Fishkin, Jeffrey Tulis, and Gretchen Ritter—invited me to be a visiting scholar for three years, during which time I also taught at the university. When I returned to the Bay Area in 2002, Bruce Cain and Nelson Polsby kindly allowed me to assume visiting scholar status at the Institute of Governmental Studies, where I was able to complete the book.

Even inside the academy, which to outsiders can appear willing to embrace just about any imaginable topic, the subject of sacrifice is not always greeted warmly. I am thus thankful to Cornell University Press for its willingness to take a risk on a book project whose central theme is anathema to mainstream political theory. Catherine Rice, my first editor at Cornell University Press, championed my work. Roger Haydon graciously picked up my project where Catherine left off. Working with Cornell University Press, which commissioned excellent and insightful comments from three anonymous reviewers, has only improved the manuscript. Finally, I am very grateful to Ann Hawthorne for her careful editing and to Susan Emanuel for her thoughtful checking of my translations of French text into English. As a courtesy to francophone readers, I have provided the French text along with all of my own translations.

I could not have written this book without the love and companionship of my partner, Ariel. Her willingness to sacrifice dozens of weekends, when she single-handedly cared for our newborn daughter Ruby, allowed me to compose this book. Although I selfishly feared that the birth of my first child might derail my writing schedule, I thankfully learned that loud, gleeful shrieks are an excellent antidote to the isolating *gravitas* of book writing. Ultimately words cannot convey how much I value everything that Ariel and Ruby have contributed to my life and work.

The Headless Republic

Introduction

Western political theory has long contemplated the problem of political foundation. Although political beginnings, past and present, have often reflected the distinctly human impulse to realize some collective version of the good life, the act of foundation itself has just as frequently been mired in blood. Thanks, in particular, to the French Revolution, modern political thought exhibits an enduring fascination with violent revolutionary change. The bloody French effort to eliminate the Old Regime illustrated to modern revolutionaries that political foundation requires blood. What is more, the formations of violence that appeared during the Revolution convinced a wide spectrum of French intellectuals that sacrifice—a public spectacle of ritual violence—was necessary for political beginnings. In his famous discussion of the nation, the nineteenth-century French historian Ernest Renan quintessentially voices this belief when he claims that all nations are constituted partly through acts of violent sacrifice.[1] In this book I examine the uniquely French debate over the role of sacrifice in the task of modern political foundation.

The French Revolution is a paradox because it unleashed violence that reflected ancient ideas about bloodshed and yet helped to give rise to one of the first modern republics. Although it is only one modality of French revolutionary violence, sacrifice appeared prominently during some of the bloodiest moments of the Revolution. Equally important, sacrificial themes—themselves inspired by French violence—framed the revolutionary understanding of political foundation. What is striking about the Revolution is that the French con-

---

1. Ernest Renan, "What Is a Nation?" in *Nation and Narration,* ed. Homi Bhabha (New York: Routledge, 1990), 19.

sistently referred to their acts of violence in sacrificial terms and used sacrificial themes to imagine different relationships between bloodshed and political beginnings. The appearance of sacrificial practices and themes during the French Revolution has been well documented by others; their theoretical significance, however, remains largely unexplored. Indeed, revolutionary sacrifice inspired an important and heretofore unrecognized theoretical debate among a diverse group of French counter-Enlightenment intellectuals. These thinkers—Joseph de Maistre, Georges Sorel, Georges Bataille—are united by their desire to understand the sacrificial origins of politics and to place sacrifice in the service of their markedly different political agendas. Their works form a distinctive, modern tradition of thought concerned with the importance of sacrificial violence for the founding of new political regimes.

In order to illuminate the theoretical significance of this French intellectual debate about sacrifice and political foundation, this book addresses three questions. Why did the French revolutionaries recuperate ancient concepts of sacrificial violence? How did this recuperation inaugurate a modern theoretical debate about the role of sacrifice in founding politics? Finally, how do Maistre, Sorel, and Bataille, writing in reaction to the violent, sacrificial founding of the French Republic, reconceptualize the relationship between sacrificial bloodshed and political instauration? The specificity of these questions reflects the fact that the history of revolutionary violence in France is unique. Along with their optimism that they could overthrow their king and establish a republic, the French revolutionaries held steadfastly to the belief that violence was an important element of their revolutionary strategy. More than a mere instrument, sacrificial violence appeared to possess moral and didactic properties, which the revolutionaries viewed as essential for converting a nation of royal subjects into republican citizens.

The revolutionary appeal of sacrificial violence can still be heard from those who approve the outcome of the French Revolution and consider the public sacrifice of King Louis XVI the central, violent, founding act of the modern French Republic.[2] Ironically, however, most of the intellectuals who participate in what I call the "French discourse on sacrificial violence" are hostile to the optimistic Enlightenment principles that supported revolutionary ideology and less sanguine than the revolutionaries about the necessity of violent sacrifice for political foundation. None of the three thinkers, Maistre, Sorel, and Bataille, finds reason to celebrate the constellation of ideas, such as scientific reason, human progress, natural rights, and democratic governance, which were codified by the

---

2. For instance, see Michael Walzer, *Regicide and Revolution* (New York: Columbia University Press, 1992).

Lumières and instituted by the French revolutionaries. Maistre, Sorel, and Bataille each maintain, albeit for different reasons, that sacrificial violence is incompatible with the task of creating political novelty. Yet their theoretical reservations about the role of sacrifice in political foundation are complicated by the fact that their written works untenably celebrate some types of sacrifice while condemning others. This oft-overlooked contradiction has encouraged generations of scholars to condemn Maistre, Sorel, and Bataille too hastily for producing only dangerous theoretical ideas. It is true that, in betraying their own pessimism about founding political sacrifice, these intellectuals reveal their theoretical shortcomings. It is also true that, at different times in their lives, they were attracted to repulsive political ideas. However, their particular theoretical emphasis on sacrificial violence reveals how an ancient, violent practice ultimately assumed an important role in modern French theory. The evolution of these theories of sacrifice also illustrates a measure of surprising theoretical cohesion among a group of thinkers whose politics are so dissimilar.

Although sacrificial violence has long been part of Western mythology, religion, and history and is perhaps the oldest form of collective violence, the term does not come very easily to modern lips. Having defined themselves in opposition to "primitive" peoples, Westerners tend to view sacrifice as irrational and barbaric. Voltaire's desire to crush superstition—*Écrasez l'infâme*—remains an important Enlightenment legacy that frames Western views on sacred violence. Furthermore, the now-dominant liberal attitude toward bloodshed makes sacrifice unpalatable. Cruel and public displays of violence have been slowly discredited and are typically considered illegitimate for conflict resolution. Most important, liberals maintain that lawful regimes do not begin in blood. Rather, they maintain that people hold conventions, write constitutions, and make contracts. The appearance of sacrifice in the West thus seems anachronistic and nonpolitical, a violent and superstitious holdover from the distant past.[3]

Current sacrificial practices in modern Western societies are mostly religious and commemorative, such as the Catholic Eucharist, Jewish Passover, and Muslim Ramadan celebrations. Although the violent destruction of scapegoats may no longer take the appearance of the fifteenth-century Spanish Inquisition or seventeenth-century Salem witch trials, the twentieth century has witnessed its share of violent scapegoating. The lynching of blacks in the American South and the genocides of Armenians, Jews, Cambodians, and Tutsis offer just a few examples. Similarly, while martyrdom may no longer appear as the violent self-sacrifice of a devout individual, such as that of the Christian Apostles, this form

---

3. For a fascinating, contemporary discussion of this topic in France, see Alain Corbin, *The Village of Cannibals,* trans. Arthur Goldhammer (Cambridge, Mass.: Harvard University Press, 1992).

of sacrificial violence has recently been adopted as a tool of regional and national liberation. Palestinian martyrs, Tamil Tigers, Chechnyan rebels, even transnational Al Qaeda terrorists have embraced different forms of martyrdom as part of distinct political, religious, and military strategies. It is tempting to associate the modern revival of martyrdom uniquely with Islamic fundamentalism and scapegoating uniquely with fascism because these ideologies appear to challenge secular liberalism with notions of theocracy or racial purity respectively. It is important to remember, however, that Islamic fundamentalism and fascism are themselves modern ideologies. Their reliance on sacred violence does not mean that the modern world has yet to jettison its premodern baggage. Rather, the appearance of scapegoats and martyrs in the twentieth and twenty-first centuries indicates that the modern world is partly constituted by ancient ideas, such as sacrifice, which have been adapted to novel political conditions.

The secular liberal distaste for sacrificial violence is based on a modern prejudice that conceives of religion and politics as two distinct, incommensurable realms. Both, however, are forms of social organization concerned with the moral conduct of human beings. From the vantage point of religion, humans act morally when they honor the distinctiveness of the sacred and profane worlds. Different forms of sacrifice—violent as well as symbolic—serve to maintain this separation. From the perspective of modern liberal politics, the sacred also has a special status. Liberal regimes enshrine their founding or constitutional principles, such as political equality or freedom. Liberal political leaders are accorded a level of security and respect that would be the envy of medieval kings. The locations of concentrated political power, such as the White House, are treated as sacrosanct. Finally, political symbols, such as flags, are imbued with sanctified power, rendering them untouchable. Consecrated religious power is thus akin to the sacred character of secular political leaders, places, and symbols. Such sacred powers also serve similar authoritative functions. Humans are more inclined to act morally or to obey when the origin of the law or religious command is hallowed. Yet, while religious leaders can always justify their power by turning to the authority of an absolute, political founders who wish to create something new in the realm of politics have no transcendental, sacred authority by which to legitimate their decisions. To the extent that modern politics, and not religion, now governs the quotidian affairs of most human beings, political authority has an even greater need than religion for a mechanism that confers sacredness on its core principles.

French history and violent practices have established sacrifice as one such mechanism. As an amalgam of Roman and Christian traditions, the French monarchy always relied on sacrificial themes and rites in order to bolster its authority. The monarchy was born when Clovis I was baptized, a Catholic cleansing ritual whose origin is sacrificial. Similarly, the monarchy perished when the French revolutionaries publicly sacrificed Louis XVI and imagined that they were purified by the king's spilt blood. French religious history is also steeped in such sacrificial traditions and events. As Ivan Strenski argues in his book *Contesting Sacrifice,* seventeenth-century Catholic theologians codified a rigid and persistent French sacrificial discourse that has helped to shape modern French views of a variety of topics, ranging from the Revolution and Dreyfus Affair to wartime patriotism and academic sociology.[4] That sacrificial ideas have so powerfully informed French royalism, republicanism, and Catholicism illustrates their ability to offer sacred support to focal points of authority. Unlike the monarchy or the church, however, the French Republic has no obvious sacred or absolute power on which to ground its legitimate use of power. For this reason, and despite the fact that public attitudes toward violent sacrifice have soured in the last two hundred years, sacrificial ideas have remained an important support for French republican authority in the modern period.

Like sacrificial practices in France and throughout the world, sacrifice in the West has an important politico-religious heritage. All three major Western religions were founded sacrificially: Judaism and Islam trace their roots to Abraham's attempted filicide; Christianity began with Jesus' crucifixion. Sacrifice—both real and symbolic—was also present at the dawn of Western politics. Ancient Greek and Roman politics were supported by a wide variety of sacrificial practices. Classical mythology and history capture this nexus of the sacrificial and political. For instance, in the mythology of ancient Greece, democratic Athens was founded after Theseus slew the Minotaur and renounced his father's royal title in favor of a representative government; and Republican Rome was born when Romulus killed his brother, Remus. Rome was later renovated, to use the Machiavellian term, when Lucius Junius Brutus committed filicide to overthrow the corrupt Tarquin monarchy, thus reestablishing the republic. In each of these religious and political examples, a new community and authority were born when people congregated around sacrificial death.

Beginning with Plato's *Republic,* Western political thinkers have struggled to understand how to found political regimes. Even Plato, who described how humans could inaugurate an ideal republic, imagined a central role for piety and sacrifices.[5] Although Plato implies that violence plays a role in the creation of

---

4. Ivan Strenski, *Contesting Sacrifice* (Chicago: University of Chicago Press, 2002).

5. In *The Republic* of Plato, Socrates tells Adeimantus and Glaucon about one aspect of the legislation required for the foundation of the city. When asked, "Then what might still remain for our legislation?" Socrates responds, "For us, nothing. However for the Apollo at Delphi there remain the greatest, fairest, and first of the laws which are given." Describing these laws, Socrates continues, "Foundings of temples, sacrifices, and whatever else belongs to the care of gods, demons, and heroes; and further, bur-

his republic, Machiavelli was the first canonical thinker to consider the problem of political foundation with violence specifically in mind. He was principally concerned with this question: Do political beginnings require legendary crimes? Machiavelli argued that legendary crimes served founders by endowing man-made authority with the sacred sense of awe historically associated with the divine. Unlike earlier political thinkers, Machiavelli viewed the problem of political foundation in anthropocentric terms: Humans who wanted to form new political communities and new sources of authority could no longer depend on absolute sources of power. Thus, founders faced a daunting task in trying to form new political communities out of a people who might be politically inexperienced or corrupt. In Machiavelli's view, the spectacular violence of the legendary crime helped founders by functionally substituting for divine right. More specifically, he realized that the legitimacy of authority is rooted in both the pure, elevated, majestic power of the king and the base, polluted, abject power of the executioner. Because legitimate power combines these contradictory yet mutually reinforcing qualities, Machiavelli believed that spectacular public executions could generate the visceral, quasi-religious sentiments that render new secular laws legitimate.

For Machiavelli, Lucius Junius Brutus served as an important example of what founders must do in order to secure their people's freedom: "Whoever takes up a tyranny and does not kill Brutus, and whoever makes a free state and does not kill the sons of Brutus, maintains himself for little time." Machiavelli argues, in part, that political founders who do not kill their chief enemies place their sovereignty at risk. In his description of Brutus' filicide, however, Machiavelli suggests that the pragmatic elimination of enemies is not the only meaning of Brutus' legendary crime. He writes that Brutus' severity "is an example rare in all memories of things to see the father sit on the tribunals and not only condemn his sons to death but to be present at their death. This will always be known by those who read of ancient things: that after a change of state, either from republic to tyranny or from tyranny to republic, a memorable execution against the enemies of present conditions is necessary."[6] The death of Brutus' sons assumes the status of a "memorable execution" because it is a sacrificial act.

---

ial of the dead and all the services needed to keep those in that other place gracious. For such things as these we neither know ourselves, nor in founding a city shall we be persuaded by any other man, if we are intelligent, nor shall we make use of any interpreter other than the ancestral one. Now this god is doubtless the ancestral interpreter of such things for all humans, and he sits in the middle of the earth at its navel and delivers his interpretations." Socrates' point is that political foundation requires a set of laws that are sacred—given and interpreted by the gods—and supported by traditional practices such as sacrifice. Plato, *The Republic of Plato*, trans. Allan Bloom (New York: Basic Books, 1968), 104–105.

6. Niccolò Machiavelli, *Discourses on Livy*, trans. Harvey C. Mansfield and Nathan Tarcov (Chicago: University of Chicago Press, 1996), 214.

Filicide is not merely punishment; it is a shocking, founding moment when a father kills his own children, destroying his private family in order to breathe life into a new political one. Membership in Brutus' newly constituted political family of citizens is sealed by Brutus' bloody display of political power, which is concentrated in the hands of a republican founder and directed against his own kin. Machiavelli admires Brutus' sacrifice for the same reason that he recommends to modern revolutionaries that they emulate the acts of the great political founders: Moses, Cyrus, Romulus, and Theseus. These figures are long remembered for their ability to give new laws and for their willingness to make the necessary sacrifices that would render their laws legitimate.

By August 1792 the French found themselves in a Machiavellian predicament. On one hand, they faced a stubborn king who embodied sacred sovereignty. On the other hand, they sought to create a new popular authority that could supplant the king's divine power. The French revolutionary program was daunting: to desacralize a king and to transfer his sacred power to the people. One of the important ways in which the French responded to this dilemma was through the practice of sacrificial violence, culminating in the regicide and the Terror. These violent episodes reveal three important ways in which the French revolutionaries embraced Machiavellian assumptions concerning sacrifice and power. First, because all political authority has a sacred quality, changes to the authoritative status of the power must also have a sacred character or origin. Second, as Machiavelli understood, the sacredness of power is simultaneously pure and abject. Therefore, sacrificial violence used to establish new forms of power must be capable of auguring both purity and abjection, which correspond to the Old Regime's king and executioner respectively. Third, certain forms of violence—sacrifice in particular—invoke, manipulate, and transform the sacredness of power, thus permitting humans to tinker—or to believe that they can tinker—with the affective qualities of political authority. Thus, the French revolutionaries engaged in sacrificial violence because they believed that it would affect how their compatriots perceived the legitimacy of political power. This belief supported the revolutionary conviction that the Republic had to be born in blood that would simultaneously cleanse the stain of monarchism and endow the people with the king's divine power.

Having associated sacrifice and political foundation in practice, the French revolutionaries encouraged the emergence of a theoretical debate about the meanings of this unique form of bloodshed. As the most important contributors to this tradition of thought, Maistre, Sorel, and Bataille collectively illustrate one of the important ways in which the French have understood political violence in the modern period. Their work is also part of a larger French discourse about sacrifice that extends across intellectual domains as varied as theology, sociology, anthropology, and history. Maistre's, Sorel's, and Bataille's work is distinctive because it forms a modern contribution to the long, unresolved debate in Western political thought about the necessity of violence for political foundation. This issue is often reduced to moral and practical concerns: Is war or rebellion justified? Will the violent destruction of one's enemies allow for freedom and equality? In contrast, Maistre, Sorel, and Bataille focus principally on issues of power and communality: How does sacrificial violence help to constitute legitimate power? Is sacrifice a foundational act in helping to form the communities that engage in politics? Above all, the French discourse on sacrificial violence is concerned with how sacrifice endows power with sacredness and participates in the formation of a community that acknowledges such newly constituted power as legitimate.

Thanks to the widespread appearance of sacrificial violence during the French Revolution, the concept of sacrifice became one of the focal points of postrevolutionary French debates about political violence. In the first chapter, I explore the historical origins of revolutionary sacrifice and examine how the revolutionaries adapted it to their unique political context. Although the revolutionaries never developed a theory of sacrifice per se, they adeptly borrowed and transformed sacrificial ideas from Roman antiquity and early Christianity. Roman political scapegoats and Christian martyrs provided the revolutionaries with historical frames of reference for sacrificial practices that participated in the formation of new communities and authorities. In seeking to found a republic, the revolutionaries engaged in a variety of sacrificial practices, which achieved different, sometimes conflicting, political effects. My examination of the evolution of revolutionary violence, from the insurrection of August 10, 1792, through the death of Robespierre in 1794, shows how sacrifice sometimes appeared to support republican foundation and sometimes to undermine its legitimacy. When the revolutionaries' use of sacrifice escalated into the Reign of Terror, it started to work against the republican aims of the Revolution, starkly illustrating how difficult it is to tether sacrifice to a particular political agenda. The goal of my analysis of revolutionary sacrificial violence is to provide a conceptual basis for understanding the postrevolutionary discourse on sacrificial violence. Sacrificial practices during the French Revolution left several generations of intellectuals convinced that political foundation required sacrificial blood. By inserting this ancient concept of violence into the first modern revolution, the French laid the cornerstone of a revolutionary sacrificial tradition whose imprint subsequent intellectuals, with their own political agendas, could not ignore.

In chapter 2, I explore the sacrificial ideas of Joseph de Maistre, the first French intellectual to transform an analysis of revolutionary violence into a theory of sacrifice. As a career diplomat for the Sardinian king, Maistre developed what remains one of the most trenchant critiques of the Revolution and Enlightenment thought. Maistre harbored a disturbing fascination with the redemptive properties of blood and considered it the locus of moral transformation. For this reason, he insists that the torrents of blood spilled during the Reign of Terror were evidence that God was working behind the backs of the revolutionaries, seeking to punish them for their hubris. Believing that the blood of the innocent redeems the sins of the guilty, Maistre offers a theoretically sophisticated account of the processes of sacrificial exchange that affect political power. Maistre is critical of the scapegoat mechanism, a sacrifice that he associates with the painfully misinformed efforts of pre- and non-Christian peoples to redeem their sins. His theory of sacrifice is reactionary, for it posits that founding violence serves only to hem human beings into a narrow sphere of political activity sanctioned by God. In his view, violence may be salutary or corrupt, but it always points human beings back to crown and scepter. Although Maistre despises the Revolution, his conservative theory of sacrifice illuminates the political significance of revolutionary sacrificial practices. Paradoxically, Maistre's criticism of revolutionary sacrificial violence also rests on a rigid and untenable theoretical distinction between Christian and non-Christian sacrifice. Like the revolutionaries, Maistre problematically maintains that sacrifice, properly understood, will generate particular moral and political outcomes. Thus, Maistre's explanation of how sacrifice fosters conservative moral regeneration unintentionally points toward more radical uses for sacrificial violence. In challenging the possibility of republican political foundation, Maistre inadvertently provides a theoretical account of the relationship between sacrifice and authority that later proves useful to Sorel and Bataille.

Between 1900 and 1910, the anarcho-syndicalist Georges Sorel adapted the sacrificial ideas practiced by the revolutionaries and critiqued by Maistre to Sorel's own political agenda. Sorel is infamous for his *Reflections on Violence,* in which he rails anarchically against the Jacobin tradition of state violence and describes why the anarcho-syndicalist revolution requires proletarian violence. Although Maistre and Sorel have been labeled bloodthirsty intellectuals, both are also deeply skeptical of the revolutionary applications of sacrifice. Not only are these thinkers united by their hostility toward scapegoats; they also share an allegiance to the Christian sacrificial tradition and, in particular, to the power of martyrs to forge communities. In chapter 3, I argue that Sorel's notion of sacrifice builds upon Maistre's by placing an even stronger emphasis on bloodlessness and symbolism. Sorel's concept of proletarian violence is modeled on first- and second-century Christian martyrs whose self-sacrifices illustrate the congregational power of sacred bloodshed. In demonstration of the novelty of his thought, Sorel agues that martyrdom possesses the unique capacity to inspire revolutionary fervor through the formation of myths, which are just as politically transformative as the bloody sacrifices that gave rise to them. Thus, Sorel rejects the tradition of revolutionary violence in which the state is the principal sacrificial agent, but on grounds that are also hostile to Maistre's disturbing fascination with bloodshed.

While Sorel's concept of sacrifice may be less bloody and threatening than Maistre's, Sorel cannot avoid falling into the same theoretical trap as his predecessor in the French discourse on sacrificial violence. A modern form of sacrifice, proletarian violence aims at breathing revolutionary life and moral vigor into the working-class movement. With the martyrdom of workers, however, the anarcho-syndicalist movement benefits from the same sacred properties of violence as did the French revolutionaries from their own bloody sacrifices. In other words, Sorel's critique of the Jacobin tradition of state violence fails because he denigrates the agent without criticizing the bloodshed itself. Sorel simply transposes the consecrating properties of bloodshed to the proletariat, claiming that violence—monopolized in the proper hands—can transform politics positively. Sorel's concerns about the use and abuse of French revolutionary bloodshed do not ultimately prevent him from seeking to identify a truly revolutionary form of sacrificial proletarian violence.

In chapter 4, I examine how the renegade surrealist Georges Bataille used the sacrificial ideas developed by his predecessors to challenge the basic premise of the French discourse on sacrificial violence. Although Bataille agrees with Maistre, Sorel, and the French revolutionaries that sacrificial violence can be adapted to modern political settings, Bataille disputes the historical association of sacrifice with political foundation and authority. Maistre, Sorel, and the French revolutionaries sought to place sacrifice in the service of moral revolutions in order to ground new forms of politics and legitimate power. For Bataille, however, human liberation requires not better politics, achieved through violent political foundation, but rather the sacrificial dismantling of the constitutive elements of modern political activity. Taking aim at liberalism and utilitarianism in particular, Bataille pursues an idea of revolutionary sacrifice that liberates human beings from all forms of servility, including morality, authority, identity, community—the whole modern political enterprise. Bataille argues that revolutionary liberation requires the retrieval of sacrificial activities that subvert rational, useful, and productive modes of thought and action—anything that transforms human beings into things. Rather than producing something that the sacrificer can use, such as power rendered sacred, Bataillian sacrifice generates an ecstatic experience of self-loss. In Bataille's view, sacrifice must free humanity from politics, not support, establish, or reestablish it. Bataille thus envisions that unproductive sacrificial activities will give birth to a metapolitical community paradoxically defined by its permanent lack of foundation. In this way, Bataille uses the works of Maistre and Sorel to repudiate the basic assumptions of the French discourse on sacrificial violence.

Bataille's radical reformulating of political sacrifice reveals what is at stake in using sacrificial violence to found politics. During the 1930s, Bataille increasingly distanced sacrificial practices from the realm of politics because he was fearful that founding violence would generate fascism rather than freedom. On the eve of World War II, Bataille extended this logic as far as it would go, imagining that sacrificial violence would achieve ecstatic liberation if it were practiced in the bedroom or on and through the text. Although Bataille never evinces any reticence about violence or cruelty, I argue that he ultimately realized that sacrifice practiced in either a French revolutionary, Maistrian, or Sorelian fashion led to tyranny. Bataille's contribution to the French discourse on sacrificial violence is thus ironical. On one hand, he pushes the idea of sacrificial violence to its logical conclusion by arguing that the sacrifice of another being for the sake of political change cannot generate anything useful or productive. On the other hand, the legendary sacrificial crime—to borrow again from Machiavelli—permanently alters the sacrificers as well as the basis upon which they can form a community with others. Thus, Bataille recognized that seeking political change through sacrifice permanently destabilizes the basic elements of modern Western politics.

Although Bataille lays bare the risk of using sacrificial violence to found politics, he also succumbs to the same temptation as his predecessors who condemned the use of sacrifice by others, but wished to harness it for themselves. Bataille criticizes the French revolutionaries, Maistre, and Sorel for placing sacrifice in the service of authoritarian structures of power. Like the other members of the discourse on sacrificial violence, however, Bataille never abandons the idea that sacrificial violence is a sacred, spectacular form of bloodshed that plays a vital role in the formation of human communality. During the Cold War, Bataille uncharacteristically developed this position into a quasi-scientific, general theory of political economy. Representing a systematic critique of utilitarianism, this postwar theoretical work illustrates Bataille's effort to find contemporary examples of sacrificial loss that will save the modern world from the dangers of political sclerosis and the possibility of nuclear annihilation. In setting sacrifice to work, Bataille contradicts his prewar claims about the absolute uselessness of sacrifice. At the same time, he also demonstrates the sublime appeal—the attraction and danger—of adapting ancient ideas about violence and loss to modern political conditions. It was precisely this particular quality of sacrificial violence that originally attracted the French revolutionaries, leading them to inaugurate the discourse on sacrificial violence.

Defining sacrifice is difficult because of the ambiguity inherent in violence. Violence is generally defined in terms of physical injury or harm to subjects and objects. Violence directed against humans involves injury to or constraint of the body and mind. Against objects, violence entails damage or destruction. Metaphoric violence, the broadest aspect of the definition, includes innumerable symbolic, culturally specific notions of harm.

The modern meaning of violence is limited and, unfortunately, confused by the fact that it is distinguished from "force," which today is often used to mean legitimate violence. Because there are various, irreconcilable concepts of right, there is also irresolvable debate about the difference between force and violence. In the ancient world, however, the concept of violence retained the ambiguity eschewed by the modern world. *Vis*, "force," is the root of the Latin *violentia*, "violence," collapsing the distinction between legitimate and illegitimate bloodshed. *Violentus* denotes "acting with (unreasonable) force towards others, violent, savage, aggressive."[7] In this case, "unreasonable" describes not the illicitness or illegality of a violent act, but rather its disproportionate, extraordinary, or distinctive quality. This definition of *violentus* is negative and thus departs from the more ambiguous meaning of *vis*, which retains a positive quality. In addition to signifying the use of physical strength to compel or constrain vigorously as well as the unlawful use of force, *vis* also implies binding force or authority.[8] *Vis* thus encompasses the essential uncertainty of violence, the fact that it can be "good" or "bad," depending on the context.

A subcategory of violence, sacrifice is etymologically an act that renders holy or sacred. If rendering sacred entails a process of setting apart from the quotidian or profane, then sacrificial violence is a paradoxical practice: it is a form of violence capable of breaking and forming distinctions or erasing and drawing boundaries. This definition is counterintuitive because the modern view of violence exclusively associates it with the breaking down of social distinctions, chaos, mayhem, disruption, anarchy, loss of control, and the like. In contrast, sacrificial violence involves a double movement; it transgresses limits in order to inscribe or reinscribe them. What is more, this is not necessarily a conservative operation. The purpose of sacrifice is not limited to the restoration of a particular order, limit, boundary, or status quo. The function of sacrifice is contingent upon *how* it "makes sacred." Some sacred things are pure, elevated, divine, majestic, and absolute; others are impure, debased, demonic, abject, and inassimilable. When *violentia* denotes the capacity to transgress, pollute, or profane things that are pure or sacred, it captures only the negative aspect of the violent dou-

---

7. P. G. W. Glare, ed., *Oxford Latin Dictionary* (Oxford: Clarendon Press, 1982), 2068.
8. Ibid., 2074–75.

ble movement of sacrifice. Viewed from the standpoint of force or legitimate violence, sacrifice holds the potential to generate a positive sacredness, which mimics the legitimacy of political power. In this respect, sacrifice describes a variety of practices that transform the negativity of violence into something socioculturally acceptable.

Like any other social phenomenon, violence has normal and exceptional manifestations. Socially acceptable violence does not call attention to itself or to its author; it is woven into the fabric of everyday life. Exceptional, spectacular, or transgressive violence creates a tear in that fabric and, in so doing, sets its authors and their victims apart from their fellow human beings. This separation by dint of violence is the essence of the sacrificial mechanism and the reason why such bloodshed is considered sacred.

A process of collective destruction, sacrificial violence is often ritualized or culturally prefigured. Although this book is concerned with the meanings of human sacrifice in a modern political context, sacrifice has, more often than not, involved animal, vegetable, and inanimate objects. Ritual sacrificial practices and their meanings are typically inherited from the past and are usually invoked only in particular circumstances. As the very term implies, ritual sacrifice is anticipated, orchestrated, and socially acceptable; like Mass or potlatch, it is a symbolic form of violence that conforms to a regularized set of expectations. The participants in the ritual know what kind of violence will take place; they know how that violence will be conducted, and by whom; most important, they know what category of victim (prisoner of war, woman, racial or religious minority, etc.) will be selected. Although the actual function of ritual sacrifice may remain a mystery to those who practice it, its total meaning is predetermined. Thus, ritual sacrifice can be compared to a game of chance: the rules may not be written down, but they are fixed. These rules govern the selection of the victim, even though the specific victim and the actual outcome remain unknown. Finally, like games of chance, sacrificial rites can have various outcomes, a reflection of their "success" or "failure."

Sacrifice is not always ritually prescribed. Two factors separate spontaneous sacrificial violence from its ritual cousin: the absence of agreement about sacrificial legitimacy and procedure. Without ritual prescription—knowing whom, when, and how to kill—communities that spontaneously sacrifice inevitably find themselves deeply divided about the reasons for and methods of killing. Indeed, in such cases, sacrifice may simply heighten communal conflict. While ritual sacrifice expresses the rigidity and hierarchy of the social order that it serves, spontaneous sacrifice has no specific allegiance to any set of cultural symbols or social distinctions. Spontaneous sacrificial violence is potentially revolutionary when it symbolically manifests sociocultural meanings and symbols that compete with dominant, traditional ones. Disconnected from an orchestrated and authorized set of practices, spontaneous sacrifice can, through violence, open a space of contestation that serves to challenge status quo views and practices. It is a telltale sign that a community in crisis is pregnant with a new political order.

Sacrificial violence tends to appear during periods of crisis, when upheaval, either human or natural, threatens the calm and predictability of everyday life.[9] Such crises typically involve violence and cultural degeneration. The steady collapse of political regimes, religious schisms, ethnic conflicts, or natural disasters have the potential to provoke violence between people who may have no formal, effective, or legitimate ability to mediate conflict. Such crises provoke a collapse of the formal rules and informal cultural distinctions that structure people's quotidian interactions. Seemingly fixed distinguishing characteristics, such as social status, religious affiliation, and political allegiance, become ambiguous, causing cultural disorientation, fragmentation, and bloodshed. During the French Revolution, for example, evidence of such cultural collapse was ubiquitous. Attacks against feudal institutions and representatives blurred the distinction between the previously rigidly defined social orders, especially between the nobility and the bourgeoisie.[10]

In French history, the term "sublimity" has often been used to describe the transforming or dynamic qualities of sacrifice. It may be possible to explain the rationality of sacrifice, but such explanations will always stand in stark contrast to the passionate, frenzied feelings produced by the collective experience of violent loss. Ironically, it is one of the French Revolution's most vociferous critics, Edmund Burke, who best illuminated the idea of sublime violence.[11] Burke, however, never intended his concept of the sublime to describe the unauthorized, transgressive violent practices that occurred during the French Revolution. In his view, sublimity captured the terrifying emotional impact of sovereign violence, which was deployed by kings or states for the sake of maintaining their power. In *A Philosophical Enquiry into the Origin of Our Ideas of the Sublime and Beautiful,* Burke writes: "Whatever is fitted in any sort to excite the ideas of pain, and danger, that is to say, whatever is in any sort terrible, or is conversant about terrible objects, or operates in a manner analogous to terror, is a source of the sublime; that is, it is productive of the strongest emotion which the mind is capable of feeling." Published more than twenty years before the French Revolution, Burke's meditation on sublimity was inspired by the execution of the

9. This point is argued strongly by René Girard in *Violence and the Sacred,* trans. Patrick Gregory (Baltimore: Johns Hopkins University Press, 1992).

10. See Alexis de Tocqueville, *The Old Regime and the French Revolution* (Garden City, N.Y.: Doubleday Anchor, 1955), 78.

11. Although Edmund Burke may be the first to offer a formal definition of sublimity in terms of sacred violence, the use of the word "sublime" to describe violent acts significantly predates Burke's eighteenth-century definition.

French regicide Damiens in 1757, a gruesome public execution that illustrated the terrible power of the monarch over the body of the condemned. Burke insightfully recognized that such executions displayed both the attractive and repulsive qualities of bloodshed. Although that play of emotions could excite a feeling of delight, it was also highly unstable: "When danger or pain press [*sic*] too nearly, they are incapable of giving any delight, and are simply terrible; but at certain distances, and with certain modifications, they may be, and they are delightful, as we every day experience."[12] Burke's point is that the delightful feelings invoked by the sight of terrible suffering are contextual. As an expression of royal sovereignty, violence is both sublime and a positive support of the monarch's power. Burke never imagined that sublimity could also be produced by the violent revolutionary activities of the lowly, marginal, or abject.[13]

During the French Revolution, sacred terms of exchange, such as catharsis, expiation, and redemption, were typically used to describe the effects of sacrifice. These forms of exchange are useful for thinking about the power of sacrifice to evoke intense ambivalent emotions and to resolve them in ways that bond communities together. Briefly investigating these concepts also helps to clarify the relationship between the sacred and sublime. Catharsis, which is of Greek origin and means purification or cleansing, describes the purging of emotional tension through an aesthetic experience, such as a tragic play. Certain sacrifices serve a cathartic function by allowing their participants to share in a sublime and dramatic spectacle of violent loss. Expiation, which comes from the Latin *expio,* originally described the purification of that which is defiled, namely, purgation through sacrifice. Expiation also involves a notion of exchange insofar as it means to make amends for a moral wrong. More so than catharsis, expiation captures the sense of unity, balance, and harmony that is achieved through a sacrificial settling of accounts. In other words, to expiate sin requires a sacrifice that will reestablish the lost balance between good and evil. Finally, the word "redemption" comes from the Latin *redemptio,* which refers to sacrifice in a religious and economic sense. As a religious term, redemption suggests a sacrificial act of release from sin or death. Under Christian influence, redemption describes the state of being unburdened, rescued, or delivered from sin, a spiritual transaction that involves the purchase of collective innocence with Christ's crucifixion. Redemption can also describe economic exchange, such as the release of

---

12. Edmund Burke, *A Philosophical Enquiry into the Origin of Our Ideas of the Sublime and Beautiful and Other Pre-Revolutionary Writings* (1759) (London: Penguin, 1998), 86.

13. I thank Ann Banfield for her insight that Burke associates sublimity with elevated power and not with what he calls the *canaille,* or the lowly rabble. That the French revolutionary *canaille* produced the very sublime effects that Burke associated with French kings is certainly an ironic example of revenge against one of the revolutionaries' greatest critics.

the debtor from the demands of the creditor or, more specifically, the purchase of one's military discharge. Together, catharsis, expiation, and redemption demonstrate the importance of violent exchange for the achievement of sacred effects, such as purification or salvation. These concepts also capture the variety of ways in which sacrificial exchange fosters psycho-spiritual transformation.

Because sacrifice possesses the ability to render things sacred or holy by invoking the paradoxical qualities of sublimity, it serves as a powerful device for both the disruption and demarcation of time and space. These bounding notions are indispensable for political life because they mark the beginning, end, and scope of authority.[14] According to Victor Turner, "The notion of sacrifice as marking a terminus, both *to* and *from*, and providing a limit between periods of time and portions of space, is well developed in both ancient Roman and postexilic Jewish societies."[15] In the past, sacrifice has been used to set a beginning and an end in the ceaseless flow of time by distinguishing the seasons or the different phases of human life. For instance, before the Romans adopted the Julian calendar, they numbered years *ab urbe condita,* or "from the founding of the city," an act that required Romulus' sacrifice of his brother. In the sixteenth century, Pope Gregory XIII instituted calendric reforms, which included the canonization of Jesus Christ's birth as the beginning of modern time. The authority of the church, which was established thanks to the crucifixion of Christ, continues to structure time. Sacrifice also permitted human beings to mark space by distinguishing peoples, cultures, and, later, nations from other groups who similarly marked their own spaces. The Romans institutionalized their act of foundation with the establishment of a capitol, their name for the Temple of Jupiter, where terrestrial authority received its legitimacy from sacrifices to the gods. Today, where religious conflict is pronounced, sacrifice continues to play a prominent role in the demarcation of political space.

Finally, sacrificial violence expresses particular relations of power. This insight was developed with particular acuity by Friedrich Nietzsche, for whom sacrifice plays a significant role in his genealogy of Western morals. In *On the Genealogy of Morals,* Nietzsche argues that the crucifixion of Jesus Christ is the culmination of a slave revolt against aristocratic morality.[16] Nietzsche deeply

14. In her excellent study of French revolutionary festivals, Mona Ozouf argues that festivals helped to "rebaptize" individuals as citizens and make the new republican social bond "manifest, eternal and untouchable." In essence, revolutionary festivals allowed French subjects to participate in the inauguration of a new form of authority. Mona Ozouf, *Festivals and the French Revolution* (Cambridge, Mass.: Harvard University Press, 1988), 9.

15. Victor Turner, "Sacrifice as Quintessential Process: Prophylaxis or Abandonment?" *History of Religions* 16, no. 3 (1977), 202.

16. Friedrich Nietzsche, *On the Genealogy of Morals,* trans. Walter Kaufmann and R. J. Hollingdale (New York: Vintage, 1969), 35.

laments this revolt because it puts human beings on a self-sacrificial path toward nihilism. He writes: "the Christian faith is a sacrifice: a sacrifice of all freedom, all pride, all self-confidence of the spirit."[17] In *Beyond Good and Evil*, Nietzsche explains how certain sacrificial practices reflect the deference or obedience of the spiritually weak to the strong. For Nietzsche, such unequal relations of power are not in and of themselves bad. The problem, however, is that some sacrificial practices, such as those embraced by Christianity, weaken the human spirit by rendering it servile. Nietzsche argues that this deleterious effect is caused by three different but related forms of sacrificial cruelty: (1) sacrificing human beings to one's god; (2) sacrificing one's strongest instincts—one's "nature"—to one's god; and (3) sacrificing God himself. In each case, humans sacrifice what they love—their fellows, their "natures," their god—in the hope of receiving some kind of balance, reward, or spiritual return, such as salvation. According to Nietzsche, however, humans who so sacrifice themselves unwittingly destroy the transcendental fictions—God, truth, morality, eternal love, and so on—that have historically defined what it means to be human. It is in this respect that Nietzsche criticizes Christianity for driving modern human beings toward nihilism.[18]

Nietzsche uses economic language to explain how the logic of sacrificial nihilism reaches its conclusion. In Nietzsche's view, Christian sacrifice involves a paradoxical exchange: those without power—spiritual debtors—engage in sacrifice in order to obtain divine goodwill or credit. Despite their expectation of divine beneficence, the more that debtors sacrifice to their god, the more power they relinquish. At its apex, Nietzsche's sacrificial economy becomes inverted when humans imagine that God, the eternal creditor, would actually sacrifice himself in order to release guilty human beings from their debt. This final sacrifice of a god fosters the spiritualization and moralization of human weakness, a permanent and dangerous state of perpetual obedience and self-torture. Nietzsche thus identifies the birth of an unhealthy sacrificial economy, which contributes to the rise of civilization, understood as a pacified organization of denatured, guilty, and repressed human beings. In the future, however, Nietzsche imagines that these weak beings will once again find their place in a healthy sacrificial economy, whereby they will "be subordinate by nature and have to sacrifice themselves" to those with noble souls.[19]

By interpreting sacrifice in terms of power, Nietzsche illustrates how politics is embedded in violent sacrificial exchange. While Nietzsche is obviously quite critical of Christian sacrificial politics because it renders human beings servile,

17. Friedrich Nietzsche, *Beyond Good and Evil*, trans. Walter Kaufmann (New York: Vintage, 1989), 60.
18. Ibid., 67.
19. Ibid., 215.

he also expresses a certain admiration for the capacity of sacrifice to transform or invert the values that humans cherish. If, as Nietzsche claims, the crucifixion of Jesus Christ is the culminating act of a slave revolt, it is also, therefore, a political sacrifice whose effect is twofold: a successful challenge to what Nietzsche calls "aristocratic" morality as well as a symbol that reinforces this new regime of values. In a word, Nietzsche considers the sacrifice of Christ to be a revolutionary act. At the same time, however, the institutionalization of the church is illustrative of how a revolutionary sacrifice, which immediately transforms the existing world of human values, can quickly become a support for a particular status quo. Christ's crucifixion thus exhibits one kind of violent economy in which certain forms of exchange structure unequal, hierarchical relationships. In this case, Christ offers redemption in exchange for obedience. Nietzsche's dim view of this exchange reflects his sensitivity to the effect of sacrificial politics on human agency and autonomy.

From a political standpoint, two general forms of sacrifice stand out among the myriad of others: scapegoats and martyrs. Scapegoats and martyrs are quintessentially political because they are often victims of collective violence and, thus, public sacrifices. Both are historically associated with the formation of communities and the aggregation of peoples. Over time, humans have also intertwined these forms of sacrifice with concepts of justice. For instance, in the modern world, scapegoats are innocents accused of crimes; martyrs, too, are innocents who die for righteous causes or ideals. This modern understanding of scapegoats and martyrs parallels the modern view of violence as distinguished from force. Just as violence means illegitimate harm, scapegoats are defined as wrongful victims. Similarly, just as force is justified as morally acceptable harm, martyrs are lauded for having sacrificed themselves in the name of a cherished idea or movement.

During the French Revolution, sacrificial violence might have proved historically or politically irrelevant were it not for the fact that the Revolution's scapegoats and martyrs were so numerous and so often extraordinary. Beginning with Michel Le Peletier, who was assassinated on the eve of the regicide of Louis XVI, the revolutionaries celebrated their martyrs in cultish fashion, using figures such as Jean-Jacques Rousseau and Jean-Paul Marat to highlight the importance of sacrifice for republican principles. Thanks to the Reign of Terror, which targeted thousands of aristocrats and clergymen, partisans of the crown also rallied around their own martyrs in order to sustain the inequalities of the Old Regime. In addition to commemorating their martyrs, the authors of the Revolution made much ado about spilling the impure blood of their enemies in order to sanctify the Republic. This language reached a crescendo when the newly formed National Assembly debated whether to kill the ultimate representative of the monarchy, Louis XVI. Because he was undoubtedly the most extraordinary of the Revolution's sacrificial victims, Louis Capet remains either a legendary republican scapegoat or royalist martyr. Unlike other monarchies, France never possessed any rituals by which kings were killed. Louis's death was thus a spontaneous sacrifice of an extraordinary victim, which marked a break in the seemingly uninterrupted flow of French history. To paraphrase Michael Walzer, a king can survive a thousand assassinations but not one execution.[20] Walzer's point is that, unlike assassination, the French regicide broke with the myths of the monarchy itself and thus became a founding gesture for a new political regime. That the French revolutionaries considered the regicide of Louis XVI to be foundational highlights both the importance of extraordinary sacrificial victims and the unique way in which those victims' lives are taken.[21]

Although William Tyndale coined the term "scapegoat" in the sixteenth century, it refers to one of the oldest forms of sacrificial violence. The Old Testament presents the scapegoat as a purifying sacrifice that bonds communities by uniting them around their founding principles. Called "the goat for Azazel," the scapegoat was expelled into the wilderness on the Day of Atonement by ancient Jewish priests who sought to dispel the iniquities of the Jewish community.[22] This sacrificial model continues to inform a conservative view of scapegoats, which holds that they appear during crises, when the arbitrary yet culturally sanctioned distinctions between right and wrong become confused or obscured. According to this logic, the function of the scapegoat is to resolve communal crisis through a sacrificial economy based on two principles: substitution and exchange. Substitution occurs when a particular community chooses a victim or object to be its symbolic surrogate.[23] The selection of a surrogate simultaneously entails an exchange, whereby the sacrificial victim embodies the community's negativity. By ostracizing (symbolic death) or destroying the scapegoat, the community marshals sacrificial violence for the sake of purification or moral renewal. Scapegoats thus permit the members of a community to experience cathartically the relaxation and restriction of its own moral codes, a process that has a clear social function: it bonds the members of a community by allowing

20. Walzer, *Regicide and Revolution*, 5.

21. One could argue that the trial and death of Louis XVI were anything but extraordinary because Louis XVI was tried not as a king but as a citizen. Citizen Louis Capet, however, was merely a strategic revolutionary fiction that permitted his judgment in a court that would otherwise have no jurisdiction—no legitimacy—to judge a sacred being. The derogation of Louis XVI to the status of "a citizen like all others" (*un citoyen comme les autres*) was symbolic only of the Revolution's efforts to desacralize the king. When he was beheaded, Louis Capet was undoubtedly Louis XVI. For further discussion of the trial and death of Louis XVI, see ibid.

22. Leviticus 16:8–26.

23. René Girard has codified this conservative interpretation of scapegoats into a full-fledged theory of sacrificial substitution. See Girard, *Violence and the Sacred*, 101–102.

them to share in the violent sacrificial destruction of their own surrogate. This vicarious experience reaffirms the moral bonds around which the community was originally constituted.

Modern notions of guilt and innocence have obscured the originally ambiguous or sacred character of scapegoats. In the modern world, where justice systems prevail, guilt is established procedurally. When courts find an individual guilty, that finding typically justifies the individual's punishment. In contrast, modern scapegoats are viewed as the innocent victims of vigilantism; scapegoating scandalizes modern sensibilities because the punishment of an innocent person seems unjust. Like modern justice systems, scapegoating involves a procedure for determining who shall be punished, but without concern for guilt or innocence. As described in Leviticus, the scapegoat of ancient times is neither guilty nor innocent. God instructed the Jewish priests to select two identical goats for the sacrificial rite of atonement. Lots determined which goat was to be killed in the sanctuary for God and which was to be released into the desert for Azazel, a demonic spirit.[24] Chance selects the scapegoat because the twin animals are, like humans, both good and evil and thus sacrificially interchangeable. An animal incapable of moral action, the goat is "innocent" or "pure." Less apparent are the goat's evil qualities, which are captured by a host of mythic images: satyrs and Satan are often depicted with cloven hooves, horns, and goatees. One archaic meaning of the term "goat" is "licentious man."[25] In Christian theology, when St. John the Baptist referred to Christ as the "Lamb of God," he dispensed with the ambiguous sacrificial symbolism of the goat found in the Old Testament. Indeed, in the New Testament, goats represent oppressors and wicked men.[26] Finally, some scholars argue that the original Greek meaning of the word "tragedy" is "goat-song."[27] If accurate, this etymology suggests that the cathartic experience of tragic drama may have a sacred origin in the sacrificial catharsis effected by the selection and sacrifice of a scapegoat. The association of tragedy and scapegoats also underscores the ambiguous character of the sacrificial victim and the important role played by the sacrificial rite/ tragic play in resolving that ambiguity.

The modern insistence on the innocence of the scapegoat obscures the sac-

24. Although there is a debate regarding the meaning of the term "Azazel," which is literally translated as "removal," biblical scholars generally agree that it refers to a demon that inhabits the desert.

25. There are additional negative meanings associated with the word "goat." For example, the goat moth exudes an unpleasant odor. Goat's bane is a poisonous plant. A "goat house" is an obsolete term for a brothel. The phrase "to get someone's goat" describes the act of angering, annoying, or irritating. Finally, calling someone "a goat" implies foolishness.

26. Ezekiel 34:17, 39:18; Matthew 25:33.

27. Walter Burkert, "Greek Tragedy and Sacrificial Ritual," *Greek Roman and Byzantine Studies* 7 (1966), 87–121. In this article, Burkert explores the sacrificial origins of Greek tragedy.

rificial dynamics at play in this form of violence. From the perspective of the participants, the killing of the scapegoat is not murder, a term that describes illegitimate violence. Rather, the selection of the scapegoat is either prelegitimated by a ritual plan or autolegitimated by its participants. The scapegoat's guilt or innocence is a function of the sacrificial process that guides the scapegoat's selection, not a precondition of it. Sacrificial victims initially possess ambiguous qualities. It is their selection that establishes their "guilt," not their "guilt" that encourages their selection. The double movement of the sacrificial process occurs when the scapegoat is ostracized or destroyed, thus transforming, through violence, the victim's "guilt" into the community's "innocence." This destruction of another human being is, like capital punishment, an extraordinary violation of the basic prohibition—shared by a wide variety of cultures—against taking a human life. Ritually sanctioned or spontaneously enacted, killing scapegoats transforms how people perceive the outcome of their violence, which may not have any obvious significance until it is organized according to opposing categories, such as guilt and innocence. The politics of the scapegoat mechanism are thus a direct reflection of its ability to confer "guilt" or "innocence." Finally, scapegoats establish moral distinctions by means of a dialectic that structures the sacrificial economy of substitution and exchange. When the community selects its scapegoat, it constructs and externalizes its own negativity. This opposition between the community's positiveness and the scapegoat's negativity is resolved by the scapegoat's destruction, the negation of the negation. With the elimination of the scapegoat, the community returns to itself.

Martyrdom is the second important form of political sacrifice to appear during the French Revolution. Like scapegoats, martyrs bond communities and establish moral distinctions in ambiguous circumstances. Martyrdom, however, is a more recent concept of sacrifice. The term "martyrdom" is derived from the ancient Greek word *martys,* which means "witness." Ancient Greek authors used *martys* to denote someone who renders an authoritative account or, more simply, assumes the role of an onlooker or spectator. Evidence from ancient Greek texts also suggests that *martys* has a legal significance. In *The Laws,* for example, Plato uses the accusative plural form of *martys* to explain procedure in capital cases: "Having followed this procedure three times, after giving due consideration to the evidence and witnesses [*martyras*], each judge should cast a sacred vote."[28] According to Plato, the testimony of a Greek martyr or witness ought to influence judicial decisions concerning executions. Beyond the "sacrifices" that witnesses must sometimes make in order to bring their account of the truth to light, the conduct of the ancient Greek *martys* is not explicitly sacrificial.

28. Plato, *The Laws,* trans. Trevor J. Saunders (Harmondsworth: Penguin, 1978), 359.

With the birth of Christianity, the meaning of the word *martys* changed. Rather than capturing the authoritative and/or legal testimony of a witness or the action of a spectator, "martyr" denoted one who suffered or died for his or her religious beliefs. Preserving the original meaning of the word, the apostles were considered martyrs because they had witnessed the life and death of Jesus Christ, an experience so powerful that it compelled them to testify about it to others. As a result of the apostles' persecution, however, martyrdom soon became associated not with witnessing or testifying about the truth, but rather with suffering for it. Whereas the testimony of the Greek martyr might have led to another's execution, the Christian martyr suffered and died for his own testimony. Today, martyrdom commonly denotes those so convinced of a particular truth that they would rather die for it than renounce or betray it.[29] Although martyrs do not necessarily choose their fate, they are distinguished by their willingness to sacrifice themselves. The fact that the modern world so commonly associates sacrifice with self-denial—the underlying principle of martyrdom—is testament to the powerful influence of Christianity on the Greek martyr.[30]

As sacrificial acts, scapegoating and martyrdom are sometimes indistinguishable. Indeed, they can be viewed as opposite sides of the same coin because of disagreement about what the violent death of a hatred or adored figure means. While it may be possible in theory to isolate the self-sacrifice of martyrs from the sacrificial victimization of scapegoats, violence in the real world rarely conforms to such tidy distinctions. One group's vilified scapegoat is often another's heroic martyr. Scapegoats and martyrs are thus ideal-typical concepts whose meanings become blurred when actual violence generates multiple forms of contestation. This ambiguity also illustrates the two respects in which sacrifices are political: (1) the form of the violence itself structures or restructures power relationships between sacrificer and sacrificed; and (2) the meaning of sacrificial

29. Both Judaism and Islam conceive of martyrdom in this way. The Arabic word for martyr, *Shaheed*, has been the subject of much debate since the Palestinian uprising against the Israeli state began using a military form of martyrdom, or "martyrdom operations." While the concept of *Shaheed* has a multitude of historical meanings, including bearing witness, its most recent incarnation collapses the distinction between self-sacrifice and sacrificing others. "Suicide" bombings are, to be sure, a form of self-sacrifice in the service of deeply held beliefs. At the same time, however, they are military strategy and, as such, a new meaning of the term "martyr."

30. It is true that notable acts of political martyrdom occurred and were recorded before the birth of Christianity. Examples of pre-Christian martyrdom include the story of Ahiqar, Socrates' death, Euripidean tragedies, and Pericles' funeral oration. In addition, there are several Jewish stories of martyrdom that predate the birth of Christ, such as Second Maccabees and the Book of Daniel. Jan Willem van Henten and Friedrich Avemarie, *Martyrdom and Noble Death* (London: Routledge, 2002), 1–43. Nevertheless, as van Henten and Avemarie argue, "there is considerable consensus that the meaning 'martyr' of *martys* occurs only in Christian literature from 150 CE or later." Ibid., 2. Van Henten and Avemarie's point is that, despite the descriptions of pre-Christian martyrdom, the transformation of the Greek witness (*martys*) into one who dies "a specific heroic death" (martyr) occurs through Christian practices and literature.

violence is a subject of dispute, which means that the dominant and weak interpretations have different political values.

As violent expressions of communal power, scapegoating and martyrdom participate in the inauguration or renovation of the "primitive" agreement that grounds political communities. This agreement is not contractual in the liberal sense of the term. Rather, it is a nonrational, chthonic union that is susceptible to the sublime—attractive and repulsive—force of sacred violence. In "Sacrifice as Quintessential Process: Prophylaxis or Abandonment?" Victor Turner explains why ritual concepts such as sacrifice are useful for fostering the social unity upon which all communities depend:

> Almost any way of structuring a society—tribal, feudal, oriental despotic, bureaucratic, etc.—into hierarchical or segmentary arrangements of corporate groups, levels of authority, statuses, and roles, produces conflicts, either through defects in social engineering or through the disparity between men's aspirations and achievements, leading to frustration, jealousy, envy, and covetousness, and other "deadly sins" of social structure. Ritual concepts such as pollution, purification, sacrifice, etc., emerge from the recognition that social groups, in the course of time, get increasingly clogged by these negative sentiments, so that if there is any sense of generic human communality at the foundation of the group it becomes harder to find as people identify themselves more and more with their statuses and their ambitions to rise in status and power.[31]

Turner argues that sacrifice permits human collectivities to cope with the "negative sentiments" that accumulate as a result of hierarchical social structures. His point about the origin of sacrificial rites is political: the distribution of power in *any* society—ancient or modern—produces conflict, which, in turn, finds an outlet in sacred practices. Turner overemphasizes the extent to which sacrifice serves as a valve for the release of social pressure. Sacrifice has too many different modalities and meanings to be reduced to one function. At the same time, however, Turner makes clear that one important function of sacrifice is the reduction of conflict, which he characterizes as the fostering of "generic human communality." Unlike René Girard, who limits the role of sacrifice to the reduction of intracommunal violence, Turner recognizes that sacrifice is also a ritual stage upon which communities play out social, political, and economic conflicts, sometimes with the intention of renovating them, sometimes with the goal of reconfiguring them altogether.[32]

In claiming that sacrifice fosters communal unity, Turner assumes a distinct

---

31. Turner, "Sacrifice as Quintessential Process," 196–197.
32. See Girard, *Violence and the Sacred*.

political attitude toward sacrifice. This attitude hinges upon his recognition that sacrifice is an ambiguous and process-oriented form of violence that alternates between structure and chaos. According to Turner's terminology, sacrifice is, on one hand, a prophylaxis, which functions to maintain, reinforce, or construct socio-moral boundaries. In this form, sacrifice is highly ritualistic, a preventive talisman against communal disaggregation and harm. On the other hand, Turner writes that sacrifice "may be an indicator of the dissolution of all structural *fines* or boundaries, an annihilator of artificial distances, restorative of communitas however transiently."[33] In contrast to prophylactic sacrifice, this description of sacrificial "abandonment" captures the capacity of sacrifice to dissolve the bounding limits of social life. Together, these opposing sacrificial impulses illustrate that the sacrificial process is not, strictly speaking, a movement to or from an ordered society. Instead, the sacrificial process contains opposite movements—consistent with Nietzsche's Apollonian and Dionysian forces—that contribute in different ways to communal unity and coherence. Describing this double movement, Turner writes:

> In the sacrifice of abandonment, the classical theological notions of sin, redemption, and atonement all find their places as phases in a process which seeks personal and social renewal through the surgical removal, interiorly in the will, exteriorly by the immolation of a victim, of the pollution, corruption, and division brought about by mere participation in the domain of social structure. Sacrifice is here regarded as a *limen,* or entry into the domain of communitas, where all that is and ever has been human and the forces that have caused humanity to be are joined in a circulation of mutual love and trust. In the sacrifice of prophylaxis, structure certainly is cleansed, but left intact; here enlightened self-interest prevails.

Turner's sacrificial process holds in tension and displays opposing violent impulses. The sacrifice of abandonment restores a "primitive," undifferentiated unity to the sacrificing community; the prophylactic sacrifice instantiates moral frameworks and structural bonds. According to Turner, prophylactic sacrifice "employs the metaphor of death to establish or reestablish structures of society and culture, with which orderly life may be lived." Thus, the prophylactic sacrifice captures the dominant meaning of martyrdom, which uses the "metaphor of death" to highlight a set of ideals or particular way of life. In contrast, the sacrifice of abandonment generally maps to scapegoats, in whose destruction communities cathartically participate. Finally, Turner reveals that sacrifice is not exclusively a reaction to crises, to the natural or human forces of dissolution. Sacrifice can also serve to set in motion disunifying forces in order to es-

33. Turner, "Sacrifice as Quintessential Process," 212–213.

tablish power relations on a new basis. For Turner, sacrifice is ultimately a potent structuring, restructuring, and "destructuring" force capable of bonding
communities.[34]

Turner's political attitude toward sacrifice is instructive for thinking about the
French Revolution, which encompassed such a variety of sacrificial practices.
Paradoxically anachronistic and modern, these practices formed a sacrificial
process through which different segments of French society alternately sought
political protection and dissolution. In the hands of the revolutionaries, who
were self-consciously aware of their intention to transform French politics radically, sacrifice came to serve both functions. The revolutionaries used sacrifice
to demolish the Old Regime and to shore up the new Republic. The instrumental use of sacrifice during the French Revolution illustrates that there is no
conservatism intrinsic to the sacrificial mechanism. Echoing Nietzsche, it also
demonstrates that ancient ideas of communal violence can participate in as well
as mask modern political struggles for power. Those who dismiss the sacrificial
practices of the French revolutionaries as anachronistic barbarism fundamentally miss how those selfsame acts contributed to the dissolution and establishment of political obedience. According to this violent tradition, which has such
powerful roots in ancient Western politics and religion, authority and community begin with neither the word, the deed, nor the contract. Instead, in the beginning, there is only sacrificial blood.

34. Ibid., 213, 215.

CHAPTER I

French Revolutionary Violence
and the Logic of Sacrifice

In the beginning, there was blood. At least, the French revolutionaries derived this political lesson from a selective reading of Roman and Christian history. Looking for guidance in their sacrilegious plan to end the French monarchy, the revolutionaries discovered that ancient sacrificial crimes appeared necessary for the successful founding of new political regimes. The cult of Roman antiquity, which so animated revolutionary thought and practice, provided a clear illustration of the sacrifices required of republican founders and citizens. Indeed, the bloodshed that led to the founding of the Roman Republic informed both Saint-Just's claim that "the Revolution begins when the tyrant ends" and Robespierre's similar declaration that "Louis was king and the Republic is founded."[1] Christ's crucifixion also supplied the revolutionaries with a religious model of martyrdom, illustrating the psychosocial impact of communal sacrificial violence. During the Terror, for instance, the French referred to executions by guillotine as the "Red Mass"; before his execution, the revolutionary Camille Desmoulins exclaimed, "I am thirty-three years old, a critical age for revolutionaries, the age of the *sans-culotte* Jesus when he died."[2] Together, the Roman and Christian sacrificial traditions informed French revolutionary violent practices and served as the cornerstone of a modern French theoretical debate about sacrifice and political foundation.

Ancient Rome and early Christianity profoundly influenced how the French

---

1. Quoted in Michael Walzer, *Regicide and Revolution* (New York: Columbia University Press, 1992), 71, 131.

2. "J'ai trente-trois ans, âge critique pour les révolutionnaires, âge du sans-culotte Jésus quand il mourut." Quoted in Henri Sanson, *Sept générations d'exécuteurs, 1688–1857*, 6 vols. (Paris: Dupray de la Mahérie, 1862), vol. 5, 38, 225. Unless otherwise indicated, English translations are mine.

conducted and interpreted revolutionary violence. Though often considered the preeminent moment of founding violence, the regicide of Louis XVI was in fact only one of several episodes of sacrifice that occurred during the Revolution. The insurrection of August 10, 1792, the September Massacres of 1792, the Reign of Terror, and the execution of Robespierre were also sacrificial and, as such, important in shaping French ideas about violent political foundation. More specifically, these episodes illuminate how the French people and their leaders—especially the Jacobins—interpreted the violence that they were witnessing and in which they were participating. The revolutionaries, however, did not translate their interpretations of violence into sophisticated theoretical claims about the meaning of sacrifice. Indeed, there was no revolutionary theory of sacrifice. Instead, the Revolution produced only sacrificial practices and interpretations, which later became the source of a unique theoretical debate about the role of sacrifice in modern politics.[3] This chapter is an attempt to characterize the nature of that revolutionary imprint.

Historical Origins of French Sacrificial Violence

The sacrificial violence that occurred during the French Revolution was rooted in two separate but related historical traditions. The first was Roman, a civilization to which the French revolutionaries felt a strong connection and from which they learned how sacrifice contributes to both political and personal transformation. The French derived a unique understanding of political scapegoats from the story of Junius Brutus, which illustrates one important narrative of this Roman tradition. Centuries of French Catholicism provided an alternative sacrificial lesson. Christ's crucifixion demonstrated how martyrdom transformed blood sacrifice into a redemptive experience that fostered the birth of a universal, transcendent community. Symbolic Christian sacrificial rites, such as baptism and Holy Communion, provided the French with an important frame of reference for their violent rituals. When the French revolutionaries adapted these traditions to the task of founding the French Republic, they laid the first building blocks for a modern theory of sacrificial violence.

Catholicism figures prominently in shaping the meanings of sacrifice in France. Ivan Strenski, who has written extensively on this subject, describes the particular French Catholic notion of sacrifice in this way: "This ideal of sacri-

---

3. Although I am concerned with theories of sacrificial violence, I want to signal that there is a rich historical literature on sacrifice that is also inspired by the Revolution and the regicide of Louis XVI. There is an excellent discussion of sacrifice in French historiography in Susan Dunn, *The Deaths of Louis XVI* (Princeton: Princeton University Press, 1994).

fice was not the calculated, prudent, 'giving of' part of one's life or treasure typical of bourgeois morality. It was, rather, a total annihilating surrender of the self, a complete 'giving up' of oneself. Sacrifice served thereby to achieve expiation for sin."[4] According to Strenski, this annihilative, expiatory notion of sacrifice has been dominant in France since the seventeenth century, when a school of Catholic thought, known as the Ecole Française de Spiritualité coalesced to defend the eucharistic sacrifice from Protestant attacks. In seeking to establish the historical evolution of this sacrificial vein of Catholic thought, however, Strenski collapses the distinction between sacrificing oneself and another. During the French Revolution, Strenski argues, this Catholic notion of sacrifice shaped the constitutional church's revolutionary interpretation of Jesus as well as the devout republican ideals of Parisian Jacobins, such as Saint-Just and Robespierre.[5] This claim is correct in the narrow sense that the French adapted Catholic notions of martyrdom to both pro- and antirevolutionary purposes. Catholicism shaped how both the French revolutionaries and their opponents interpreted martyrdom, the quintessential form of Catholic self-sacrifice. Yet the sacrifice of revolutionary enemies is a different matter. Strenski's collapsing of this distinction becomes apparent in his discussion of Lucius Junius Brutus and his descendent Marcus Brutus. Junius Brutus, who Strenski mistakenly argues killed the Roman King Tarquin, assumed a mythic status in the revolutionary imagination because he killed his two traitorous sons in order to found the first Roman Republic.[6] Committing a similar act of political violence, Marcus Brutus assassinated Julius Caesar in order to save that republic. "In both cases," writes Strenski, "the self-sacrificing acts of 'Brutus,' whether to establish the first Roman republic . . . or to attempt to save its successor from the rise of Julius Caesar, the moral lesson of sacrifice for the community is the same." Calling filicide and regicide "self-sacrificing" makes sense only if one interprets sacrifice in a nonannihilative and, thus, non-Catholic way. In ordering the death of his sons, Junius Brutus "gave of" himself qua father for the sake of the existence of the Roman Republic.[7] Such "self-sacrifice" has little in common with Jesus' crucifixion—if, indeed, it is appropriate to call Brutus' act self-sacrificial at all.

Although they emphasize different aspects of sacrificial violence, the Chris-

---

4. Ivan Strenski, *Contesting Sacrifice* (Chicago: University of Chicago Press, 2002), 4.

5. In contrast to the church of France, which was authorized by the pope, the constitutional church refers to the quasi-Catholic religious institution officially recognized by the Constituent Assembly in 1791.

6. Brutus forced King Tarquin into exile, giving him the opportunity to conspire against the new republic with Brutus' sons.

7. In the first part of his book, Strenski distinguishes between sacrifice that involves "giving of" and "giving up." He argues that the former is a partial, calculated, prudent sacrifice "typical of bourgeois morality"; the latter, a "total annihilating surrender of the self." *Contesting Sacrifice*, 32, 4.

tian and Roman traditions have much in common. Both present sacrificial perspectives on foundation. The Christian view is celestial and takes the form of
the *corpus mysticum;* the Roman is terrestrial and contributes to the foundation
of the Roman Republic. These traditions proved useful to the revolutionaries
for interpreting sacrificial violence as a form of public spectacle and an agent of
sociopolitical transformation. To his witnesses, Jesus illustrated the virtue of
martyrdom and its contribution to the formation of a new Christian community. Similarly, Brutus' filicide exemplified the ultimate duty of the Roman republican citizen. Together, Brutus and Jesus offer images of founding sacrifices:
one who kills for the sake of a new political regime, and one who dies for the
sake of a new spiritual community. These figures also exemplify the familial nature of political sacrifice, as both involve a father's taking his son's life. While the
Roman tradition highlights the role of the father qua sacrificer, the Christian
tradition focuses on the son qua sacrificial victim. Finally, both traditions present compelling images of political death: killing or dying for one's political
community.

Despite these similarities, the Roman and Christian sacrificial traditions did
not commingle harmoniously during the revolutionary period, because of a
long-standing, historical tension. At France's foundation, Roman political ideas
were subordinated to Christianity. Before becoming the first French king, Clovis was the hereditary pagan monarch of a Gallo-Roman territory stretching
between Reims and Tours. In 492 C.E. Clovis married Clothilde de Bourgogne,
a Catholic, who persuaded him to convert. That conversion, which involved the
rites of Mass and baptism, facilitated the political transition from Roman sovereignty to the creation of something entirely new: French monarchical rule.[8]

Both of these Catholic rituals were symbolically sacrificial. Defined by the
Roman Catechism as "the sacrament of regeneration by water in the word,"
baptism is a regenerative rite that employs holy water to achieve spiritual purification. Similarly sacrificial and purifying, Mass involves the eucharistic rite,
an ingestion of the blood and flesh of Christ for the sake of renewing the sacred bond between individuals and the *corpus mysticum.* Clovis' participation in
these rites—his conversion—led to the constitution of a new source of authority and a new state entity, both embodied in the king.

Christian sacrificial rites supported the sacred character of the French monar-

---

8. The word "baptism" comes from the Greek *bapto,* "to dip in water." As the first and most important Catholic sacrament, baptism signifies cleansing the soul of sin and regeneration of the dead. "Baptism is the sacramental representation of the death and resurrection of Jesus Christ. By this action the
person baptized dies to sin and is regenerated with the life of God or grace." *New Catholic Encyclopedia*
(New York: McGraw-Hill, 1967), 62. Although the baptismal rite is not literally sacrificial, i.e., violent, it
is foreshadowed by circumcision in the Old Testament and thus refers to a metaphoric violence.

chy, establishing the nexus of religious and political power upon which the divine right of kings rested. The enduring strength of the sacrificial origin of the French monarchy is graphically illustrated by the revolutionaries' intentional desecration of the royal tombs in the Abbey of Saint-Denis. The revolutionaries vandalized the abbey on several occasions during the Revolution, symbolizing their hostility toward the monarchy and the church. In December 1792, when the periodical *Les Révolutions de Paris* published the following exhortation to further destruction, it captured the sacrificial language used to describe French kings:

> While we are in the process of effacing all vestiges of royalty, how is it that the impure remains of our kings repose still intact in the former Abby of Saint-Denis?
>
> On the 22nd of September 1792, the day after the abolition of royalty and the establishment of the Republic, why didn't the *sans-culottes* from August 10th go to Saint-Denis to make the executioner exhume the vile bones of all the proud monarchs, who from the bottom of their tombs still seem today to defy the laws of equality; Louis XIV, Louis XV await their successor there in peace? One would say that the Revolution respected them . . . The heaped up stones of the building consecrated to their burial should not remain.[9]

The peril to the Revolution posed by the royal bones entombed at Saint-Denis illustrates the sacred authority of long-dead kings. The revolutionaries desecrated the abbey in order to neutralize the sublime power of royal bones. That power originated with Saint Denis himself, who, according to legend, first brought Christianity to Paris. The abbey commemorates Saint Denis's martyrdom in 270 C.E., notable because, after being decapitated, he came back to life and then carried his head to the spot where the abbey stands. Thus, sacrificial violence had originally consecrated the abbey, giving it a sacred power that the revolutionaries considered threatening and wished to destroy. It is for this reason that *Les Révolutions de Paris* recommended the desecration of the royal tombs: the success of the legal abolition of royalty depended upon the elimination of its sacred authority.

Because French monarchical authority was born with Clovis' conversion, and thus with a symbolic purging of the sacred Roman traditions that Clovis had once worshipped, the French revolutionaries could not depend upon the church to sanctify their political aspirations. The destruction of the Abbey of Saint-

9. Quoted in Emmet Kennedy, "The King's Two Bodies: Monuments, Mausoleums, and Museums of the French Revolution," in *The French Revolution in Culture and Society,* ed. David Troyansky, Alfred Cismaru, and Norwood Andrews Jr. (New York: Greenwood, 1991), 7. The *sans-culottes* were Parisian partisans of The Mountain (*La Montagne*), a loose coalition of the most radical revolutionaries led by Danton, Marat, and Robespierre.

Denis, as well as the revolutionaries' attempt to replace Catholicism with an equally sacred, civil religion, illustrates the depth of revolutionary anger toward the alliance of crown and scepter. They also illuminate why, in the revolutionary imagination, this anger emerged in the guise of a brotherhood indignant at the privileged rule of their royal and ecclesiastic fathers. In order to wage their battle against the sacred French monarchy, the authors of the French Revolution instead recuperated the very tradition upon whose rejection the French monarchy was founded. Scholars of the Revolution, such as Hippolyte Taine and François-Alphonse Aulard, have firmly established that the revolutionaries developed a cult of Roman antiquity in their quest for inspiring examples of ancient republicanism.[10] This recuperation offered the revolutionaries the company of Roman republican founders and dutiful citizens who were engaged in political sacrifice. It also allowed the French to imagine that they could displace their political fathers by removing a despotic king and founding a republic.

One of the ancient figures whom the French revolutionaries placed in their most important pantheon of heroes was Junius Brutus. Paradoxically, this Roman founding father helped them to envision the creation of a political world without fathers, a fraternal republic. A model of republican virtue, his bust adorned the National Assembly and Convention. The French often substituted his name for their children's birth names. Cities regularly held festivals in his honor. The name Brutus was even used to connote sincerity (e.g., "I swear on Brutus' head").[11] In his discussion of the books read by the French revolutionaries, Harold Talbot Parker claims that *collège* students such as Camille Desmoulins, as well as other revolutionaries, were encouraged to appreciate Brutus, "not because he gave liberty to Romans but for his stoicism in sacrificing his relatives (his two sons and Tarquin) for his love of country."[12]

As recounted by Livy, Brutus' story is a fascinating account of sacrificial violence that begins with the violation of a taboo: King Tarquin's son rapes Lucretia, a married woman. To protect her family's reputation and the honor of her husband, she commits suicide, a socially unsanctioned and thus destabilizing violent death. Brutus swears on her spilt blood that he will rid Rome of the tyrant Tarquin, who did not commit the rape but must take responsibility for it as the biological and political father. Livy also recounts an additional reason for Brutus' hatred of Tarquin: in an effort to consolidate his power as king, Tarquin

10. See Harold Talbot Parker, *The Cult of Antiquity and the French Revolutionaries* (Chicago: University of Chicago Press, 1937); and David H. J. Larmour, "History Recreated or Malfunctioned Desire?" in Troyansky, Cismaru, and Andrews, *The French Revolution in Culture and Society*.

11. "Je jure sur la tête de Brutus." Parker, *The Cult of Antiquity*, 139, 143, 179. See also Patrice Higonnet, *Goodness beyond Virtue* (Cambridge, Mass.: Harvard University Press, 1998), 138.

12. Parker's claim is confusing because King Tarquin was not sacrificed per se; he was banished from Rome. Parker, *The Cult of Antiquity*, 32.

killed Brutus' brother, a member of the Roman political elite. Thus, two familial dishonors—Brutus' brother's murder and Lucretia's rape—provoked a Roman political crisis that, in turn, inspired Brutus to seek revenge against the king.
Using the crisis to call Roman subjects to arms, Brutus banished the king and
his family from Rome, inaugurating the republic.

In the midst of this political turmoil, several noblemen, including Brutus' two
sons, conspired with the exiled King Tarquin to restore the monarchy and secure their privileges.[13] The plot revealed and the sons found guilty of treason,
the responsibility for the conspirators' punishment fell to the newly appointed
consul Brutus. The execution of the sons, a public and spectacular ritual overflowing with political significance, illustrates the scapegoat mechanism at work.
The sons represent a monstrous combination of republican lineage and monarchist sympathy, whose sacrificial resolution symbolically purifies the new republic. As father and founder, Brutus participated in a violent drama whose goal
was to refocus the locus of Roman authority from the royal to republican father. In his history of Rome, Livy describes the scene of the sons' execution:
"Throughout the pitiful scene all eyes were on the father's face, where a father's
anguish was plain to see."[14]

The story of Brutus culminates in the sacrificial resolution of ambiguous authority and identity. Traitorous sons, allied with a kingly father against their natural one, vividly illustrate the dangers faced by the new Roman Republic. Are
they subjects or citizens? Will they ultimately obey the paternal founder or King
Tarquin? When he oversees his sons' executions, Brutus uses the scapegoat
mechanism in order to demonstrate the singular importance of his political fa-
therhood. In contrast, Tarquin is merely exiled. It is worth recalling that the biblical scapegoat involved two animals, one of which is exiled, the other killed.
The sacrifice of the sons resolves the ambiguity of republicans aligned to the
crown by treating them not so much as individuals but as surrogates for the king.
With "all eyes . . . on the father's face," Romans witnessed a sacrifice whose ultimate goal was to confer on Brutus the same sacred authoritative power possessed by the exiled but still-living king.

The French revolutionaries' interpretation of the Brutus story provided them
with an important lesson in the violent theater of political foundation. Brutus'
filicide, awesome yet dreadful, focused all eyes on the father qua founder and illustrated what a founder must be prepared to do in the event of political resistance. The sons' deaths also highlighted Brutus as a model of republican virtue.

13. Livy writes: "Longing for that licentiousness, now that the privileges of all were equalized, they
complained that the liberty of others had been converted to their slavery." Livy, *The History of Rome*, trans.
William A. M'Devitte, vol. 4 (London: G. Bell and Sons, 1911), 82.

14. Quoted in Hanna Pitkin, *Fortune Is a Woman* (Berkeley: University of California Press, 1984), 59.

Brutus' actions demonstrate, however, that the subordination of private interest to public good, a virtue often associated with peaceful forms of civic sacrifice, can also be expressed violently.[15] By supervising the execution of his sons, Brutus illustrates the double meaning of this sacrifice: an expression of the lawful duty of a Roman consul and the terrible deed of a founding father. Through the example of Brutus, new Roman citizens gather around the violent display of their own legitimate power.

The figure of Brutus allowed the French revolutionaries to take comfort in the fact that they were not the first republicans to dispose of a monarch violently. However, from the revolutionary perspective, Brutus was not the most recent antimonarchical republican hero. In the previous century, the British had held a criminal trial for King Charles I, found him guilty of treason, and cut off his head. Although the French revolutionaries could have adopted the British regicides in lieu of Brutus as their chief source of historical inspiration, they were roundly displeased by the politics surrounding the death of the English king. To begin with, Cromwell's authoritarian aspirations made him an unlikely republican hero. As Jean-Baptiste Maihle stated in his speech concerning the merits of trying and punishing Louis XVI, "Unfortunately, the Commons was ruled by the genius of Cromwell, who himself desired to be king under the title Protector; and the ambition of Cromwell would have been crushed beneath the heel of a national convention."[16] Maihle would not celebrate the British regicides, because they called no national convention, the only political body whose sovereignty might have "crushed" Cromwell's lofty, antirepublican aspirations. Moreover, even hesitant revolutionaries with royalist sympathies such as Charles-François-Gabriel Morisson had difficulties with the British model. In his defense of the banishment of Louis XVI, Morisson declared: "England caused the head of the criminal Charles Stuart to fall upon the scaffold, and yet England is still subjected to a king. Rome, on the other hand, was more generous and merely exiled the Tarquins; and Rome for many years enjoyed the happiness of being a republic." Morisson wanted to spare the king's life because he perceived the British regicide as a political failure: it did not secure a lasting republic. Finally, even the Jacobins—those calling vociferously for the execution of Louis XVI—were disinclined to praise the British. Since the Jacobins wanted

---

15. This virtue was fundamental to Robespierre's revolutionary vision, which often blurred the distinction between violent and nonviolent virtue: "The duty of every man and citizen is thus to work together, as much as he can, toward the success of this sublime enterprise, by sacrificing his particular interest to the general interest." ("Le devoir de tout homme et de tout citoyen est donc de concourir, autant qu'il est en lui, au succès de cette sublime entreprise, en sacrifiant son intérêt particulier à l'intérêt général.") Maximilien Robespierre, Œuvres complètes de Robespierre, le défenseur de la constitution, vol. 4 (Paris: Librairie Félix Alcan, 1939), 110.

16. Quoted in Walzer, Regicide and Revolution, 106.

to execute Louis XVI without trial, there was little reason to invoke the arguments of British revolutionaries. Robespierre exclaimed: "In what republic was the need to punish the tyrant a subject for the courts? Was Tarquin called before the bar?"[17] The French revolutionaries may have sympathized with the spirit of the British regicide, but they did not like its leadership, form, or outcome. For these reasons, as well as the historical animosity between France and Great Britain, there was little interest in Paris in looking across the Channel for revolutionary inspiration.

On August 27, 1792, just two weeks before the National Assembly suspended the power of Louis XVI, Brutus' bust was brought into the Club des Jacobins. Louis Pierre Manuel, the *procureur* of the Commune, explained its significance: "It is here that the fall of kings was prepared, the fall of Louis the last. Here must repose the image of the one who was the first to want to purge the earth of kings. Sirs, here is Brutus, who will remind you of all the cases in which, to be a citizen, one must always be ready to sacrifice everything, even one's children, to the happiness of one's country."[18] Manuel's description illuminates the distinctiveness of the revolutionaries' interpretation of the Brutus story. As the first "to want to purge the earth of kings," the Roman republican Brutus provided the revolutionaries with a historical reason to brand Louis XVI a contaminating, guilty king who merited the same fate as Brutus' sons. This view, however, required that the revolutionaries conflate their political father, Louis XVI, with Brutus' sons, an interpretive sleight of hand that reflects the Revolution's unique fraternal ideology and historical circumstances. The story of Brutus is a political tragedy told from the vantage point of the father. In contrast, as Lynn Hunt has demonstrated, the Revolution generated a fraternal narrative about a revolt by the sons cum brothers against the monarchical father.[19] By sacrificially erasing the royal stain contaminating his sons, Brutus becomes a political father, a founder. Brutus' filicide is thus regicide by proxy. The revolutionary objective was similar but originated in a different part of the political family. A brotherhood, the French revolutionaries became republican founders through regicide, an act never committed by Brutus but paradoxically inspired by him.

Emblematic of revolutionary thought, Manuel's interpretation of the Brutus story prepared the revolutionaries for two different kinds of sacrifices, neither

---

17. Ibid., 118, 133.

18. "C'est ici que s'est préparée la chute des rois, la chute de Louis le dernier. Ici doit reposer l'image de celui qui le premier voulut purger la terre des rois. Messieurs, voici Brutus, qui vous rappellera à tous les instants que, pour être citoyen, il faut toujours être prêt à sacrifier tout, jusqu'à ses enfants, au bonheur de son pays." P. J. B. Buchez and P. C. Roux, *Histoire parlementaire de la Révolution française ou journal des assemblées nationales depuis 1789 jusqu'en 1815*, vol. 17 (Paris: Librairie Paulin, 1835), 182.

19. See Lynn Hunt, *The Family Romance and the French Revolution* (Berkeley: University of California Press, 1992).

of which appeared in Livy's historical narrative. First, the Roman sacrificial legacy suggested to the French that, as founders, they must be ready to "purge the earth" of their king. Although Brutus did not actually kill Tarquin, that fact did not prevent the revolutionaries from describing Brutus in regicidal terms. Nor did it offer any historical impediment to the revolutionaries' trying and killing Louis XVI. Second, Manuel also uses Brutus to illustrate that citizens must "be ready to sacrifice everything, up to [their] children, to the happiness of [their] country." Nowhere in Livy's account of Brutus is citizenship itself characterized by such a total familial sacrifice or systematic pursuit of scapegoats. Roman citizens watched the founder Brutus take his sons' lives, a sacrifice that Brutus did not intend his fellow citizens to emulate. Filtered through a revolutionary lens, however, Brutus' example of cruel virtue became an exhortation to widespread, purging sacrificial violence, such as the September Massacres and the Terror.

Because the revolutionaries sought to install a regime based on the principle of equality, they extended that principle to their ideas of founding sacrifice. When Manuel suggests that founders as well as citizens must be ready to sacrifice their children, he captures one aspect of this logic.[20] French citizens, however, were involved in creating a new political world, one without a paternal authority. Thanks to the revolutionary reconfiguration of the national family, founding brothers could not turn to sacrificial filicide in order to demonstrate good citizenship. If familial sacrifice illustrated republican virtue and heroism, then the French revolutionaries would have to engage in fratricide. Of course, in the original Brutus story, Roman citizens did not turn against one another in order to secure the founding of the republic. Rather than encouraging more bloodshed, Brutus' filicide was particularly effective because it ended additional destabilizing violence. Manuel, however, ignores the political importance of the finality of Brutus' sacrifice and instead articulates a sacrificial logic that leads to an escalation of death.

While the French revolutionaries were looking to ancient Rome for models of sacrifice that would help them to rid France of its sacred, hereditary monarch, their efforts were complicated by a competing Christian sacrificial tradition. Crucified by the Romans, Jesus of Nazareth demonstrated to the French the political significance of redemption through sacrifice. It was Jesus' charisma and

---

20. This same confusion of the duty of founders and citizens also appeared during the Italian Renaissance when, for example, the humanist Coluccio Salutati, in the early part of his life, expressed admiration for Roman Republican heroes, such as Brutus, in sacrificial terms. According to Hans Baron, "of the great citizens of the *Respublica Romana* he [Salutati] had said explicitly that their example 'excites in us, as it were, a desire of virtuous deeds and the daring to act as they did.'" Hans Baron, *The Crisis of the Early Italian Renaissance*, vol. 1 (Princeton: Princeton University Press, 1955), 95–96.

thaumaturgy, as well as his willingness to die for his radical beliefs, that allowed him to become a martyr and to serve posthumously as the founder of the new Christian spiritual community. The social unification that occurred around Jesus' death is rooted in the sacred power of Christian martyrdom, a sacrificial mechanism of purification. In giving his life in order to purify his followers of sin, the example of Jesus shows how sacrificial exchange fosters human spiritual transformation. In Jesus' case, however, the martyrdom of an extraordinary sacrificial victim generates divine authority to which humans must submit in order to be saved. In contrast, Brutus demonstrates how sacrificial victimization depletes divine authority of its sacred power, replacing it with popular sovereignty. Christian martyrdom thus fosters social congregation by attaching a metaphysical, paternal authority to the continued promise of salvation.

Christ's martyrdom symbolizes dying for a particular type of corporate, organological community that possesses a head and body. In *The King's Two Bodies,* Ernst Kantorowicz explains that medieval political theologians closely associated the secular royal body and Christian spiritual one.[21] This association was based on the secularization of the concept of the *corpus mysticum.* Originally a reference to the Eucharist, the *corpus mysticum* came to be understood as a description of the spiritual Christian community, with Jesus at the head and his followers composing the body. This understanding of the community of Christ was later secularized, transforming the king into the head of the body politic and his subjects into its corpus.[22] Because Christ died in order to give life to his spiritual body and to redeem it from sin, the church could easily consecrate any self-sacrificial act on the part of the members of the body to preserve the integrity of the whole. *Pro patria mori,* the secularization of the willingness to die for the Christian *corpus mysticum,* became a quasi-religious duty of subjects and citizens to sacrifice themselves for the good of their countries or fatherlands. This secular, political interpretation of Jesus' crucifixion thus gave rise to the concept of the political martyr who dies not for heavenly redemption, but rather for earthly immortality in the historical memory of that political community for whom the self-sacrifice was made.

The fact that royalists and French revolutionaries alike were steeped in centuries of Catholicism led both groups to conceive of revolutionary sacrificial violence in Christian terms. Unlike the Roman tradition, whose recovery and

21. Ernst Kantorowicz, *The King's Two Bodies* (Princeton: Princeton University Press, 1997), 193–206. See also Kennedy, "The King's Two Bodies."

22. As the royal councillor Gilbert de Voisins explained, "The whole nation is so to speak confounded with the king, in whose hands and under whose sovereignty it rests." Quoted in Jeffrey Merrick, *The Desacralization of the French Monarchy in the Eighteenth Century* (Baton Rouge: Louisiana State University Press, 1990), 12.

interpretation the revolutionaries could monopolize, the Christian tradition had long been associated with French royalism. Beginning with Clovis' baptism, Christ had been intimately connected to the French monarchy, rendering its kings sacred and legitimating their power. To challenge, let alone kill, a French king would thus require the undermining of the monarchical conception of the body politic, which was itself Christian in origin. For the revolutionaries, a Christian king posed a problem: by dissociating the body from the spirit of Christ, the community of Christians could thrive well after the death of its founder. Similarly, Louis XVI, who symbolized the head of France, could physically die without necessarily endangering his transcendental political body. Just as Christ's martyrdom purified the Christian community by redeeming it of sin, the French king and his loyal subjects hoped that his death would provide monarchical France with the same lasting spiritual reward.

Although Christian sacrificial ideas and rites strongly supported the sacred power of French kings, the revolutionaries adapted them to their cause. Martyrdom was the most important of their appropriations because it allowed them to transform their own dead into Christ-like sacrificial victims.[23] The first revolutionary "martyr of freedom" (*martyr de la liberté*) was Michel Le Peletier, an aristocrat-turned-revolutionary who was killed by a member of the king's Gardes du Corps on the eve of the regicide. Buried in the Pantheon and immortalized by the celebrated revolutionary painter Jacques-Louis David, Le Peletier initiated a cult of revolutionary martyrs. In his funeral oration for Le Peletier, Robespierre declared: "Citizens, Friends of Liberty and Equality, it is our responsibility to honor the memory of the martyrs of this truly divine religion whose missionaries we are."[24] Robespierre's language vividly illustrates the important connection between Christian and political martyrdom. Later in his oration, Robespierre underscores the significance of the revolutionary martyr for the perpetuation of the Revolution:

> O Le Peletier, you were worthy to die for the fatherland under the blows of its assassins! Dear and sacred shadow, receive our vows and our oaths! Generous citizen, incorruptible friend of the truth, we swear by your virtues, we swear by your fatal and glorious death to defend on your behalf the saintly cause for which you were

23. For an excellent discussion of the cult of revolutionary martyrs, see Albert Soboul's article, "Religious Sentiments and Popular Cults during the Revolution: Patriot Saints and Martyrs of Liberty," in *New Perspectives on the French Revolution,* ed. Jeffrey Kaplow (New York: John Wiley and Sons, 1965), 338–350.

24. "Citoyens, Amis de la Liberté et de l'Egalité, c'est à nous qu'il appartient d'honorer la mémoire des martyrs de cette religion vraiment divine dont nous sommes les missionnaires." Maximilien Robespierre, *Œuvres de Maximilien Robespierre, Discours, septembre 1792–juillet 1793,* vol. 9 (Paris: Bureaux de la Revue historique de la Révolution française, 1910), 257.

the apostle . . . They will remain forever engraved in our hearts, these last words through which you showed us your entire soul: "May my death, you said, be useful to the fatherland, may it serve to reveal the true and false friends of liberty, and I die content."

O Le Peletier, tu étais digne de mourir pour la patrie sous les coups de ses assassins! Ombre chère et sacrée, reçois nos voeux et nos serments! Généreux citoyen, incorruptible ami de la vérité, nous jurons par tes vertus, nous jurons par ton trépas funeste et glorieux de défendre contre toi la sainte cause dont tu fus l'apôtre . . . Elles resteront à jamais gravées dans nos coeurs, ces dernières paroles où tu nous montrais ton âme tout entière: "Que ma mort, disais-tu, soit utile à la patrie, qu'elle serve à faire connaître les vrais et les faux amis de la liberté, et je meurs content."[25]

Robespierre's eulogy communicates the religious meaning of revolutionary martyrs. He connects Le Peletier's sacrificial death to the highest republican virtues and to the continuation of the Revolution itself. By virtue of his death, Le Peletier becomes an important political symbol around which to gather the new republican nation. In helping to transform Le Peletier into a revolutionary martyr, Robespierre also links the highest expression of patriotism and noblest example of French republicanism to a particular form of sacrificial violence. Missing, however, from Robespierre's and Le Peletier's language is an indication that Le Peletier's martyrdom is redemptive. Indeed, in declaring his death "useful," Le Peletier illustrates how the revolutionary appropriation of Christian martyrdom lacks the sacrificial mechanism of exchange, which permitted Jesus' martyrdom to be redemptive. In other words, the revolutionaries did not imagine that their martyrs purified—in a spiritual sense—the republican nation. Although the revolutionaries clearly attempted to co-opt the sacrificial tradition that had historically supported royal sovereignty, they could not embrace the idea of redemption without tacitly supporting the very sacrificial mechanism upon which the king depended for his sacred power.

In bestowing two sacrificial traditions upon the revolutionaries, French history helped to shape the meaning of revolutionary sacrificial violence. The deeds of Brutus illustrated how the killing of sacrificial victims could foster the birth of a new republican regime. Christianity provided the revolutionaries with a framework for understanding how to offer their individual lives for the good of the whole nation. Together, these traditions informed the lofty language of national political assemblies just as often as they contributed to the grotesque rhetoric of violent Parisian crowds. Similarly, they structured the highly choreographed rituals of peaceful revolutionary festivals as well as the formations of

---

25. Robespierre, *Œuvres*, vol. 9, 258.

violence at spontaneous, bloody gatherings. Most important, when subjected to revolutionary interpretation, these traditions allowed the French revolutionaries to believe that a particular form of violence could be broadly applied to the task of founding a republic.

The Insurrection of August 10, 1792

The first significant episode of revolutionary sacrificial violence erupted during the summer of 1792. At that moment, anxiety about the efficacy and legitimacy of popular sovereignty had reached its apex. Although the National Assembly had secured the power to make laws under the Constitution of 1791, it continued to share sovereignty with the inviolable king, who could veto its legislation. Angry at the king's vetoing of three legislative decrees, the revolutionaries attempted a violent insurrection on August 10, 1792.[26] Much of the bloodshed that occurred during the insurrection was sacrificial, a reflection of the revolutionaries' desire to resolve the ambiguity of political power, which prevented the complete installation of the Republic. The revolutionaries specifically targeted victims whose spectacular deaths would highlight the awesome power of the people. Directed at monarchical scapegoats, the violence demonstrated a vivid power of exchange, whereby the revolutionaries imagined that sacrificial victimization would permit them to assume the king's sacred power and thus resolve the crisis of sovereignty. People who symbolized royal authority were sacrificed in ways that converted their impurity into something that the revolutionaries could consider pure, fertile, or useful. As a result of the insurrection, Louis XVI was forced to abdicate.

Accounts of revolutionary sacrificial violence have been conserved primarily in archival records and documented by several generations of historians. However, even a cursory glance at the eyewitness reports of the August insurrection or the September Massacres raises evidential problems. Written accounts from this period are generally authored by literate people who, for reasons of education and status, were more likely to be hostile to and, thus critical of, the Revolution. Although well-educated revolutionaries such as Marat were not squeamish about justifying violence in general terms, they were also

---

26. Just before the violence commenced, the king had used his constitutional power to veto three important legislative decrees, which called for the dissolution of the king's constitutional guard, the arrest and deportation of refractory priests, and the establishment of a camp of 20,000 *fédérés* near Paris. The *fédérés* were members of the republican National Guard who had come to Paris from departments throughout France. Jean Tulard, Jean-François Fayard, and Alfred Fierro, *Histoire et dictionnaire de la Révolution française* (Paris: Robert Laffont, 1987), 528.

sufficiently politically astute to avoid endorsing detailed descriptions of bloodshed. For these reasons, written descriptions of revolutionary bloodshed tend
to be either fancifully specific or purposely vague. The accounts of violence
included here come from events that were well known and widely reported.
My focus is on bloodshed that occurred in Paris between 1792 and 1794 because these formations of violence differed substantially from those outside the
city, reflecting more regional concerns about aristocratic authority.[27] Although
it is impossible to authenticate these accounts, it is not necessary that they be
historically accurate. The anecdotes and stories about sacrificial violence that
were widely circulated both during and after the Revolution illuminate the
political and historical importance of sacrificial interpretations of revolutionary bloodshed. In the realm of politics, what people believe to be true is often
more important than the truth itself. Well-disseminated revolutionary reports
of violent sacrifice—authentic or not—provide a crucial window into the
meaning of founding violence.

There is no better illustration of the lasting importance of revolutionary
sacrificial violence than the French national anthem, *La Marseillaise*.[28] Written
in April 1792 by an aristocratic officer named Claude-Joseph Rouget de Lisle,
the song's refrain captures the importance of sacrifice for the revolutionary
imagination:

> To arms, citizens!
> Form your battalions,
> March on, march on!
> May their impure blood
> Water our fields.[29]

Lisle describes citizens—members of the new French nation—gathering together to fight the enemies of the Revolution. As if engaged in crop fertiliza-
tion, the battalions water French fields with the impure blood of their enemies.
On July 14, 1792, in an address to the *fédérés* who had come to Paris for the Fête
de la Fédération, Robespierre also raised this issue of blood and impurity: "The

---

27. See Steven Reinhardt, "Ritualized Violence in Eighteenth-Century Périgord," in Troyansky, Cismaru, and Andrews, *The French Revolution in Culture and Society*; and John Markoff, "Violence, Emancipation and Democracy," in *The French Revolution: Recent Debates and New Controversies*, ed. Gary Kates
(London: Routledge, 1998), 236–276.

28. The song was first brought to Paris in July 1792 by the *fédérés* from Marseilles, who had arrived
for the Fête de la Fédération.

29. "Aux armes, citoyens! / Formez vos bataillons, / Marchons, marchons! / Qu'un sang impur /
Abreuve nos sillons." M.A. Granier de Cassagnac, *Histoire des Girondins et des massacres de septembre*, 2 vols.
(Paris: E. Dentu, 1860), vol. 1, 383–384.

Champ de Mars, my brothers, is still soiled with the blood of patriots spilled last year on July 17. It is you to whom the fatherland has reserved the care of its vengeance; the blood of the guilty must wash away the injury done to liberty."[30] Robespierre and Lisle suggest that sullied blood is purified when patriots spill it, thus placing it in the service of the Republic.[31] In suggesting that blood-fed crops feed French people, Lisle also conjures an image of cannibalism. The enduring popularity of *La Marseillaise* is evidence of the importance of these sacrificial themes for the sense of nationalism that has contributed to the longevity of the French Republic.[32]

The eruption of violence on August 10, 1792, in many ways illustrated the sacrificial themes found in *La Marseillaise*. Late on August 9, poorly armed and organized members of participating Parisian sections marched to the Tuileries, where the king and his family had resided since they were forced to leave Versailles on October 6, 1789.[33] Once inside the palace grounds, armed revolutionaries were met by the National and Swiss Guards assigned to protect the king. At first, according to some eyewitness accounts, the revolutionaries intermingled peacefully with the king's protectors. Amidst the confusion, however, someone fired a shot, precipitating hours of fighting in which dozens of revolutionaries and National Guardsmen perished; the king's Swiss Guards were massacred. No evidence suggests that the massacre was planned. Furthermore, no one could have deliberately chosen the form of violence that occurred inside and outside the palace walls. In the early hours of August 10, the king and his family escaped from the palace and took refuge at the National Assembly. In response to the insurrectionary violence and pressure from the Paris Commune,

30. "Le Champ de Mars, mes frères, est encore souillé du sang des patriotes versé le 17 juillet de l'année dernière; c'est vous à qui la patrie a réservé le soin de sa vengeance, c'est dans le sang des coupables qu'il faut laver l'injure faite à la liberté." Maximilien Robespierre, *Œuvres complètes de Maximilien Robespierre*, vol. 8 (Paris: Bureaux de la Revue historique de la Révolution française, 1910), 394.

31. What is unique about Lisle's refrain is his insistence on impure blood. In contrast, Tertullian's claim that "the blood of the martyrs is the seed of the church" emphasizes the importance of pure blood for the life of the church.

32. The refrain "qu'un sang impur abreuve nos sillons" captured the fascination of the engraver Villeneuve, who used it in at least two revolutionary etchings. In the first, Villeneuve depicts the severed head of Louis XVI with blood dripping down from the wound. At the bottom of the image are the words "His impure blood watered our fields." The second, almost identical image shows Adam Philippe Custine's severed head with droplets of blood dripping down. Custine's image is accompanied by the words "To the spirits of our brothers sacrificed by the traitor" and "His impure blood watered our fields." These images vividly illustrate the French revolutionaries' belief that violent sacrifice was an important aspect of their foundational efforts. Shown in Daniel Arasse, *The Guillotine and the Terror*, trans. Christopher Miller (London: Penguin, 1989).

33. Though originally separated into sixty sections in order to ease elections to the Estates General, Paris was later divided by the revolutionaries into forty-eight sections, each of which possessed a citizens' assembly. The assemblies were involved in local decisionmaking and were instrumental in revolutionary organization.

the Assembly voted to suspend the king's power, effectively bringing an end to more than a thousand years of French monarchism.[34]

During the insurrection, the French revolutionaries viewed sacrificial violence as an expression of their own political power. Eyewitness descriptions of the events inside the Tuileries linked violence to concepts of popular sovereignty and illustrate the revolutionary desire to adopt the king's power. Although the revolutionaries wanted to eliminate the king, they paradoxically held the monarchical belief that power emanated from a singular, transcendent entity and was expressed as a unified will.[35] Thinking of themselves in these terms, the revolutionaries justified their violence as the rightful will of a singular, abstract people to punish the king. For example, one insurrection eyewitness named Hébert wrote:

> Finally, the day of the people's vengeance had arrived. A king one hundred times foresworn, a villainous court had fulfilled the measure of their crimes. The long patience of the people was at its end, and they all rose up no longer to demand, in energetic but disdainful petitions, the discharge of executive power and the accusatory decree against a seditious soldier; but to retake its sovereignty entirely, and to make terrible use of it.

> Enfin, le jour des vengeances du peuple était arrivé. Un roi cent fois parjure, une cour scélérate avaient comblé la mesure de leurs crimes. La longue patience du peuple était à son terme et il s'est levé tout entier non plus pour demander, dans des pétitions énergiques, mais dédaignées, la destitution du pouvoir exécutif et le décret d'accusation contre un soldat factieux; mais pour reprendre sa souveraineté toute entière, et en faire usage terrible.[36]

Hébert describes how the people's vengeance, by which he means violence, achieved both the downfall of the king and the reclamation of popular sovereignty.[37] The people made "terrible use" of their sovereignty—indicating the

34. Between 1789 and 1795, the revolutionaries referred to the municipal government of Paris as the Paris Commune.

35. One finds elements of Alexis de Tocqueville's famous thesis *The Old Regime and the French Revolution* in the revolutionaries' sacrificial rhetoric. His notion that the French Revolution simply perpetuated the centralizing, bureaucratic tendencies of the monarchy can be found in the language used by the revolutionaries to describe the sacrificial appropriation of the king's power.

36. Hébert, *Grand et Véritable Détail (de ce qui s'est passé hier aux Tuileries)* (Paris: Imprimerie de la rue Ste. Barbe, près de la porte Saint-Denis, No. 5, ci-devant chez Tremblay, 1792), Bibliothèque de l'histoire de la ville de Paris, 957 044. The earnest, matter-of-fact tone of this pamphlet supplies no indication that its author is the famous Jacques René Hébert, editor of the radical revolutionary newspaper *Le Père Duchesne*.

37. Robespierre also uses the idea of vengeance in his discussions of executive power. For example,

link between violence and the power of the people—in order to retake it "entirely" from the king. Hébert voices the revolutionary perception that founding violence permitted them to wield the king's sacred authority. Hébert's account also demonstrates that the French perceived violence to be a manifestation of popular will. For them, the will of the people, like that of the king, was unified, transcendent, and sacred. Thus, popular violence was intrinsically good. This understanding of popular violence also indicates how it was possible for the French to consider collective bloodshed as constitutive of legitimacy: it was the unmediated expression of the power of a people who were not yet in complete possession of political authority.

Revolutionaries who participated in the insurrection sought out scapegoats or sacrificial surrogates for the king. One of the most famous of these sacrifices involved the murder and decapitation of an aristocratic journalist named François Louis Suleau. He was detained on the morning of August 10 for "impersonating" a republican, an accusation that reflects revolutionary anxiety about Suleau's ambiguous status. Suleau was recognized by Théroigne de Méricourt, who incited a crowd of *sans-culottes* and *fédérés* against him.[38] He and his disguised companions were beheaded in the Place de la Vendôme, again showing how sacrificial violence helps to resolve royalist / republican ambiguity. Their heads were placed on pikes and paraded around the Manège, a building where the Constituent Assembly, the Legislative Assembly, and the Convention all met at different times during the Revolution.[39] Two days later *Le Moniteur universel*

---

he writes: "In order to free themselves from the destructive power of their own sovereignty, the people will need to arm themselves once again with their vengeance." ("Il faudra que le peuple, pour se délivrer de cette puissance destructrice de sa souveraineté, s'arme encore une fois de sa vengeance.") *Œuvres,* vol. 8, 430.

38. Théroigne de Méricourt met a fate as sacrificial as Suleau's. Though a revolutionary, she was openly critical of Robespierre. During the Terror, she was, according to Michelet, who described the scene, severely punished: "The Mountain imagined a way to take away her prestige, to degrade her in the most cowardly violent way that a man can do to a women. She was walking almost alone on the terrace of the Feuillants; they formed a group around her, seized her, removed her skirts, and nude, under the crowd's derision, they flogged her like a child. Her prayers, her cries, her howls of hopelessness only increased the crowd's cynical and cruel laughter. Finally released, the unfortunate continued her howls, killed by this barbarous injury to her dignity and courage: she had lost her spirit. From 1793 until 1817, she remained ragingly mad, howling like the first day." ("Les Montagnards imaginèrent un moyen de lui ôter son prestige, de l'avilir par une des plus lâches violences qu'un homme puisse exercer sur une femme. Elle se promenait presque seule sur la terrasse des Feuillants; ils formèrent un groupe autour d'elle, la saisirent, lui levèrent les jupes, et nue, sous les risées de la foule, la fouettèrent comme un enfant. Ses prières, ses cris, ses hurlements de désespoir ne firent qu'augmenter les rires de cette foule cynique et cruelle. Lâchée enfin, l'infortunée continua ses hurlements, tuée par cette injure barbare, dans sa dignité et dans son courage: elle avait perdu l'esprit. De 1793 jusqu'en 1817 elle resta folle furieuse, hurlant comme au premier jour.") Quoted in Tulard, Fayard, and Fierro, *Histoire et dictionnaire,* 1118.

39. Ibid., 969, 1105. See also E. Boursin and Augustin Challame, eds., *Dictionnaire de la Révolution française* (Paris: Librairie Turne, Jouvet, 1893), 257, 801.

described the scene: "The indignant people wanted them [Suleau et al.] to be delivered to their vengeance. The four alone, including M. Suleau and a priest, were sacrificed, and their heads carried on the end of a pike."[40] Recognizing the extraordinary sacrificial nature of their death, *Le Moniteur universel* described, in rather matter-of-fact terms, how Suleau and his companions were delivered to the "indignant" people and beheaded. This report is significant because it captures the feelings of injustice that render the selection of scapegoats political. Deemed a victim of popular vengeance, Suleau dies because the revolutionaries wished to punish aristocrats for political crimes against the people.

Because he was an aristocrat and monarchist, Suleau could serve sacrificially as a surrogate for the king. His was a royal body around whose destruction the new, republican body politic congregated. Royalists had traditionally and organically understood the king to be the head and the people the body of the French body politic.[41] Suleau's decapitation graphically illustrated republicans' exertion of control over the very part of the body that had symbolically mastered them since Clovis was baptized. In placing the head on a pike and parading it around the seat of popular sovereignty, the Manège, republicans demonstrated their rejection of royal authority as well as their assertion of popular sovereignty.[42] Using sacrificial puppetry, the people paraded the head of an aristocrat and a priest—members of the First and Second Estates—in order to demonstrate the inversion of the flow of monarchical power. The use of the pike to parade their heads created an ocular focal point for the exhibition of this inversion and starkly demonstrated the newfound power of the common people. Royal rationality and authority could not have been as threatening when raised above the heads of the people and directed by them. Suleau's head, a sacrificial substitute for the "head" of state, belonged to the people.

The revolutionaries' targeting of scapegoats reached its climax with the massacre of the king's Swiss Guards. First used by Charles IX in 1573, the Swiss Guard was one of a hierarchy of regiments that defended the king. Along with the National Guard, they were instructed to defend the king and his family on August 10. Because the National Guard was created in 1789, however, its loyalty to the king was weak. Its members were also poor scapegoats because they

40. "Le peuple indigné veut qu'on les livre à sa vengeance. Les quatre seuls, au nombre desquels se trouvaient M. Suleau et un prêtre, sont immolés, et leurs têtes portées au bout d'une pique." *Le Moniteur universel*, no. 225 (August 12, 1792), in *Réimpression de l'ancien Moniteur*, vol. 13 (Paris: H. Plon, 1862), 384.

41. See the chapter "Corpus Reipublicae Mysticum," in Kantorowicz, *The King's Two Bodies*, 207–231.

42. The pike had been used in France since the end of the sixteenth century and had been employed by the French army until the end of the seventeenth century. It reappeared during the Revolution as a common weapon of the people and was characteristically used after 1789 to parade the heads of decapitated enemies. Tulard, Fayard, and Fierro, *Histoire et dictionnaire*, 1032.

were mostly Parisian and thus ill suited as a category of victim who might serve to unify the revolutionary brotherhood against the king. In contrast, the Swiss, who numbered between 900 and 1,000, were perfectly suited for this sacrificial role.[43] They were foreigners beholden to the king and thus easily perceived as enemies of the people. Wearing red uniforms, the Swiss were also quickly distinguished from National Guardsmen. Between 600 and 900 members of the Swiss Guard were killed on August 10; most who survived were jailed and later killed during the September Massacres.[44] The massacre followed the sacrificial logic of the scapegoat: unable to vent their violence upon its intended object, the king, the revolutionaries chose victims who best symbolized the sovereign power of the king and whose deaths could serve to unify the people.[45]

The massacre of the Swiss Guard illustrates the congregational effect of sacrificial violence. Just as Suleau's decapitation provided the revolutionaries with an opportunity to unite and demonstrate their power, the destruction of the Swiss allowed the revolutionaries to usurp and transform the royal notion of the body politic. This outcome is captured by reports that the massacre of the Swiss was accompanied by cries of *Vive la nation*, a replacement for *Vive le roi*. *Le Moniteur universel* provides one account of the context that inspired this patriotic chanting:

Near eight o'clock, the glimmer of the flames ready to die out, the approach of night, the sight of dead Swiss bodies spread out and almost naked, the spectacle of ruin and destruction of the palace apartments, the confused cries of the multitude, all filled the soul with horror and a dreadful secret.

The brief reflection that all these disasters were the work of the enemies of the revolution, still forming new plots, rendered painful and heart-rending the cry *long live the nation* that dominated the scene.

Vers les huit heures, la lueur des flammes prêtes à s'éteindre, l'approche de la nuit, la vue des corps étendus et presque nu des suisses morts, le spectacle de ruine et

43. Louis Mortimer-Ternaux, *Histoire de la Terreur, 1792–1794*, 3 vols. (Paris: Michel Levy Frères, 1863), vol. 2, 283.

44. Tulard, Fayard, and Fierro, *Histoire et dictionnaire*, 528. Some 780 soldiers, 26 officers, 50 gentlemen, 40 gendarmes, and 100 royal assistants died. The revolutionaries lost 3,000 people in the Place du Carrousel, the Tuileries Gardens, and the Place de Louis XV. Boursin and Challame, *Dictionnaire de la Révolution française*, 194–195.

45. Consider the use of fraternity in the following description of violence against the Swiss: "They were massacred wherever they could be found: yet many hid in the caves: around eighty were escorted by the National Guard to city hall. Some wanted to save their lives, but a terrible cry came forth: *Vengeance! Vengeance! They slaughtered our brothers!* It was impossible to shield them from death." ("On les massacrait partout où on pouvait les rencontrer: cependant plusieurs ont été cachés dans les caves: quatre-vingts environ furent conduits à l'hôtel-de-ville par la garde nationale. On voulait leur sauver la vie, mais un cri terrible se fit entendre: *Vengeance! Vengeance! Ils ont égorgé nos frères!* Il fut impossible de les soustraire à la mort.") *Le Moniteur universel*, no. 225 (August 12, 1792), in *Réimpression*, 384.

de destruction des appartements du château, les cris confus de la multitude, tout remplissait l'âme d'horreur et d'une secrète épouvante.

La courte réflexion, que tous ces désastres étaient l'ouvrage des ennemis de la révolution, toujours formant de nouveaux complots, rendait pénible et déchirant le cri de *vive la nation,* qui dominait sur cette scène.[46]

The sense of turmoil, made palpable by this scene of violence and destruction, culminates in the cry *Vive la nation.* The image of the dead, naked bodies of the Swiss and the smoldering cinders of the sacked royal palace contrasts sharply with the sound of voices calling for the nation's longevity. Yet this sublime paradox—the celebration of the life of a collective political entity at the literal expense of symbolic, vilified victims—is the quintessence of sacrificial violence. It is during this moment, so lucidly captured by *Le Moniteur universel,* that power attains a transcendent quality, at once horrible and majestic, giving to the people and the nation something thought to belong only to kings.

Accounts of the massacre of the Swiss Guards provide evidence of the revolutionary belief that certain kinds of bloodshed foster sacrificial exchange. These descriptions include mention of cannibalism, mutilations, and necrophilia conducted by the revolutionaries against royal bodies. Louis Mortimer-Ternaux reports that the Swiss were cut into pieces and that prostitutes performed indecent acts on the bodies of the Swiss Guards inside the queen's bedroom. He also describes a festive atmosphere of carnage and the mixing of blood and wine in the king's cellar.[47] Similarly, Granier de Cassagnac depicts scenes of revolutionaries eating the raw and roasted flesh of the Swiss, including a vivid account of one Arthur who consumed a fresh heart placed in a flaming glass of eau de vie.[48] Cassagnac also describes the furor of the Marseillais *fédérés* as being so great that they started to kill dogs when they ran out of people. In another version of this story, the author claims that the anger against the Swiss was so intense that the revolutionaries killed everyone wearing red, including two unsuspecting *fédérés* from the Orient who passed near the Tuileries.[49]

46. Ibid.

47. Mortimer-Ternaux, *Histoire de la Terreur,* vol. 2, 330–331.

48. Cassagnac, *Histoire des Girondins,* vol. 1, 530, 532–534.

49. *Collection complète des tableaux historiques de la Révolution française,* 2 vols. (Paris: Imprimerie de Pierre Didot l'aîné, 1798), vol. 1, 272. In addition to the transgressive physical violence that illustrated the transposition of royal and popular sovereignty, there were reports of transgressive, nonviolent behavior that highlighted this change. For example, Mortimer-Ternaux reports: "Street porters put on the sacred costumes and sat on the throne; ignoble prostitutes appeared in the queen's dresses, sprawled on her bed." ("Des portefaix revêtaient les costumes du sacré, s'asseyaient sûre le trône; d'ignobles prostituées se paraient des robes de la reine, se vautraient dans son lit.") *Histoire de la Terreur,* vol. 2, 331. This story illustrates the apparent fascination that French people had with the trappings of royal authority. In the context of a bloody massacre designed to repossess the king's executive power, what better way is there to

Although the killing of aristocrats on the street and the massacre of the Swiss Guards may not appear to have anything in common with Brutus' filicide, all are instances of the scapegoat mechanism. These sacrifices occurred in response to a political crisis characterized by a blurring of distinctions between emerging republicanism and disintegrating monarchism. Aristocratic scapegoats provided the revolutionaries with the ability to construct boundaries between popular and monarchical sovereignty as well as republican and royalist identity. They also helped to crystallize a new concept of the nation by gathering French people together as witnesses to violent, sublime spectacles. Like Brutus' sons, whose deaths conferred political legitimacy on Brutus, revolutionary scapegoats substituted for the king and enacted a dramatic, violent exchange whereby French citizens came to believe that sacrifice would permit them to appropriate the king's divine power. Finally, sacrifice practiced during the insurrection fitted neatly into the revolutionaries' interpretation of the Brutus story: they viewed it as a violent cleansing of aristocratic contamination whose continual, vigilant pursuit would eventually be foundational.

The tumid rhetoric used to describe the Revolution's scapegoats extended to its martyrs as well. During the insurrection, thousands of revolutionaries lost their lives inside and outside the Tuileries, providing the raw material for the appearance of martyrs, the second archetypal sacrificial victim. If revolutionary scapegoats violently orchestrated the redistribution of sovereignty from the king to republican citizens, revolutionary martyrs served propagandistically to attract French people to the cause of republicanism and to embolden their violent actions. In a remarkable passage from the *Courrier des départements* on August 18, 1792, Antoine Joseph Gorsas writes about the fallen patriots of the August 10 insurrection and their meaning for the nation as a whole:

Eight days have already passed since the fatal moment when the citizens were slaughtered; every hour, funereal hymns are sung at the coffin of a patriot sacrificed to satisfy the vengeance of tyranny; a thousand others still fight in vain against death; their last sigh is about be spent against the breast of a father or a friend; and yet the law has been mute! Vain forms, always dangerous in violent upheavals, have been invoked, and *crime breathes*! So, you want the people carried to excess? You want them to abuse their victory? Well! They will abuse it. Pushed by perfidious instigations, they will surpass the limits . . . and, when they have surpassed them, will you stop them, cold calculators? Several drops of impure blood would have sufficed for their just vengeance, but rivers of blood will be spilled.

---

display the sacralization of popular sovereignty than to dress it in the king's and queen's clothes? This form of cross-dressing, like so many of the other acts that took place during the insurrection, is indicative of the disintegration of the social boundaries maintained by the monarchy.

Huit jours se sont déjà écoulés depuis le moment fatal où les citoyens ont été égorgés; à chaque heure, des hymnes funèbres sont chantés sur le cercueil d'un patriote immolé pour satisfaire les vengeances de la tyrannie; mille autres encore luttent vainement contre la mort: leur dernier soupir est prêt à s'exhaler dans le sein d'un père ou d'un ami; et cependant la loi a été muette! De vaines formes, toujours dangereuses dans les violentes secousses, ont été invoquées, et *le crime respire!* On veut donc que le peuple se porte à des excès? On veut donc qu'il abuse de sa victoire? Eh bien! Il en abusera. Poussé par des instigations perfides, il dépassera les limites . . . et, quand il les aura dépassés, l'arrêterez-vous, froids calculateurs? Quelques gouttes d'un sang impur auraient suffi à ses justes vengeances, et des flots de sang seront versés.[50]

Here Gorsas comments on several facets of the sacrificial violence that appeared during the August 10 insurrection. He explicitly connects the sacrificial death of innocent patriots and the dangerous impurity symbolized by the remnants of the Old Regime. Martyred revolutionaries thus anchor Gorsas's call for further purifying violence. Martyrdom justifies blood sacrifice because, as Gorsas states, "the law was mute!" and "crime breathes!" The implication of Gorsas's rhetoric is that law is impotent to deal with the problem of royalist contamination. When Gorsas declares that the Revolution's enemies will drive the people to spill "streams" of their "impure blood," he recalls the refrain from *La Marseillaise.* Gorsas's sacrificial logic also indicates that only blood can satisfy the revolutionaries' need to avenge their martyred compatriots. In other words, there must be a balanced exchange of purity for contamination—a settling of accounts—before the revolutionaries can cease their substitution of sacrifice for the law.

The transgressive images of violence generated by the insurrection of August 10 are amenable to political and religious interpretation. For instance, the practice of cannibalism involves ingesting parts of a sacrificed body. During the insurrection, the consumption of the Revolution's enemies literally facilitated the absorption of their power, just as the Eucharist symbolically allows the Catholics to share in the redemptive body and blood of Christ. Although *La Marseillaise* implicitly conjures images of cannibalism without also referencing Catholic rituals, it was common for both revolutionaries and counterrevolutionaries to view cannibalism through a Catholic lens. For instance, in the following antirevolutionary passage, which Jacques Castelnau attributes to l'Abbé Morellet, a member of the Académie Française and a contributor to Diderot's *Encyclopédie,* cannibalism is linked to a "Jacobin Eucharist":

---

50. Pierre Caron, *Les Massacres de septembre* (Paris: Maison du Livre Français, 1935), 424.

When night came, it so happened that those who suppressed their terror during the day found it again in their troubled sleep. One of these men, bewildered by fever and the spectacle of the moment, threw himself, one Messidor night, from his bed to the work table, and proposed to the patriots "a new means of subsistence for the nation." He would ask for the establishment of a "national slaughterhouse based on the plans of the great artist and patriot David." In this slaughterhouse would be sold the flesh of victims of the Terror. He would call for "a law that obliges all citizens to provide for it at least once a week under the threat of imprisonment, deportation, [or] death as a suspect." Finally, he would insist that "in every patriotic festival there will be a plate of this type which would be the true communion of patriots, the Eucharist of the Jacobins!"

La nuit venue, il arrive que ceux qui ont fait taire leur frayeur durant le jour la retrouvent dans leur sommeil troublé. Un de ces hommes, égaré par la fièvre et le spectacle du moment, se jettera, un soir de messidor, de son lit à sa table de travail, et proposera aux patriotes "un nouveau moyen de subsistance pour la nation." Il demandera l'établissement d'une "boucherie nationale sur les plans du grand artiste et du grand patriote David." Dans cette boucherie sera vendu la chair des victimes de la Terreur. Il réclamera "une loi qui obligeât les citoyens à s'y pourvoir au moins une fois chaque semaine sous peine d'être emprisonnés, déportés, égorgés comme suspects." Il insistera, enfin, pour que "dans toute fête patriotique il y eût un plat de ce genre qui serait la vraie communion des patriotes, l'eucharistie des Jacobins!"[51]

This passage reveals the nexus between Catholicism, politics, and sacrifice. Although the imagery is clearly meant to cast the Jacobins as barbarians, it also invokes a sublimity whose attractive/repulsive power is similar to that of the Catholic image of Christ on the cross. Such imagery helped the revolutionaries to appropriate the sublime, sacred traditions whose political effects were monopolized by the crown.

Necrophilia has a significance similar to that of cannibalism. Accounts of revolutionary women performing sexual acts on the bodies of dead Swiss Guards suggest a desire to internalize or incorporate the virility of the king's protectors. In this case, virility implies fertility as much as courage or strength. The sacrificial character of these images is reinforced by the fact that cannibalism and necrophilia facilitate a gruesome exchange between antirevolutionary and revolutionary forces. At a more general level, this exchange involves the use of royal bodies to construct a republican one. Incidences of mutilation lend credence to

51. Jacques Castelnau, *Le Comité de salut public* (Paris: Hachette, 1941), 13–14.

this interpretation in two respects. The first, involving the retrieval of torture practices under the Old Regime, suggests a marking of royal bodies with visible signs of popular sovereignty. Michel Foucault's argument that torture is a mechanism for the state to "write" its power onto the bodies of its condemned applies here.[52] Second, mutilation symbolizes the breaking up of the singular unified royal body and its incorporation into a plural but also unified republican one. This view is supported by Louis Legendre, who, in referring to the king's trial, suggested that Louis XVI be killed and cut up into eighty-three pieces, each of which would be sent to one of the eighty-three administrative departments in France.[53] Legendre's proposal for the king's punishment illuminates the significance of sacrifice during the insurrection: the legitimacy of the new body politic was to be achieved symbolically by the cutting into morsels and ingestion—corporeal democratization—of the old one.

The consumption of human flesh, performance of sexual acts upon the deceased, and massacre of political enemies challenge long-standing Western fears concerning death and the human body. These fears are rooted in ancient associations of death with pollution and contamination, which themselves form the basis of cultural prohibitions against cannibalism, necrophilia, and mutilation. Paradoxically, this fearfulness is expressed in the modern period as disgust for public bloodshed and unreasonable suffering. By violating these basic human taboos, which have ancient roots as well as modern "rational" expressions, the French revolutionaries demonstrated the sublime character of their violence. Acts that so transgress the boundary between culturally acceptable and unacceptable behavior generate a sense of awe that is simultaneously attractive and repulsive. Described in ways that the Western imagination typically associates with "primitive" cultures and rites, insurrectionary violence assumed a transgressive mystique that symbolically challenged the sacred, Christian authority of the king. Sacrifice permitted the French revolutionaries to mimic the sanctified aura of the crown because it created the same couplet of abjection and purity that rendered the king's authority legitimate. In this way, the revolutionaries harnessed sacrificial exchange for the sake of political foundation.

The August 10 insurrection illustrates the emergence of a sacrificial economy whose abandonment of death taboos and logic of exchange guided the violent practices of the French revolutionaries. This economy had an instrumental

---

52. Michel Foucault, *Discipline and Punish*, trans. Alan Sheridan (New York: Vintage, 1979), 3–69.

53. "They should put him to death, cut him into eighty-three pieces, and send him like that to the eighty-three departments." ("Qu'on le mette à mort, qu'on le coupe en quatre-vingt-trois morceaux, et qu'on l'envoie ainsi aux quatre-vingt-trois départements.") Quoted in Louis Sébastien Mercier, *Le Nouveau Paris* (Paris: Mercure de France, 1994), 186, 1419. Legendre was a master butcher and, at one point, a Convention deputy.

component: sacrificial acts against ambiguous and contaminating royal symbols helped to coerce the National Assembly into stripping Louis XVI of power. In this respect, sacrifice resembles other forms of political violence used as tools to achieve some end. However, sacrifice also helped the revolutionaries to discredit the king and to purify republican political identity. By targeting surrogates of the monarch, the revolutionaries used scapegoats to gather and anoint the new republican community as well as to distinguish between republicans and royalists. Sublime spectacles such as the sacrifice of Suleau and the Swiss Guards served to clothe popular vengeance with majesty, allowing the will of the people to attain the same quality of fear and respect as that of Louis XVI.

A Sacrifice of Conservation: The September Massacres

Although the September Massacres occurred less than a month after the insurrection, they display a different modality of sacrifice as a reflection of a changed set of popular concerns and political anxieties. Insurrectionary sacrifice had contributed to the task of founding a French republic by reorienting French perceptions of legitimate power. In contrast, the September Massacres involved vigilante sacrificial acts that substituted for juridical procedures. Between approximately September 2 and 9, 1792, small bands of French revolutionaries broke into Parisian jails and slaughtered more than 1,000 prisoners. This violence was highly ritualized and formal, often appearing in the guise of a tribunal. The revolutionaries who participated in the massacres described their actions in terms of vigilante justice. Rather than symbolically asserting the legitimacy of popular sovereignty, the September Massacres demonstrated the punitive function of sacrifice. Sacrifice practiced during the insurrection functioned to contest monarchical power; its appearance during the September Massacres served to guard coalescing republican authority. In this respect, the September Massacres are akin to torture practices under the Old Regime, which were used to enforce divine right. The appearance of punitive sacrifice indicates that the instigators of the September Massacres recognized the Republic's legality as well as their "right" to play the same sacrificial role as the king's executioner.

The suspension of the king's power had placed France's political future in the hands of the revolutionaries. Yet their ability to create a viable republic was threatened by internal and foreign hostility to the Revolution. The revolutionaries were haunted by rumors of a vast prison conspiracy and fearful of the invading Prussians, who laid siege to Verdun on August 29. In contrast to the crisis of authority that had inspired the insurrection, the issues that precipitated the September Massacres were related to national security and identity. By the end of August 1792, these concerns translated into profound anxiety about the membership of the new republican nation.[54] Habituated to thinking about revolutionary events in familial terms, Parisians framed their fears of a prison conspiracy and foreign invasion in terms of threats to women and children. In particular, Parisian men departing for the Prussian front feared that thousands of revolutionary enemies, imprisoned in and around Paris after August 10, would escape and kill their "innocent" families.[55] In *Les Massacres de septembre,* Pierre Caron explains that rumors of a prison conspiracy existed before the massacres began and that their tempo increased during the massacres thanks to wide circulation by the revolutionary press.[56] On September 2, the day Verdun fell to the victorious Prussians, small groups of *sans-culottes* and *fédérés* broke into Parisian prisons and commenced a systematic liquidation of their inhabitants. Within a week more than 1,000 prisoners were brutally killed. Although many were petty criminals, there were also significant numbers of political prisoners, such as nobles and clergymen.

Eyewitness and historical accounts of the September Massacres characterize the violence similarly to that of the insurrection. There were reports of cannibalism and festivals of carnage as well as descriptions of violent, drunk men mixing blood and wine.[57] Revolutionary newspapers published inflated numbers

---

54. In the most thorough and least polemical analysis available, Pierre Caron argues that the massacres are best explained by what he calls "collective mental preparation" ("une préparation mentale collective"). *Les Massacres de septembre,* 469. He elaborates: "We believe we have established that it was a question of a mass act, resulting not from organized coordination, but from a collective mental preparation, in which it is vain to try to discern the interplay of individual and group initiatives." ("Nous croyons avoir établi qu'il s'agit d'un acte de masse, résultant non de préparatifs, mais d'une préparation mentale collective, dans laquelle il est vain de vouloir discerner le jeu des initiatives d'individus et mêmes de groupes.") This "preparation" is, according to Caron, a product of the fears caused by the Prussian invasion and the related rumors circulating around Paris of a prison conspiracy. Caron links this "mental preparation" to the concept of sacrifice when he writes: "Associated with the willingness to create security by the sacrifice of the enemies of the state is the idea that it is necessary to observe a minimum of forms." ("A la volonté de créer, par le sacrifice des ennemis de la chose publique, la sécurité, s'associe l'idée qu'il faut observer un minimum de formes.") Ibid., 469, 473. Caron clearly recognizes the link between popular sovereignty and violent sacrifice when he observes that state enemies were sacrificed in order to achieve security. What he does not discuss, however, is how the nature of those sacrificial acts reinforced the concept of sovereignty that authorized them.

55. The consequence of this fear is summed up by Antoine Joseph Gorsas in his newspaper, *Courrier des departments,* no. 4 (September 1792): "While more than a hundred thousand citizens flew to arms in order to proceed to the borders, a hundred thousand others, or rather all of Paris, led the way to the prisons filled with brigands with the intention of sacrificing all of them to public safety." ("Pendant que plus de cent mille citoyens volaient aux armes pour se porter aux frontières, cent mille autres, ou plutôt tout Paris, se sont rendus aux prisons encombrées de brigands avec l'intention de tout sacrifier à la sûreté publique.") Quoted in Gustave Gautherot, *Septembre 1792: Histoire politique des massacres* (Paris: Gabriel Beauchesne, 1927), 13.

56. Caron, *Les Massacres de septembre,* 149–150.

57. Cassagnac, *Histoire des Girondins,* vol. 2, 182, 199.

of victims, contributing to the idea, which circulated during the insurrection as well, that an extraordinary number of people were killed and that excessive violence was used.[58] Such exaggeration underscores the revolutionary conviction that violence and republican legitimacy were intimately connected: the greater the number of perceived victims, the more likely it was that the Republic would be successfully founded.

Although the French revolutionaries targeted scapegoats during both the August 10 insurrection and the September Massacres, the latter involved a more sophisticated and formalized ritual. Unlike the more public, spontaneous, and mass-based violence of August 10, the September Massacres were conducted inside prisons by relatively small groups of armed men. Revolutionaries who participated in the insurrection targeted victims who symbolized royalty, such as Suleau or the Swiss Guard. In contrast, the *septembriseurs,* as those who participated in the massacre were called, focused their violence on a more general category of revolutionary enemy. Finally, in many of the prisons, the revolutionaries created ad hoc tribunals to mete out summary justice, a ritual completely absent from the insurrection. It is in this respect that the September Massacres were unique: they demonstrated a collapse of the distinction between republican justice and sacrificial violence.

The violence of the September Massacres reflects the fact that the French revolutionaries perceived their political situation through a sacrificial lens. They viewed the still-living king, as well as his real and imagined supporters, as sources of dangerous contamination. Although the Republic had secured its legitimacy and begun the process of constitutional framing, the revolutionaries themselves remained deeply skeptical that such a political entity could survive without first purifying the Revolution of its contaminating enemies. In a report in the *Journal universel,* Xavier Audouin captures this sacrificial logic: "As I am finishing this article on the meeting, all of Paris has risen up; it is necessary, cry the citizens, that we get rid of all the enemies from within . . . Picks and sabers will suffice to throw down the counterrevolutionaries from within: here is the moment to achieve the Revolution, and to rid ourselves of the scoundrels who pollute the earth."[59] Audouin expresses the surprising claim that Parisians can finish the Revolution by eliminating its contaminating enemies. In suggesting that sacrificial violence can complete the foundation of the Republic, Audouin reveals

58. At the time of the massacre, some published accounts of the number of dead reached 10,000 people. Caron, *Les Massacres de septembre,* 76.

59. "Au moment où je finis cet article de la séance, tout Paris est levé; il faut que nous nous débarrassions, s'écrient les citoyens, de tous les ennemis du dedans . . . Les piques et les sabres suffiront pour jeter bas les contre-révolutionnaires du dedans: voilà le moment d'achever la Révolution, et de nous débarrasser des scélérats qui souillent la terre." Quoted in ibid., 451–452.

the mesmerizing power of sacrificial logic. With no mention of popular sovereignty or vengeance, Audouin appears unconcerned with the legitimacy of the
Republic. Instead, violence has a more concrete goal: the elimination of revolutionary enemies. This conception of revolutionary violence revives the connection between citizens and sacrificial violence that led Manuel, drawing from
the story of Brutus, to claim "one must always be ready to sacrifice everything,
up to one's children, to the happiness of one's country."

During the insurrection, sacrificial violence helped the revolutionaries to resolve the ambiguity of political power that was simultaneously royal and republican. When sacrifice took place in Parisian prisons, it too was administered
for the sake of resolving an ambiguity, but this time between friend and enemy.[60] Prisons provided the revolutionaries with an ideal solution to a thorny
problem of distinction: How did one identify an enemy of the republic? While
Swiss Guards and Prussians were easily identifiable scapegoats, many of the revolution's "internal" enemies were hidden from plain view. Prisons, however,
contained numerous identifiable revolutionary enemies such as aristocrats,
royalist sympathizers, Swiss Guards, and refractory priests. There were also hun-
dreds of common-law criminals, including thieves, counterfeiters, and prostitutes.[61] By virtue of being in jail, both common-law and political prisoners
assumed the same marginal status relative to the nation. By definition, prisoners are socially marginal because they have ostensibly violated some social or
legal norm. In *The Crowd and the French Revolution*, Georges Rudé notes that
the revolutionaries labeled this social class "les gens sans aveu," or "people without the oath," an indication that they had not sworn an oath to the Republic.[62]
In the case of political prisoners, such as priests and nobles, their marginality
was compounded by their social exoticness: they originated in distinct historical estates and were endowed with privileges that placed them outside the republican nation. As enemy aliens, prisoners were thus perfectly suited human
sacrifices for absorbing, through violence, the revolutionary fear of enemy subversion.

Inside prison walls, the *septembriseurs* ritualized sacrifice, illustrating an important transformation of revolutionary violence. The bloodshed typically be-

---

60. The Nazi jurist Carl Schmitt argues that the friend/enemy distinction is the foundation of all
politics: "The specific political distinction to which political actions and motives can be reduced is that
between friend and enemy." *The Concept of the Political* (Chicago: University of Chicago Press, 1996), 26.

61. Caron, *Les Massacres de septembre*, 99–102. "Refractory priests" refers to those clergy who refused
to administer the civil oath mandated by the revolutionary government.

62. Quoted in Brian Singer, "Violence in the French Revolution: Forms of Ingestion/Forms of Ex-
pulsion," in *The French Revolution and the Birth of Modernity*, ed. Ferenc Feher (Berkeley: University of
California Press, 1990), 154.

gan with the ritual formation of a "court," composed of up to twelve men, who assumed the roles of judge, jury, and executioner. These "tribunals" attempted to establish the guilt or innocence of prisoners by interrogating them about their personal histories and role in the Revolution. Prisoners found "guilty" were often immediately executed; those found "innocent" were sometimes granted their freedom. In setting up these courts and attempting to determine guilt, the revolutionaries demonstrated a concern with the formalism of republican justice. Without formal rules or procedures, however, these tribunals expressed unmitigated popular sovereignty, namely, revolutionary vigilantism. A simulacrum of judicial procedure and punishment, the September Massacres sought not to establish republican order by challenging and reorienting the symbols of monarchical power. Instead, the *septembriseurs* hoped to consolidate republican power by ritualizing the sacrificial purification of revolutionary enemies and thus to cleanse the republican body politic of human contamination. Rather than helping to create something new, such as a republic based on legitimate popular sovereignty, this sacrificial behavior sought to protect an existing republican authority from real and imagined threats.

The form of sacrifice that appeared during the September Massacres harkened back to the Roman and Christian sacrificial traditions. In the case of Roman sacrifice, Brutus oversaw the execution of his sons after they had been found guilty of treason. The founding of the Roman Republic thus involved a formal, legitimate judicial process followed by a sacrificial execution. In contrast, the *septembriseurs* substituted sacrificial finality for judicial formality. Without the law's support, the authors of the September Massacres simply repeated their sacrificial gestures in an effort to assuage republican insecurity through ritual purification. In this way, the September Massacres exemplified the unique revolutionary interpretation of the Brutus story, according to which citizens demonstrate their virtue through sacrificial repetition.

The September Massacres also included elements of the Christian sacrificial tradition. Some eyewitnesses reported that prisoners were given an unusually appetizing "Last Supper" before the massacres began.[63] In a twisted revision of Holy Communion, there are several versions of a story concerning Mademoiselle de Sombreuil, who was forced to drink a glass of blood in order to secure the freedom of her imprisoned father.[64] This story refers to the Eucharist, a

---

63. Buchez and Roux, *Histoire parlementaire de la Révolution*, 407.

64. This story resembles that of the king who was forced by the revolutionaries to drink a glass of red wine to the health of the new nation on July 20, 1792. In this case, wine, symbolizing blood and used during Communion, became the blood of the new nation being absorbed by the body of the old. Tulard, Fayard, and Fierro, *Histoire et dictionnaire*, 908.

commemoration of the Christian spiritual community through symbolic sacrifice and cannibalism. Finally, in his account of the massacre, Mathon de la Varenne explains how he was forced to take an oath on an altar of corpses:

> I crossed Ballets Street, which was covered on each side by a triple row of people of both sexes and of all ages. Reaching the end, I recoiled in horror upon noticing in the gutter a pile of corpses, soiled with mud and blood, on which I was forced to take an oath. A cutthroat had climbed on top and animated the others. I articulated the words that they demanded of me, when I was recognized by one of my old clients who was perchance passing by. He answered me, embraced me a thousand times, and got the very same massacrers to take pity on me.

> Je traversai ainsi la rue des Ballets, qui était couverte de chaque côté d'une triple haie de gens des deux sexes et de tous les âges. Parvenu au bout, je reculai d'horreur en apercevant dans le ruisseau un monceau de cadavres nus, souillés de boue et de sang, sur lesquels il me fallut prêter un serment. Un égorgeur était monté dessus et animait les autres. J'articulais les paroles qu'ils exigeaient de moi, quand je fus reconnu par un de mes anciens clients, qui sans doute passait par hasard. Il répondit de moi, m'embrassa mille fois, et apitoya en ma faveur les massacreurs mêmes.[65]

Varenne's experience suggests that the *septembriseurs* needed to adopt Christian rituals in order to highlight the sacred character of their required oath. Much in the same way that witnesses swear on Bibles in courts of law, Varenne was forced to take a republican oath at an altar of soiled bodies. In this specific case, the altar was comprised of "les gens sans aveu," the class of people considered outside the new national body and thus available for sacrifice. Varenne's vow is a reflection of the revolutionary belief that sacrificial violence was a consecrating act for republican legitimacy and identity. It is also a grisly illustration of how a new nation is formed on the bodies of the old.

The most renowned, gruesome sacrifice during the September Massacres involved Princess Marie-Thérèse de Savoie-Carignan de Lamballe. A confidante and servant to Marie-Antoinette, the princess escaped with the royal family to the National Assembly on August 10 and was imprisoned with them in the Temple until her transfer to another prison on August 19. All the accounts of the princess' death claim that she was asked to take an oath to liberty and equality and to denounce the royal family, all of which she refused to do.[66] Like Suleau

---

65. Quoted in Cassagnac, *Histoire des Girondins,* vol. 2, 411.

66. Mortimer-Ternaux, *Histoire de la Terreur,* vol. 3, 270. In another account, she is forced to give the oath at an altar of dead bodies, adding a religious element to the sacrifice. Camille Nash, *Death Comes to the Maiden* (London: Routledge, 1991), 127.

during the insurrection, she was beheaded by the revolutionaries, who paraded her head up to the Temple so that the royal family could see it.[67] It is not accidental that Lamballe and Suleau met the same sacrificial fate. In both cases, the people brought the heads of well-known royalists to places where the concentration of republican power outweighed that of the monarch. When Suleau's head was brought to the Manège, the king was hiding inside the building newly dedicated to the National Assembly. Similarly, at the Temple, the revolutionaries displayed the princess' head to the king who had been incarcerated by the republican government. In both instances of decapitation, parade, and display, the people chose a substitute for the king. By showing Lamballe's head to Louis XVI and his family, the revolutionaries conveyed their sovereignty and demonstrated, rather prophetically, that the only way to eradicate royal sovereignty was to remove its head.

Separated by only weeks, the August 10 insurrection and the September Massacres illustrate two different applications of sacrifice that share a similar logic. During the former, the revolutionaries engaged in spontaneous acts of sacrificial violence against victims "stained" by royalty. A violation of long-standing Western taboos, this sublime violence permitted the revolutionaries to benefit from a process of sacrificial exchange through which they transferred the unified, transcendent, and sacred power of the king to the people. In contrast, the September Massacres occurred after the legal powers of the king had been suspended and the Republic formally established. Unlike those who participated in the insurrection, the *septembriseurs* selected broad categories of sacrificial victims, subjecting them to mock judicial proceedings and punitive sacrifice. Prisoners were treated as an amorphous enemy who posed a general threat to the survival of the Republic, not a specific impediment to the establishment of popular sovereignty. Despite these differences, however, the September Massacres demonstrated the same sacrificial logic as the insurrection: the use of ritual violence to convert the impure, contaminating sources of social and political power into something useful to the Republic. Reflecting a changed political context and anxieties unique to rumor-filled Paris, the September Massacres initiated an effort to police sacrificially the definition of the new republican body politic. A nexus of the sacrificial and judicial, the massacres proved to be a rehearsal for the application of sacrificial logic to the problem of political consolidation.

---

67. The Temple, an ancient monastery in the center of Paris, was nationalized during the Revolution and served as a prison for the king and his family.

The Regicide of Louis XVI

The regicide of Louis XVI was the most extraordinary sacrifice of the Revolution because Louis was no ordinary being. In a singular body, he represented both God and the French people. Under normal circumstances, the king's death would do no harm to the French body politic, for even when the king is dead, his transcendent life is celebrated with the declaration "Long live the king." When the French revolutionaries decided to try Louis for treason, they embarked on a battle against this sacred royal power. During the trial, Louis invoked his inviolable right not to be judged by his subjects. In response, the revolutionaries referred to the king as Louis Capet in order to remind the French that all are equal in a republic. The revolutionaries ultimately subjected the king to the same death as common criminals: the guillotine. As he mounted the scaffold and prepared to die, however, Louis tried to shape the meaning of his sacrifice in ways that would perpetuate the monarchy. While the revolutionaries believed that the regicide would help to found and sanctify the republic, royalists viewed his death as a great martyrdom capable of extending the sacred power and glory of the French monarchy.

The regicide was the violent founding act of the French Republic. As a political event, the regicide had no precedent in French history because, unlike other monarchies, France had no ritual tradition of killing kings. Despite the fact that Louis died in the same manner as thousands of his former subjects, his execution was a sacred act. Neither the public sacrifices of aristocrats and royal guards nor the sacrificial massacres of political prisoners could effectively discredit Louis's divine right. On January 21, 1793, when the new nation sacrificed the embodiment of the old, it mounted a successful challenge to this divine authority through a violent process of sacred exchange. As a religious event, however, Louis's execution posed a grave threat to the Revolution. Because Louis XVI derived his power from God, the king's execution was tantamount to Christ's crucifixion, and thus a repetition of founding crime. Viewed as a martyr, Louis could redeem his subjects, providing a spiritual basis for a resurgent monarchism.

In keeping with Kantorowicz's claim that kings have two bodies, Louis's execution conjured two opposing sacrificial images. These images were based on the revolutionaries' and monarchists' attempts to portray the king as a "guilty" scapegoat and "innocent" martyr, respectively. Turning the king into a guilty sacrificial victim accomplished two goals. First, it allowed the French people to judge the king, whose inviolability otherwise rendered illegitimate any formal legal judgment against him. Second, by subjecting the king to a sacrificial process, the revolutionaries could invoke their own sacred power in order to capture the king's. The catharsis of the regicide would then leave the revolutionaries purified and renewed, able to wield kingly power without its corrupting effects.

Killing a French king, however, also required the undermining of the Christological concept of the body politic, an idea that anchored the royalist perception of the king as a great martyr for the French people. By rallying behind an "innocent" kingly martyr, royalists hoped to convert the king's death into a redemptive device that would permit the reestablishment of the throne. In this way, the regicide would achieve the opposite political effect of that expected by the revolutionaries. Cleansed of the sin of regicide by the king's "innocent" death, the French would participate in the restoration of the sacred Christian principles that supported the monarchy. The sacrifice of the king would thus be the salvation of the Old Regime, not the founding act of a new one.

Well aware of the sacrificial tradition from which he derived his power, Louis participated in his own martyrdom by announcing it to the French people. According to the executioner Charles-Henri Sanson, the king exclaimed, moments before his death, "Frenchmen, you see your king ready to die for you. May my blood cement your happiness. I die innocent of all of which I am accused."[68] These few sentences contain the necessary elements of Christian martyrdom. The king self-consciously recognizes that his death is a sacrifice for the French people. He offers his ephemeral physical body, symbolized by his blood, for his eternal corporate body, which encompasses the whole the French nation. Like Christ, who was perceived to have died innocently on the cross, the king died "innocently" on the scaffold in order to redeem the French people for the sin of bringing the Revolution. In proclaiming his innocence, the king also powerfully affirmed his connection to the church and thus to the religiously sanctioned social and political hierarchies contested by the Revolution. The deep historical connection between crown and scepter was underscored by Louis's priest, who on the scaffold was reported to have taken the king's confession and then to have said to the condemned monarch: "Sire . . . resign yourself to this last sacrifice by which you will more closely resemble the God who will reward you for it."[69] Acknowledging the king's divinity, the priest confirmed that the sacred power of the monarch could, by virtue of his sacrifice for the French people, extend itself beyond the grave.

Despite the king's effort to be a martyr, the French monarchy ended precisely

---

68. "Français . . . vous voyez votre roi prêt à mourir pour vous. Puisse mon sang cimenter votre bonheur. Je meurs innocent de tout ce dont on m'accuse." Quoted in Sanson, *Sept générations d'exécuteurs*, vol. 3, 478.

69. "Sire . . . résignez-vous à ce dernier sacrifice par lequel vous ressemblerez davantage au Dieu qui va vous en récompenser." Ibid., 477.

the way it began: by baptism. The French became royal subjects when Clovis was baptized with holy water; they became republican citizens when they baptized themselves in the king's blood. Like holy water, the king's blood was sacred. Although the revolutionaries considered the king to be traitorous, corrupt, and contaminating, they also imagined his spilt blood to have precisely the opposite characteristics. Camille Desmoulins wrote in *Histoire secrète de la Révolution* that the king's blood would "seal the decree which declares France a republic," illustrating that he viewed royal blood as pure and binding, like the king's official stamp authorizing the Republic.[70] Similarly, on January 26, 1792, Louis Marie Prudhomme remarked in his journal *Les Révolutions de Paris:* "The blood of Capet, shed by the sword of the law on the 21st of January 1793, washes from us a stain thirteen hundred years old. We became republicans only on Monday the 21st, and not till then had we the right to consider ourselves a model for neighboring countries."[71] Prudhomme also imagined the king's blood to be pure and thus able to cleanse republican bodies of the monarchist "stain." He explains how the blood of the monarch, violently released from his body by the "sword of the law" (i.e., the guillotine), "washes" away the political symbolism of the king's physical body. With the elimination of the king's corpus, new, cleansed republican bodies emerge. Through the conduit of the king's purified blood, the sacred authority of the royal body was transferred to the many republican ones.

Immediately after Louis XVI was executed, his blood became a source of intense public fascination. Some eyewitnesses to the regicide observed that French people soaked up the king's blood with their clothing and tried to obtain physical mementos of the fallen monarch, such as locks of his hair. In a particularly vivid account of this frenzy, Baudrais writes:

> One citizen even climbed onto the guillotine, and thrusting his bare arm deep into Capet's blood, which had flowed in abundance, took handfuls of clots and three times sprayed the watching crowd, who thronged forward under the scaffold so that each might receive a drop on the forehead. "Brothers," cried the citizen, "we have been told that the blood of Louis Capet would be upon our heads. Well, so be it! How often did he not soak his hands in our blood! Republicans, the blood of a king brings good fortune!"[72]

70. Quoted in Arasse, *The Guillotine and the Terror*, 61.
71. Ibid., 61–62.
72. Ibid., 61–65. Arasse is skeptical of Baudrais's description, remarking that he "was no doubt taking too literally the sacred connotations of speeches made in the Assembly." Arasse may be correct to point out Baudrais's exaggeration, but Arasse also clearly illustrates that many revolutionaries viewed the royal execution in Christian and baptismal terms. Furthermore, he offers evidence of the public's fascination with the king's blood and personal items in chapter 2, "The Death of the King."

This description of the anointing of the Republic offers remarkable insight into the sacrificial nature of the king's execution. Although it was patriotic brothers who killed the king, the republican sacrifice, with its familial metaphors, is reminiscent of Brutus' filicide. Mixing sacrificial traditions, the citizen who showers his compatriots with blood inverts Clovis' baptism, thus invoking Christian sacrificial rites. The crowd is sprayed three times, a dramatization of the connection between the Holy Trinity and the republican one of liberty, equality, and fraternity. This use of Catholic purification and initiation rites to found the French Republic illustrates how the revolutionaries co-opted the Christian symbols of royal sovereignty. Baudrais's account of the regicide thus marries elements of Christian sacrifice with those of Rome, revealing the novelty of the modern French sacrificial tradition.

The significance of the king's execution for the foundation of the republic was not lost on the authors of the Revolution. In their view, the regicide ended the sacred mystique that had long supported French monarchical power. By desecrating the king, sacrificial violence fostered the emergence of republican power and identity, just as it had started to do during the August 10 insurrection. Unlike this previous episode, however, the regicide offered the French revolutionaries the appearance of finality. With Louis beheaded and the monarchy crushed, it appeared to revolutionaries such as Robespierre that the sacrifice of the king had accomplished a foundational act: "The tyrant has fallen under the sword of the law. This great act of justice has dismayed the aristocracy, destroyed royalist superstition, and created the republic. It imparts tremendous character to the National Convention and renders it worthy of the confidence of the French people."[73]

Robespierre describes the fruits of the regicide: the establishment of authority and the consolidation of identity. Before the king's execution, the insurrection and September Massacres had anticipated these outcomes. With the drop of the guillotine's blade, the French violated the most dangerous political taboo, marking a fundamental transition in time, space, and meaning with a sublime sacrificial spectacle. Louis XVI was sacrificed for a new body politic authorized by popular sovereignty and composed of republican citizens. Gathered around the decapitated body, the French people admired the king's power even as they took possession of it. The king's sacrifice marked the culmination of a largely uncoordinated process by which the French retrieved ancient sacrificial ideas and incorporated them into their radical political designs. Despite all the his-

---

73. "Le tyran est tombé sous le glaive des lois. Ce grand acte de justice a consterné l'aristocratie, anéanti la superstition royale, et crée la république. Il imprime un grand caractère à la Convention nationale, et la rend digne de la confiance des français." Maximilien Robespierre, *Œuvres complètes de Robespierre*, vol. 5 (Gap: Imprimerie Louis-Jean, 1961), 227.

torical interpretations and revisions of the Revolution, Louis's extraordinary death remains the central founding act of the modern French Republic.

From Foundation to Conservation: The Reign of Terror

The infamous Reign of Terror began shortly after the regicide. The most extreme period of revolutionary bloodshed, the Terror has added its name to the modern lexicon of violence, describing secret police, social paralysis, paranoia, excessive violence, and unchecked state power. The Terror marks the first time in history that the practice of sacrificial violence became formalized and routine. An extended repetition of the regicide, yet marked by sacrificial formations common to the September Massacres, the Terror involved the public guillotining of revolutionary enemies in an effort to purify the newly founded republic. Camille Desmoulins underscores this view when he describes the guillotine as a tool of national purification: "With every passing year the national representation grows purer."[74] Despite the revolutionaries' wish that the guillotine perform this sacrificial function, evidence from the Terror suggests that it achieved precisely the opposite effect: rather than purifying the Republic of its enemies, the guillotine was quickly perceived as its greatest source of contamination. The Terror ultimately demonstrated that the repetition of sacrificial violence emphasizes the repulsive negativity of sublime violence, a phenomenon that first appeared during the September Massacres.

The Terror exhibited many of the same sacrificial formations found during earlier revolutionary bloodshed. Just like the violence of August 10, the Terror remained a public spectacle, which initially attracted large crowds. Republican control of enemies' severed heads continued to be an important performative ritual during executions. According to Henri Sanson, "Since the people became partial to torture, they demanded that we show them the heads, which the guillotine had just knocked down. The movement of pity that momentarily softened the multitude dissipated with the life of the victim, and a thousand voices called for the complement to the spectacle."[75] Additionally, the Terror borrowed ritual components from the September Massacres, such as the use of judicial

74. Arasse, *The Guillotine and the Terror*, 78.
75. "Depuis que le peuple devenait friand de supplices, il exigeait qu'on lui montrât les têtes que la guillotine venait d'abattre. Le mouvement de pitié qui, pendant un instant, avait attendri la multitude s'en était allé avec la vie du patient, et mille voix réclamaient le complément du spectacle." Sanson, *Sept générations d'exécuteurs*, vol. 3, 426. Sanson's grandfather, Charles-Henri Sanson, recounts the story of how, on the occasion of the first execution by guillotine at the Place du Carrousel, he asked his assistant to raise the severed head of the victim. Upon doing so, the assistant fell backward as a result of what the

proceedings and absurdly general criteria for the selection of victims. Finally, the regicide lent to the Terror the politico-religious symbolism that had allowed the revolutionaries to believe that violence facilitated political anointment and transformation.

The Terror's perpetuation of sacrificial violence, however, occurred in a novel legal context. In contrast to preregicidal and regicidal violence, the Terror was legally sanctioned by the republican state. Although certain elements of the Terror—secret police, summary judgment, and public executions—existed before the regicide, it was not until the creation of the Revolution Tribunal (March 10, 1793), the establishment of the Committee of Public Safety (April 6, 1793), and the fall of the Girondins (June 2, 1793) that the Terror fully commenced. The Terror passed its first major legal hurdle with the passage of the Law of Suspects on September 17, 1793, which defined the enemies of the state so broadly that virtually anyone could be arrested. It reached its legal apex with the Law of 22 Prairial (June 10, 1794). By broadening the definition of "suspects" and eliminating all procedural formality from the courts, this law systematized the ritual elements of the September Massacres, ensuring the state's victims quick, summary justice.

The Terror legalized sacrifice in order to regenerate the sacred basis of state legitimacy, which originated during the regicide. The goal of the Terror was to preserve the Republic through punishment, not to challenge the sacred symbols and representatives of royal power. Sacrificial violence practiced during the insurrection and September Massacres sought to generate legitimacy because the Republic lacked legality. These sacrificial episodes used violence to create a reverential sense of awe, the positive, attractive aspect of sublimity. As such, they mimicked the moral feelings invoked by sacred events, such as religious activities and ritual ceremonies of state. Once legal and placed in the service of a fragile Republic, however, sacrifice generated a sacred dynamic that was contaminating rather than purifying. By seeking to produce the sacredness of authority—its legitimacy—while maintaining its legality, the revolutionaries collapsed the necessary distinction between pure and abject power, turning sacrifice against the Republic. François Furet sheds light on this curious reversal when he argues that the Terror created a surfeit of legitimacy, purchased at the expense of all legality:

---

grandfather describes as a "sudden apoplexy" ("apoplexie foudroyante"), killing the assistant. Even the executioners were not habituated to the spectacle of violence demanded by the onlookers. Ibid., 426–427.

Revolutionary power depends for its survival on the constant projection of an image that shows it to be wholly consubstantial with, indeed, equivalent to the "people"; if ejected from that symbolic position, it yields to the group or the leader who, in denouncing it, restores the consubstantiality and equivalence that have been endangered. The Revolution had no legality, only a legitimacy . . . After the fall of Robespierre it lost all legitimacy; all it had left was legality (even when it violated it).[76]

According to Furet, the Terror attempted to create a perfect identity between the people and its representatives. Because state legitimacy was based on an ever-fluctuating "will of the people," violence became the means by which the state maintained this "consubstantiality," and thus its legitimacy. Furet, however, underestimates the extent to which the French perceived the Terror as legal violence and thus subversive of state legitimacy. When sacrifice became an expression of the law itself, not only did it lose its creative force; it became a fetter on the process of political foundation. Before the regicide, sacrifice could serve as an expression of popular sovereignty because it was not legal. Afterward, however, sacrificial violence was impotent to legitimize a government whose authority already rested upon legality. Thus, Furet is not entirely correct when he argues that "the Revolution had no legality, only a legitimacy." Rather, because the Revolution had legality during the Terror, its use of sacrifice undermined its legitimacy.[77]

The Terror subverted state legitimacy by circulating powerful feelings of sacred negativity among the French. In his fascinating analysis of the guillotine, Daniel Arasse ascribes a religious quality to the Terror: "The Terror consisted very largely in the ritual repetition of this initial sacrifice [the king], and the guillotine, 'ensign of so many a massacre,' in Cabanis's words, was able to assume the status of the altar at which the new religion was celebrated."[78] Religious rituals typically invoke divinity in order to provide their participants with a life-affirming, transcendent experience. In contrast, as the Terror escalated, the use of the guillotine to celebrate the "new religion" transformed the extraordinary spectacle of public sacrifice into something utterly malevolent. Instead of asso-

76. François Furet, *Interpreting the French Revolution,* trans. Elborg Forster (Cambridge: Cambridge University Press, 1981), 74.

77. Jean-Clément Martin also argues that there is a connection between revolutionary violence and legitimacy. He claims that, in suspending the transcendent legitimacy of political power, the Revolution created a weak state that relied on violence in order to maintain order. The Terror, representing the apex of this expression of violence, was thus a political expedient, replacing legitimate power. Martin's position contrasts with my argument that, in the early part of the Revolution, sacrificial violence was constitutive of political legitimacy. Jean-Clément Martin, "Un bicentenaire en cache un autre repenser la terreur?" *Annales historiques de la Révolution française,* no. 3 (1994), 517–526.

78. Arasse, *The Guillotine and the Terror,* 73.

ciating sacrificial violence with purity and cleanliness, the French began to perceive the Terror in terms of radical contamination. Henri Sanson captures this perception in his citation of a section of his grandfather Charles-Henri Sanson's journal:

> 3 Floréal. Great citizens and good men follow one another continuously to the guillotine. How many of them will it yet devour? Those who govern us should nevertheless realize that this daily butchery has become quite odious. The boors of the guillotine have themselves lost their intensity and their rage, and as for the real citizens, it was nothing like in Pluviôse. When the tumbrels arrive, it is as if the plague were passing by: doors, shop windows, all are closed, the street is deserted; when we cross it with our following of howlers and furies, one would say that we are entering the city of *Sleeping Beauty*.

> 3 floréal. Les grands citoyens, les hommes de bien se succèdent sans interruption à la guillotine. Combien en dévorera-t-elle encore? Ceux qui nous gouvernent devraient cependant s'apercevoir que cette boucherie quotidienne est devenue bien odieuse. Les goujats de la guillotine ont perdu eux-mêmes de leur chaleur et de leur rage, et quant aux véritables citoyens, c'est bien autre chose qu'en pluviôse. Lorsque les charrettes arrivent, c'est comme si la peste allait passer: portes, fenêtres boutiques, tout est clos, la rue est déserte; quand nous la traversons avec notre suite d'aboyeurs et de furies, on dirait que nous entrons dans la ville de *la Belle au Bois dormant*.[79]

Sanson describes the pernicious effects of repetitious sacrificial violence: the French began to treat the guillotine as a harbinger of the plague, an experience that the executioner describes as akin to a fantasy. The bloody machine used by the revolutionary government to eliminate its enemies became a source of contamination in the eyes of its principal audience. Intended to purify the republican body of aliens and enemies, the Terror served only to sully the newborn regime.

Maximilien Robespierre as Scapegoat

The ninth of Thermidor, Year II (1794), is well known to all French people as the day when the republican dictatorship ended with the fall and execution of its principal author, Maximilien Robespierre. Less obviously, the ninth of Thermidor also marks the second and final "regicide" of the French Revolution. If

---

79. Sanson, *Sept générations d'exécuteurs*, vol. 5, 111.

the sacrifice of Louis XVI desecrated the French monarchy and transferred its sacred power to the Republic, the execution of Robespierre repeated the legendary crime for the sake of social peace. This time, however, the "regicide" of Robespierre resolved political ambiguity created when the king lost his head. The first regicide left unanswered the question of whether the king had died a sacrifice for the new republic or a martyr for the Old Regime. That ambiguity was compounded by the fact that the revolutionary government viewed its power in monarchical terms and exercised it despotically. In other words, it appeared to many of the French that the execution of the king had served only to create a monstrous regime that looked like a republic but acted even more tyrannically than a monarchy.

As the Terror intensified and became increasingly despised, all eyes shifted to the man who once symbolized the greatness of the Revolution. Like the king, but unlike most of the thousands of victims who perished during the Terror, Robespierre was an extraordinary victim. A highly visible leader of the revolutionary government, Robespierre acted as if he were above the laws, which he had helped to create. Even worse, his single-minded effort to purge the Revolution of its enemies had unleashed a torrent of violent contamination that ultimately congealed around him. Unable to orchestrate the use of sacrificial violence in order to gather and bond new republican citizens, Robespierre became one of the final victims of that sacrificial logic. More than any other leader of the Revolution, Robespierre wanted to die for the people. Ultimately, he did, but according to conditions completely different from those which he had imagined.

As Robespierre became increasingly obsessed with his own death, he articulated the quintessential republican founder's fantasy: to die for the people. Robespierre wanted to perish a revolutionary martyr, immortalized for eternity like his friend Le Peletier and his rival Marat. Because, however, he considered himself a much greater man than those who had passed before him, he imagined an epic martyrdom through which he would take his rightful place among the most famous martyrs in Western history. In his *Lettres à ses commettants,* Robespierre writes:

> Read history, and you will see that the benefactors of humanity were its martyrs. Aegis is condemned by the Ephesians for having wanted to reestablish the laws of Lycurgus; Cato cuts out his entrails, the second Brutus is reduced to plucking his own life after having taken the tyrant's; the son of Mary expires under the blows of tyranny; Socrates drinks the hemlock; [Algernon] Sidney dies on the scaffold.

> Lisez l'histoire, vous verrez que les bienfaiteurs de l'humanité en furent les martyrs. Agis est condamné par les éphores pour avoir voulu rétablir les lois de Li-

curgue; Caton déchire ses entrailles, le second des Brutus est réduit à s'arracher la
vie après l'avoir enlevée au tyran; le fils de Marie, expire sous les coups de la tyrannie; Socrate boit la ciguë; Sydnei meurt sur un échafaud.[80]

Comparing his own fate to the tragic deaths of past saviors, Robespierre imagined the company he would keep after dying for the well-being of the French
Republic. He wanted to sacrifice his life for republican citizens in precisely the
same way that Louis XVI hoped to shed his blood for royal subjects. Ironically,
Robespierre hoped that martyrdom would grant him immortality, a distinction
that he desperately wanted to forbid the king. Illustrating how the revolutionaries mixed their sacrificial traditions, Robespierre sought to blend his Roman
sacrificial credentials with Christ's.

"Everyone dies," writes Robespierre, "including the heroes of humanity and
the tyrants who oppress it—but in different conditions."[81] Robespierre did not
believe that he would die according to the same conditions as the king, but he
nonetheless imagined himself to be kingly and divine. A representative of the
people, Robespierre understood that he did not possess two bodies, one
ephemeral, and the other immortal. Yet Robespierre placed himself at the center of a fabricated divinity when he gathered Paris together to celebrate his civil
religion, the Cult of the Supreme Being, just one month before he died. In his
famous speech introducing the idea of the Cult of the Supreme Being, Robespierre began to speak like Louis XVI: "I am French; I am one of your representatives . . . O sublime people! Receive the sacrifice of all my being; happy is
the one born among you! Happier still is he who can die for your happiness!"[82]

This passage remarkably parallels the king's last words. Robespierre asserts his
nationality and uses a possessive pronoun to describe his representation of the
French people. Similarly, the king begins his final address with the word
"Frenchmen" and, with a possessive pronoun, reminds them that he is their king.
Robespierre offers the French his "being," the king his blood. Both recognize
the sacrificial nature of their martyrdom. Moreover, both recognize that their
sacrifice is for the happiness of the French people. The two sacrificial statements, however, depart on the issue of innocence. The king declares himself in-

---

80. Robespierre, Œuvres, vol. 5, 114.

81. "Tout meurt, & les héros de l'humanité & les tyrans qui l'oppriment; mais à des conditions dif-
férentes." Robespierre, Œuvres complètes, vol. 10 (Paris: Presses Universitaires de France, 1967), 182.

82. "Je suis Français, je suis l'un de tes représentants . . . O peuple sublime! Reçois le sacrifice de tout
mon être; heureux celui qui est né au milieu de toi! plus heureux celui qui peut mourir pour ton bonheur!" Ibid., 445. Before he died, the king exclaimed: "Frenchmen, you see your king ready to die for
you. May my blood cement your happiness. I die innocent of all that I have been accused of." ("Français
. . . vous voyez votre roi prêt à mourir pour vous. Puisse mon sang cimenter votre bonheur. Je meurs innocent de tout ce dont on m'accuse.")

nocent of the charge of traitorousness. Robespierre—widely known as the Incorruptible—believes himself to be innocent in his capacity as founder, representative, and citizen. Finally, unlike the king who used the formal *vous,*
reminding the French of his royal, paternal authority, Robespierre uses the informal *tu,* communicating to his revolutionary brothers that he is their equal.

Just as the revolutionaries refused to grant Louis XVI his innocence, they also
came to disbelieve Robespierre's. The French recognized that one of the principal architects of the Terror had betrayed the very principles for which he hoped
to give his life. His innocence betrayed by his brutality, Robespierre was transformed in the eyes of his compatriots. Hoping to offer the Revolution a redemptive closure, to die for the citizens an innocent and virtuous republican,
Robespierre instead became a scapegoat, blamed for everything wrong with the
Revolution. Robespierre describes this transformation:

> They said to the nobles: it is he alone who has abolished you; at the same time,
> they said to the patriots: he wants to save the nobles; they said to the priests: it is
> he alone who pursues you; without him you would be peaceful and triumphant;
> they said to the fanatics: it is he who destroys religion; they said to the persecuted
> patriots: it is he who commanded it [persecution] or who does not want to pre-
> vent it. They accused me of everything whose causes I could not prevent, in say-
> ing: Your fate depends on him alone. Men stationed in public places were
> fomenting this system every day; it occurred where the Revolutionary Tribunal
> meets, where the country's enemies expiate their crimes; they were saying: there
> are the unfortunate condemned; who in the world is the cause of it? Robespierre.
> They were particularly attached to proving that the Revolutionary Tribunal was a
> court of blood, created by me alone, and that I completely directed the massacre
> of all the good people as well as all the rascals, for they wanted to incite against me
> every kind of enemy.

> On disait aux nobles: C'est lui seul qui vous a proscrits; on disait en même temps
> aux patriotes: Il veut sauver les nobles; on disait aux prêtres: C'est lui seul qui vous
> poursuit; sans lui vous seriez paisibles et triomphants; on disait aux fanatiques: C'est
> lui qui détruit la religion; on disait aux patriotes persécutés: C'est lui qui l'a or-
> donné ou qui ne veut pas l'empêcher. On me renvoyait toutes les plaintes dont je
> ne pouvais faire cesser les causes, en disant: Votre sort dépend de lui seul. Des
> hommes apostés dans les lieux publics propageaient chaque jour ce système; il
> y en avait dans le lieu des séances du Tribunal révolutionnaire, dans les lieux où
> les ennemis de la patrie expient leurs forfaits; ils disaient: Voilà des malheureux
> condamnés; qui est-ce qui en est la cause? Robespierre. On s'est attaché partic-
> ulièrement à prouver que le Tribunal révolutionnaire était un tribunal de sang, créé
> par moi seul, et que je maîtrisais absolument pour faire égorger tous les gens de

bien et même tous les fripons, car on voulait me susciter des ennemis de tous les genres.[83]

Robespierre illuminates the sacrificial construction of "guilt," whereby the French have molded Robespierre into a scapegoat by blaming him for all of their misfortunes. Although Robespierre wanted to die like a martyred king, he soon recognized that his fate would instead be identical with that of a kingly scapegoat. When Louis XVI died on the scaffold, however, his historical access to the Christian sacrificial tradition complicated the meaning of his death, making it difficult for his sacrifice to bond a newly formed and deeply divided nation. In essence, Louis was the scapegoat of an aristocratic society in the throes of a social and political revolution. In contrast, Robespierre was the scapegoat of a republic seeking to reaffirm the principles of its recent birth. Unlike January 21, 1793, the ninth of Thermidor 1794 brought a universally hated figure to the scaffold.

The French revolutionaries believed that the regicide would peacefully inaugurate the new Republic. Sacrificial ideas borrowed from the Romans and early Christians, as well as sacrificial practices that appeared during the August 10 insurrection and the September Massacres, led the revolutionaries to believe that political foundation required the spilling of sacrificial blood. Even after the Republic was founded, sacrificial logic pointed to violence as a fount of republican legitimacy and identity. This ideology culminated in the regicide of Louis XVI, whose highly symbolic death, like a tapestry, wove together different facets of French sacrificial ideas and practices. The French revolutionaries were cognizant that a particular form of violence had played a significant role in the birth of the French Republic, but they did not fully understand its meaning or use. The Terror illustrates this misunderstanding as the French revolutionaries employed sacrifice as a violent and counterproductive instrument for the conservation of the state.

Although Robespierre's death brought an end to the vicious cycle of sacrificial violence that characterized the French Revolution from 1792 to 1794, it only heightened the peculiar French fascination with and intellectualization of this form of bloodshed. The French revolutionaries sent their former king to the guillotine in an effort to consecrate their novel political project, to make holy a republic that challenged the sacred authority of the king. The French also sent their most famous revolutionary leader to the guillotine because he, unlike the king, belonged to the very political body from which and for which he was sacrificed. Robespierre's death offered his compatriots no redemption,

83. Ibid., 558.

only solace for the lamentable fact that bloody execution and political constitution, combined, promote social ties that bind. In a poem written only a few
months before he died and preserved by his sister Charlotte, Robespierre expresses this sentiment with striking clarity:

> The sole torment of the just, at his last hour,
> And the only one that will tear me apart,
> It is to see, while dying, the pale and somber desire
> To distill shame and infamy on my brow,
> To die for the people and yet be abhorred for it.

> Le seul tourment du juste, à son heure dernière,
> Et le seul dont alors je serai déchiré,
> C'est de voir, en mourant, la pâle et sombre envie
> Distiller sur mon front l'opprobre et l'infamie,
> De mourir pour le peuple et d'en être abhorré.[84]

84. Quoted in Jean Bernard, *Quelques poésies de Robespierre* (Paris: Imprimerie R. Thoms, 1890), mi-
crofilm, Bibliothèque National de France, 8 Ye 2605.

CHAPTER 2

Joseph de Maistre and the Politics
of Conservative Regeneration

In September 1792, just as the Reign of Terror was beginning to unfold, Joseph de Maistre fled his home in Chambéry, then part of the kingdom of Piedmont-Sardinia, in an effort to avoid the invading French troops. Both before and after his exile, Maistre assiduously followed revolutionary events with fascination and increasing concern. As the Revolution radicalized and became more violent, his tentative and skeptical enthusiasm for certain aspects of it gave way to a deep hostility. Maistre came to reject every conceivable facet of the Revolution, an attitude that he articulated in a sophisticated and trenchant critique titled *Considérations sur la France*. In certain respects, his analysis of the Revolution was typical of a conservative eighteenth-century thinker. Maistre passionately defended monarchism and Catholicism, the political and religious pillars of hierarchy, order, and faith. Revolutionary excesses left no doubt in Maistre's mind that a secular republic could never rule France successfully. He was particularly dismayed by the spectacle of revolutionary violence. In his view, the regicide of Louis XVI was the greatest crime committed by the French in their effort to found a new political regime. For this collective sin, God punished the French by subjecting them to the Terror.[1] It was by way of this providential interpretation of the French Revolution that Maistre became the first French intellectual to offer a theoretical critique of sacrificial violence in the service of political foundation.

---

1. Although Maistre was devoutly Catholic throughout his life, his religious beliefs were strongly influenced by his participation in "illuminist" French Freemasonry as well as by the mystical writings of Saint-Martin. For further information on this subject, see Antoine Faivre, "Maistre and Willermoz," and Jean Rebotton, "Josephus à Floribus," in *Maistre Studies,* ed. and trans. Richard Lebrun (Lanham, Md.: University Press of America, 1988). Additional scholarship on Maistre's religious influences can be found in Richard Lebrun, *Joseph de Maistre: An Intellectual Militant* (Kingston, Ont.: McGill-Queen's University Press, 1988), 53–69, 143.

Although the French Revolution inspired Maistre's theoretical reflections on violence and sacrifice, his inquiry into the meaning of sacrificial bloodshed is framed by larger, theological concerns. "There is," writes Maistre, "a *satanic* character to the French Revolution that distinguishes it from everything that we have seen, and perhaps from anything that we will see."[2] According to Maistre, the Revolution was an extraordinary act of political evil that combined elements of human folly as well as divine intervention. Paradoxically, however, Maistre contends that the purpose of revolutionary violence was to regenerate the morality of the French people, leading them from republican sin to monarchist salvation. This providential reading of revolutionary events is rooted in Maistre's belief that some forms of violence are salutary. More specifically, he makes two claims about the regenerative capacity of violence. Divinely sanctioned punitive violence expiates a victim's guilt by spilling his or her blood. Conversely, Maistre argues that divinely authorized sacrificial violence redeems a guilty collectivity by spilling a victim's "innocent" blood. This sacrificial logic is precisely that which Louis XVI invoked on the scaffold moments before his execution. In short, Maistre turns revolutionary violence against the instauration of the French Republic by calling upon the Christian sacrificial tradition and tying it to a political theology of conservative regeneration. By refusing to abandon the idea that certain forms of sacrifice participate in the violent regeneration of morals, however, Maistre unintentionally generates a theoretical justification for the revolutionary practices of violence that he despises and thus anticipates the work of the twentieth-century radicals Georges Sorel and Georges Bataille.

Maistre argues that revolutionary violence achieves moral restoration only when it is an expression of divine punishment. In Maistre's opinion, the French needed violent purification because they suffered from cultural and moral decadence. He maintained that late eighteenth-century French society suffered from a corrupt clergy, bad political leaders, and sophistical *philosophes,* all of whom contributed to a monstrous, anti-Catholic, antimonarchical revolution. The violence of the Terror thus punished the French for straying from king and church. God's retribution also worked secretly: while they thought they were dismantling the Old Regime in order to build a new republic, the revolutionaries were actually participating in a divine tragedy in which they would be the principal victims. As the core of this tragedy, the Terror served the purpose of conservative moral regeneration by applying violence to the restoration of the social and political equilibrium disturbed by the regicide.

Despite his reactionary perspective, Maistre's theological evaluation of the

---

2. "Il y a dans la Révolution française un caractère *satanique* qui la distingue de tout ce qu'on a vu, et peut-être de tout ce qu'on verra." Maistre, *Ecrits sur la Révolution* (Paris: Quadrige/Presses Universitaires de France, 1989), 132.

French Revolution allows him to consider the politics of sacrifice in a modern light. Maistre condemns the scapegoating conducted by the French revolutionaries, calling it a violent, anti-Christian consequence of political foundation. The revolutionaries imagined that republican foundation required sacrificial victims whose sublimity would desacralize the king and confer legitimate power to the people. In contrast, Maistre argues that scapegoating is always a degenerate sacrificial practice that results from a fundamental misunderstanding about how sacrifice redeems. By undertaking a theological critique of revolutionary violence, Maistre illuminates the revolutionaries' distinctly modern dilemma: human political foundation without divine intervention. Maistre's response to the revolutionaries—and Machiavelli—is that lasting, legitimate sovereignty always begins through miraculous political creation. Human beings cannot make politics; they can, however, regenerate decadent politics by spilling blood. Political regeneration is a moral enterprise that involves war, punishment, and martyrdom, the only form of sacrifice that receives Maistre's approval. As the first to theorize revolutionary bloodshed, Maistre challenges the political efficacy of sacrificial victimization and states unequivocally that sacrifice cannot be placed in the service of modern political foundation.

Although Maistre believed that the French Revolution was doomed to fail, he never abandoned the idea that certain forms of sacrifice are politically and religiously useful. In this respect, Maistre repeated the mistake of the French revolutionaries. Thanks to their recognition of the important role of sacrifice in French Catholicism as well as their fascination with Roman antiquity, the French revolutionaries imagined that a variety of sacrificial practices would help them to found a republic. While Maistre is explicit in his hatred of political scapegoating, which the revolutionaries learned from the Romans, Maistre continues to celebrate the value of self-sacrifice—both real and symbolic—for the perpetuation of monarchism and Catholicism. This attempt to distinguish "good" sacrifice from "bad" demonstrates Maistre's unwillingness to abandon the sacrificial dynamics that had originally motivated the French revolutionaries. By attributing to certain forms of violent sacrifice the same regenerative and redemptive ideas as the revolutionaries, Maistre actually contributes to the modern, political appeal of martyrdom. Maistre also subverts his critique of the Revolution by claiming, in effect, that sacrificial violence operates just as the revolutionaries expected it would.

Maistre's conception of sacrifice illustrates the self-subverting nature of his theoretical critique of the Revolution. Maistre conceives of sacrifice in sacred terms and recognizes that, historically speaking, it possesses an intrinsic ambiguity that structures the meaning of the ritual destruction of human beings. In his slim work on sacrifice, *Eclaircissement sur les sacrifices,* Maistre reveals this ambiguity etymologically: "We see here why the word *sacred* (SACER) was taken in Latin in good and bad senses, why the same word in Greek (ΟΣΙΣ) signifies equally that which is holy and that which is profane."[3] The etymology of "sacred" suggests that both the Greeks and Romans imbued their sacrificial victims with sacred ambiguity: guilty criminals and innocent victims possessed both positive and negative sacred attributes. According to Maistre, ancient sacrificial rites resolved this sacred ambiguity through a process of exchange, which permitted the destruction of an innocent victim to purify a guilty community. In sacrificing humans to the gods in a pre-Christian world, the ancients sought to harness the expiatory power of this violent metamorphosis.

Despite his appreciation of sacred ambiguity, Maistre attempts to maintain a strict moral divide between different forms of sacrifice. For instance, even though Catholicism taught Maistre that all human sacrifice or scapegoating is an abomination conducted by depraved people, he praises martyrdom because it models Christ's crucifixion. This rigid distinction between sacrificial victimization and self-sacrifice is sometimes obscured in Maistre's oeuvre, where he appears to glorify human sacrifice, suggesting that it is a necessary aspect of the human experience.[4] Similarly, when Maistre discusses different forms of violence, such as the Terror, he often refuses to characterize them as sacrificial despite their being amenable to such interpretation. Thus, reading Maistre's work on sacrifice requires an appreciation of the tension between his dogmatic Catholicism and pessimistic realism. When Maistre argues that violence is endemic to the human condition and that sacrifice—human sacrifice—is one of its principal, redemptive modalities, he illustrates this tension. If humans act violently, they must do so for a good reason, even if their violent conduct is morally repugnant. This attitude ultimately frames Maistre's critique of French revolutionary violence, which depends on his ability to maintain this strict but fragile moral divide.

Maistre's understanding of guilt and innocence offers another illustration of his need to maintain strict moral delineations between different forms of vio-

---

3. "On voit ici pourquoi le mot *sacré* (SACER) était pris dans la langue latine en bonne et en mauvaise part, pourquoi le même mot dans la langue grecque (ΟΣΙΣ) signifie également ce qui est saint et ce qui est profane." Joseph de Maistre, *Eclaircissement sur les sacrifices*, in *Sur les sacrifices* (Paris: Pocket, 1994), 35. Maistre's use of the word *éclaircissement*, or "enlightenment," in the title of his work on sacrifice is ironical. Maistre intended his study of sacrifice to counteract the destructive influence of Enlightenment philosophy, which looked to reason in order to unmask the superstitions that enslave human beings. Maistre's idea of enlightenment is more accurately a notion of Christian revelation and, thus, precisely the opposite of what the *philosophes* had in mind.

4. This glorification is especially in evidence in Joseph de Maistre, *Les Soirées de Saint-Pétersbourg, ou Entretiens sur le gouvernement temporel de la Providence*, 2 vols. (Paris: Editions de la Maisnie, 1980), vol. 2.

lence. In Maistre's view, humans are intrinsically guilty, a condition that they have sought to ameliorate throughout time. Indeed, Maistre argues that, from ancient sacrificial rites to the emergence of Christianity, humans had destroyed the innocent in order to redeem the guilty. This sacrificial idea, which Maistre calls "dogma of reversibility," tolerates no equivocation regarding matters of guilt or innocence. In order for a guilty collectivity to be redeemed, the sacrificial victim must be innocent. This logic contrasts sharply with that of the French revolutionaries, who reversed Maistre's position in two respects. First, in the revolutionary imagination, the sacrificial victim is often a guilty scapegoat whose destruction offers a variety of communal benefits, such as purity, power, and identity. Second, whereas the revolutionaries established the guilt of their victims through the sacrificial process, Maistrian sacrifice begins with innocent victims, not ambiguous ones. It is for this reason that Maistre rigidly distinguishes between different types of violence, such as punishment, war, and sacrifice. Unable to conceive theoretically of an ambiguous victim, Maistre must instead delineate forms of violence suitable for the innocent and the guilty.

Finally, in keeping with his Manichaean perspective on violence, Maistre argues that some forms of bloodshed regenerate human beings while others contribute to their decline. Maistre borrows the concept of regeneration from Catholicism and imbues it with political significance obtained from its role in the French Revolution. Unlike the revolutionaries, who viewed sacrificial regeneration as an agent of political transformation, however, Maistre strips it of creativity. In Maistre's hands, regeneration retains the ability to achieve moral transformation but only in a conservative, spiritual, and Catholic sense. Regenerative violence punishes the revolutionary *homme nouveau,* morally restoring him to the status of a royal subject.[5] In this respect, violence is a spiritual palliative that heals the soul by hemming the mind and body into a narrow space of divinely sanctioned activity. Although Maistre is uniquely interested in preserving the authority of the Catholic church and monarchy, he agrees with his revolutionary archenemies that violence has a regenerative capacity. He disagrees with them, however, concerning the political operation of violence. For Maistre, even though it is preposterous that violence can make citizens from subjects, he willingly accepts that bloodshed can lead misguided, sinful citizens back to the moral and political framework of the traditional three Estates.

Maistre's critique of the French Revolution and its violence is theoretically fragile because it is so dependent on Catholicism. Every time Maistre attempts

---

5. *L'Homme nouveau* means "new man." For a discussion of the concept of regeneration and *l'homme nouveau,* see Mona Ozouf, *L'Homme régénéré* (Paris: Gallimard, 1989), 116–157.

to distinguish between "good" and "bad" violence, innocence and guilt, regeneration and decadence, he relies on the moral absolutism of church dogma. This reliance becomes starkly evident when, for instance, Maistre argues that only divinely sanctioned bloodshed contributes to moral regeneration. The French revolutionaries themselves illustrate the weakness of this position when they claim either that their violence has divine approval or that revolutionary bloodshed needs no god to be regenerative. The former position reflects the attitude of all religious zealots; the latter captures the theoretical approach of Machiavelli and all modern, secular revolutionaries. By clutching at the regenerative power of violence and sacrifice under a religious banner, Maistre ultimately cannot avoid lending a helping theoretical hand to those who, in a different context, would do the same for diametrically opposite political ends.

Reactions to Maistre's reflections on violence and sacrifice have varied widely. Some scholars have dismissed his work as the ravings of a religious fanatic obsessed with blood. Others have sought to portray Maistre as a protofascist. More recently, a few intellectuals have tried to mold Maistrian ideas into the building blocks of a poststructuralist critique of power and ideology.[6] Maistre's work is essential to this study because he is the first French intellectual to offer a comprehensive theory of sacrifice. Thanks to this contribution, Maistre has shaped terminologically and conceptually the French debate about sacrifice and political foundation that continued well after his death. Although revolutionary rhetoric and symbolism captured the idea that sacrifice could mold French subjects into republican citizens, Maistre deserves credit for recognizing the sociological and political implications of such regeneration through violence.

6. For a discussion of those who consider Maistre bloodthirsty and his thought irrational, see Isaiah Berlin, "Joseph de Maistre and the Origins of Fascism," *New York Review of Books* 37, nos. 14–16 (September 26, October 11 and 25, 1990); or idem, *The Crooked Timber of Humanity* (New York: Vintage, 1992), 91–96. Berlin argues that Maistre's ideas anticipate modern fascism. Richard Lebrun discusses the anglophone reception of Maistre, which has been largely negative thanks to early and mid-twentieth-century works like Harold Laski's *Studies in the Problem of Sovereignty* (1917) and Roger Soltau's *French Political Thought in the Nineteenth Century* (1931). See Lebrun's "Maistre in the Anglophone World," in *Joseph de Maistre's Life, Thought, and Influence*, ed. Richard Lebrun (Montreal: McGill-Queen's University Press, 2001), 66–83. Most important for the contemporary study of Maistre are a small group of intellectuals whose essays, books, and translations have significantly enhanced scholarly awareness of Maistrian thought. This group includes Lebrun and Jean-Louis Darcel, both of whom have published numerous works on and translations of Maistre and were instrumental in the publication of *La Revue des études maistriennes*. Also noteworthy for elucidating Maistre and defending him against his critics are Graeme Garrard, "Rousseau, Maistre, and the Counter-Enlightenment," *History of Political Thought* 15 (spring 1994), 97–120; and Owen Bradley, *A Modern Maistre* (Lincoln: University of Nebraska Press, 1999). Bradley and Garrard highlight Maistre's anticipation of modern and postmodern ideas.

Reflections on the Vitality of Blood

Maistre's concept of violence is rooted in blood. Because blood gives the body life, Maistre conceives of violence as an attack upon the life of a human being and, therefore, upon his or her blood. He draws this association between life and blood directly from the Old Testament: "Only you shall not eat flesh with its life, that is, its blood" (Genesis 9:4) and "The life of the flesh resides in the blood" (Leviticus 17:11).[7] To underscore the significance of the biblical position on blood, Maistre references an eighteenth-century physiologist, John Hunter, who claims in *Treatise on the Blood, Inflammation and Gunshot Wounds* that blood is alive ("vivant").[8] When life and blood are equated, violence requires bloodshed. Even a cursory glance at Maistre's work reveals his fascination with the myriad of ways in which blood can be spilt. War, human sacrifice, punishment, and martyrdom are the most common formations of violence addressed by Maistre. Each, however, spills blood according to different moral conditions. Some forms of violence are moral, and thus beneficial; others are immoral, corrupt, and thus forbidden.

Following the teachings of the medieval Christian theologian Origen, Maistre reasons that if blood is life, it must also be the repository of the soul.[9] Blood is thus a living substance in both a physical and a spiritual sense. Since blood possesses metaphysical qualities, Maistre argues, it must also be the locus of the degradation from which all souls suffer. Guilt for original sin thus resides in the blood: "Therefore man being guilty through his *sensuous principle*, through *his flesh*, through *his life*, the curse fell upon the blood."[10] Because blood is alive and home to the guilty soul, its spillage has moral consequence. Under circumstances sanctioned by God, when it flows out of the body, blood holds the promise of purification. Bloodshed fosters the health of the body and the expi-

7. In *Eclaircissement sur les sacrifices,* Maistre mistakenly cites Leviticus 13:7 as the origin of the sentence. *Sur les sacrifices,* 29.

8. John Hunter, *Treatise on the Blood, Inflammation and Gunshot Wounds* (London, 1794). Quoted in Maistre, *Sur les sacrifices,* 30.

9. Quoted by Maistre, Origen claims: "And we believe that this soul of the flesh resides in the blood." *Sur les sacrifices,* 25. Furthermore, in *Origen,* Rowan Greer writes: "The body is not integral to the definition of a human being, who is a soul or incorporeal nature making use of a body . . . Rather, the body is a sign of the fallen state of the soul . . . if the body is a sign of the state of the soul, it is a punishment that the soul has brought upon itself. And since the punishment is also an operation of God's providence, the body functions in a remedial way to drive the soul back to God. From one point of view the body cuts the soul off from God and blocks its vision. From another point of view it is the vehicle whereby God reveals Himself and through which the soul moves toward God." *Origen,* trans. Rowan Greer (New York: Paulist Press, 1979), 15.

10. "L'homme étant donc coupable par son *principe sensible,* par *sa chair,* par *sa vie,* l'anathème tombait sur le sang." Maistre, *Sur les sacrifices,* 29.

ation of the soul. Violence is thus a salutary agent of moral change for both individuals and collectivities because it eradicates, purifies, and instructs, depending on the circumstance. In this respect, its capacity for moral instruction also holds political significance because it shapes human judgments concerning the achievement of a good life.

Maistre's metaphysics of blood allows him to interpret political violence in ways that uniquely suit his politics. For instance, Maistre argues that bloodshed is essential for bringing moral health to individuals who suffer from corruption, vice, or decadence. He writes: "First, when the human soul lost its resilience through the indolence, incredulity, and gangrenous vices that follow from an excess of civilization, it can be retempered only in blood."[11] Drawing a connection between blood and the human soul, Maistre suggests that bloodshed reinvigorates the life force (soul) dampened by civilization's corrupting influences. The reference to "an excess of civilization" illustrates Maistre's belief that bloodshed is "naturally"—by virtue of blood's intrinsic properties—equipped to reverse the morally perverse cultural decadence brought by Enlightenment arts and sciences. As Maistre understands it, violence heals the deleterious moral effects of reason in the service of human perfectibility. Maistre also carries this rather individualistic understanding of violent regeneration to the political level. "We know," he writes, "that nations never reach the highest point of grandeur of which they are capable except after long and bloody wars."[12] Violence thus achieves both individual and collective moral reinvigoration thanks to its ability to purify elements of the guilty soul.

"Balance" is the precise word that Maistre uses to describe the purpose of salutary violence in his theodicy. All injustice or evil finds compensation. Although the revolutionaries subscribed to a similar logic of violence, they believed that violence punished the sin of aristocratic privilege. In contrast, Maistre argues that violence is "good" only when human sovereigns and God use it punitively in order to foster a perpetual settling of accounts between good and evil. Maistre borrows this Manichaean symmetry directly from Christianity:

> Christianity clearly shows us a different balance. On one side all the crimes, on the other all the satisfactions; on this side, the good works of all men, the blood of martyrs, the sacrifices and tears of innocence accumulating without end in order to balance the evil that, since the origin of things, spills into the other basin its poi-

11. "D'abord lorsque l'âme humaine a perdu son ressort par la mollesse, l'incrédulité et les vices gangreneux qui suivent l'excès de la civilisation, elle ne peut être retrempée que dans le sang." Maistre, *Ecrits sur la Révolution,* 119.

12. "On sait que les nations ne parviennent jamais au plus haut point de grandeur dont elles sont susceptibles qu'après de longues et sanglantes guerres." Ibid.

sonous streams. In the end, salvation must win, and in order to accelerate this universal work, whose expectation *makes all beings groan,* it suffices that man want it.

Le Christianisme nous montre bien une autre balance. D'un côté tous les crimes, de l'autre toutes les satisfactions; de ce côté, les bonnes oeuvres de tous les hommes, le sang des martyrs, les sacrifices et les larmes de l'innocence s'accumulant sans relâche pour faire équilibre au mal qui, depuis l'origine des choses, verse dans l'autre bassin ses flots empoisonnés. Il faut qu'à la fin le salut l'emporte, et pour accélérer cette oeuvre universelle, dont l'attente *fait gémir tous les êtres,* il suffit que l'homme veuille.[13]

According to Maistre, the universe is host to an omnipresent violence that works constantly to balance the scales of good and evil. Individuals and nations, as well as political and religious institutions, all risk disorder at the hands of evil. All can be "healed" by virtue of salutary violence.

The capacity of violence to achieve a cosmic balance between good and evil is particularly important given the imperfectability of human nature. Maistre conceives of human beings as naturally frail, deeply flawed creatures. Their capacity to live a good life is entirely contingent upon their ability to act morally, consistent with principles of divine justice. Because of their bodily impulses, hubris, ignorance, and, most important, original sin, Maistre argues, humans are destined to suffer perpetually. History also broadly demonstrates that the human condition is comprised of misery, conflict, and death. Maistre maintains that humans contribute to their wretched condition through immoral action, vice, and corruption. Such evil, as Maistre would call it, leads periodically to the moral decline of individuals and whole societies. In Maistre's view, such human decadence always fosters social disorder and political instability. Consequently, only violent intervention by God can remedy these bouts of decadence, which threaten to destroy entire nations.

In order to achieve moral renewal, God requires blood, a demand that Maistre often conveys through the metaphor of a surgeon. Just as human surgeons sometimes counsel their patients to undergo difficult, painful procedures in order to save their lives, Maistre believes that God does the same for moral evils. Pushing the parallel to its logical conclusion, Maistre writes:

These surgical instruments, whose sight makes us grow pale, the saw, the trepan, the forceps, the lithotome, etc., were undoubtedly not invented by some evil genius of humanity: Indeed! These instruments are in the hands of man for the healing of physical evil, what physical evil is, in the hands of God for the extirpation

13. Maistre, *Soirées,* vol. 2, 207–208.

of real evil . . . In the sensuous as in the higher order, the law is the same and as old as evil: THE REMEDY FOR DISORDER WILL BE PAIN.

Ces instruments de la chirurgie, dont la vue nous faire pâlir, la scie, le trépan, le forceps, le lithotome, etc., n'ont pas sans doute été inventés par un génie ennemi de l'espèce humaine: eh bien! Ces instruments sont dans la main de l'homme, pour la guérison du mal physique, ce que le mal physique est, dans celle de Dieu, pour l'extirpation du véritable mal . . . Dans l'ordre sensible comme dans l'ordre supérieur, la loi est la même et aussi ancienne que le mal: LE REMÈDE DU DÈSORDRE SERA LA DOULEUR.[14]

As a surgeon, God uses pain, suffering, and the spilling of blood to cure human beings of their moral ailments. Although human nature prohibits complete moral purification, Maistre believes that violence can fundamentally improve the moral condition of humanity. One aspect of this logic is clearly sacrificial: the experience of divine violence restores spiritual health. The omniscient God-surgeon knows exactly what part of the individual or political body to remove in order to save the whole. Paradoxically, this logic is also scientific and rational: God precisely deploys sacred violence against the human race in the same way that scientific knowledge permits a surgeon to remove a life-threatening tumor.

Maistre's divine surgeon attempts to strike a balance between pain and moral health, an equilibrium that would seem to mitigate violence. In Maistre's view, however, the violence experienced by the human race comes without reserve. Using another organic metaphor, Maistre describes this overflowing, salutary violence: "What one sees clearly enough is that the human race can be considered as a tree which an invisible hand continually prunes, and which often benefits from this operation. In truth, if one were to touch the trunk, or if one were to *overprune,* the tree could perish: but who knows the limits of the human tree?"[15] Once again, Maistre blends sacrificial logic and scientific rationalism as he describes the precision of divine arboriculture. In claiming that only God knows how much the human species can be pruned, Maistre approaches a concept of violence without reserve. Such violence is essential to the human condition because it serves as a bulwark against the ever-present human capacity for evil.

The French revolutionaries also imagined that violence checked vice and corruption, allowing for the achievement of a moral equilibrium. Revolution-

14. Ibid., 131–132.
15. "Ce qu'on voit assez clairement, c'est que le genre humain peut être considéré comme un arbre qu'une main invisible taille sans relâche, et qui gagne souvent à cette opération. A la vérité, si l'on touche le tronc, ou si l'on coupe en *tête de saule,* l'arbre peut périr: mais qui connaît les limites pour l'arbre humain?" Maistre, *Ecrits sur la Révolution,* 118–119.

ary leaders, such as Robespierre, shared a version of Maistre's belief that violence exists without reserve. Robespierre, however, also imbues violence with a
creative capacity, as he demonstrates in this passage:

> The times that ought to have given birth to the greatest marvels of reason were
> also sullied by the last excesses of human corruption. The crimes of tyranny ac-
> celerated the progress of liberty, and the progress of liberty multiplied the crimes
> of tyranny, by redoubling its alarms and furors. Between the people and its ene-
> mies, there was a continual reaction whose progressive violence carried out in just
> a few years the work of several centuries.

> Les temps qui devaient enfanter le plus grand des prodiges de la raison devaient
> aussi être souillés par les derniers excès de la corruption humaine. Les crimes de la
> tyrannie accélérèrent les progrès de la liberté, et les progrès de la liberté multi-
> plièrent les crimes de la tyrannie, en redoublant ses alarmes et ses fureurs. Il y a eu,
> entre le peuple et ses ennemis, une réaction continuelle dont la violence progres-
> sive a opéré en peu d'années l'ouvrage de plusieurs siècles.[16]

Robespierre describes a balance struck between revolutionary violence and
counterrevolutionary corruption whose product is politically progressive. Here
a violent dialectic serves the purpose of moral purification and creates a new
form of politics, republicanism. Although Maistre's concept of violence illustrates a similar dialectical tension between evil and its violent remedy, it lacks
any component of creative sublation. For him, excessive violence forms an iron
cage from which humans cannot escape on their own volition. Thus, viewed
from a Maistrian standpoint, the Terror illustrates divine violence without reserve in the service of monarchism. The guillotine clips morally degraded
branches from the human tree, eliminating political threats to republicanism.
This idea of violence without reserve will reappear in the twentieth-century
works of Sorel and Bataille, who strip away its association with an active, omnipresent God.

Looking for a violent, salutary alternative to the French Revolution, Maistre
turns to the Spanish Inquisition in order to illustrate how violence fosters the
moral health of a body politic. Maistre's choice of the Inquisition to expound
upon the virtues of violence amounts to a direct attack against *lumières,* such as
Voltaire, who considered the Inquisition a quintessential example of fanatical
religious intolerance. In *Lettres sur l'inquisition espagnole,* Maistre argues that
Spain, in cooperation with the Catholic church, was perfectly justified in per-
secuting, expelling, and killing Jews because "near the end of the fifteenth cen-

16. Robespierre, *Œuvres complètes,* vol. 10 (Paris: Presses Universitaires de France, 1967), 168.

tury, Judaism had thrown down such deep roots in Spain that it threatened to suffocate entirely the national plant."[17] Maistre argues that the survival of the Spanish nation required the eradication of Jewish cultural weeds. More precisely, Judaism threatened the distinct moral fiber of the Spanish people: "If the nation [Spain] has conserved its maxims, its unity, and the public spirit that saved it, it owes its success entirely to the Inquisition."[18] Violence during the Inquisition permitted the Spanish to defend and preserve their national moral character. Maistre thus regards the Inquisition as a preemptive use of violence in the service of moral and cultural preservation.

In defending the Spanish Inquisition, Maistre revises his concept of unmitigated violence so that it encompasses both divine and human bloodshed. Both are political, but the latter is directly applicable to international affairs: "*Never could great political evils, never especially could violent attacks carried out against the body of the state, be prevented or repelled except by equally violent means.* This ranks as one of the most incontestable political axioms."[19] Maistre derives a principle of Realpolitik from his theodicy: states must use violence in preemption of and in proportion to the violence used against them. Just as in the universe, violence in the political realm must achieve harmony. In addition to operating as a practical recommendation for statecraft, Maistre's "political axiom" has metaphysical significance. The idea that only violence can repel violence reinforces Maistre's view that bloodshed is physically and morally ambiguous: it both destroys and reestablishes the order of things. In this respect, even political violence is sacred. The setting of violence against violence also suggests that political violence contributes to metaphysical stasis. Both individual order (sin balanced by redemption) and sociopolitical order (revolution balanced by terror) are achieved through bloodshed. Blood is thus the unit of exchange that animates Maistre's sacred, violent economy.

Maistre's analysis of the Spanish Inquisition illustrates the importance of preemptive, regenerative violence that economically guards against a nation's committing a great crime. In Maistre's view, a French Inquisition would have ultimately served the same function of moral regeneration as the Terror, but without "that horrible effusion of human blood."[20] Maistre conceived of re-

---

17. "Vers la fin du XVe siècle, le Judaïsme avait jeté de si profondes racines en Espagne, qu'il menaçait de suffoquer entièrement la plante nationale." Joseph de Maistre, *Lettres à un gentilhomme russe sur l'inquisition espagnole* (Lyons: Librairie Catholique Emmanuel Vitte, n.d.), 4–5.

18. "Si la nation a conservé ses maximes, son unité et cet esprit public qui l'a sauvée, elle le doit uniquement à l'Inquisition." Ibid., 66.

19. "*Jamais les grands maux politiques, jamais surtout les attaques violentes portées contre le corps de l'état, ne peuvent prévenues ou repoussées que par des moyens pareillement violents.* Ceci est au rang des axiomes politiques le plus incontestable." Ibid., 6.

20. Maistre, *Ecrits sur la Révolution*, 113.

generation as a "natural" return to basic Catholic and monarchical principles because bloodshed purified human beings of their original and social guilt. Ironically, however, the revolutionaries imagined that violent regeneration would allow for the moral and political conversion of oppressed French subjects to free republican citizens. From their perspective, the violence of the Terror eliminated the stain of monarchism, thus ending a form of government that had stripped human beings of their natural rights. Although Maistrian regeneration refers directly to a redemptive process of moral purification through bloodshed, it operates in much the same way as revolutionary regeneration. Yet, thanks to his peculiar, Catholic understanding of blood's properties and his view that God's will shapes all human activities, Maistre can boldly maintain that violent regeneration leads only to his preferred political outcomes. Maistre illustrates this thinking when he links this idea of regeneration to punitive bloodshed: "It cannot too often be repeated that men do not lead a revolution; it is the revolution that uses men. It is well said *that it takes off by itself.* This phrase signifies that Divinity has never shown itself in such a clear manner in any human event. If it employs the vilest instruments, it is to punish in order to regenerate."[21] In claiming that the Terror punished and then regenerated the French people, Maistre transforms revolutionary sacrifice into divine punishment, revaluing the Jacobin understanding of the Terror. The violence used by the French revolutionaries to found a republic instead redeems the sinful French and restores their beleaguered monarchy. Maistre easily alters the revolutionary idea of moral regeneration by replacing republican morality with his rigid Catholicism. This theoretical strategy is weak and problematic, however, because it ultimately leads Maistre to provide a counterrevolutionary justification for the bloodshed that he despises. What is more, Maistre can make this strategy work only if he artificially maintains a strict delineation between sacrifice and punishment. Even though Maistre's concept of regeneration clearly makes use of a sacrificial logic of purification, he carefully argues that punishment, not sacrifice, restores the health of nations. Maistre never uses the word "sacrifice" to mean moral regeneration through blood in either *Considérations sur la France* or *Lettres sur l'inquisition espagnole.*

Maistre's concept of violence serves as the basis for his critique of the French Revolution. According to his worldview, there are only two general forms of violence: those that lead to decadence and those that foster conservative moral

---

21. "On ne saurait trop le répéter, ce ne sont point les hommes qui mènent la révolution, c'est la révolution qui emploie les hommes. On dit fort bien quand on dit *qu'elle va toute seule.* Cette phrase signifie que jamais la Divinité ne s'était montrée d'une manière si claire dans aucun événement humain. Si elle emploie les instruments les plus vils, c'est qu'elle punit pour régénérer." Ibid., 98.

regeneration. It is the latter that Maistre considers salutary, redemptive, and, thus, essential to human beings after the Fall. By acting upon the blood, morally regenerative violence also proscribes any attempt at political artifice, any effort to depart from the political and religious institutions sanctioned by God, because it constantly works to punish and purify those who undertake such endeavors. Maistrian regeneration through violence thus forbids revolutionary attempts at political foundation.[22] However, Maistre's effort to deny the French revolutionaries the fruits of their violence demonstrates how theoretically difficult and dangerous it is to turn regenerative bloodshed against one form of politics and in favor of another.

Violence in a Maistrian World

In recognizing that revolutionary violence is sacred, but resisting perceiving it as ambiguous, Maistre faces two theoretical difficulties. The first concerns Maistre's claim that only certain types of violence are salutary. Because he considers violence to be such an essential part of the human condition, Maistre must explain why some forms of violence corrupt and debase human beings, while others foster moral health. Maintaining this elusive distinction is essential to Maistre's ability to restrict regenerative violence to the pursuit of his political agenda, for without it, the role that Maistre assigns to salutary violence can be co-opted by those who wish regenerative bloodshed to serve alternative ends. Second, Maistre's hostility toward political foundation is linked to the remedial

22. Although Maistre considers all acts of political foundation to be divine and thus beyond the ability of mere mortals, he does not believe, as Owen Bradley argues in his dissertation, that "all beginnings are low and violent." "Logics of Violence: The Social and Political Thought of Joseph de Maistre," vol. 2 (Ph.D. diss., Cornell University, 1992), 376–377. It is important to make a distinction between Maistre's claim that political foundation has no intrinsic legitimacy and the idea that such beginnings must be mired in blood. In Maistre's view, foundation succeeds when God sanctions the pure sacred power of the founder. While it is true that this sacred right, transferred to kings, maintains itself though the impure, sacred, and regenerative violence of the executioner, Maistre never argues that political foundation itself requires a founding crime. Indeed, in *Against Rousseau*, Maistre explicitly makes this argument: "The Sacred Scriptures show us the first king of the chosen people, elected, and consecrated by an immediate intervention of the divinity; the annals of every nation in the world assign the same origin to their particular governments. Only the names change. All, after following the succession of their princes back to a somewhat remote epoch, finally arrive at those mythological times whose true history would instruct us much better than all the others. All show us the cradle of sovereignty surrounded by miracles; always divinity intervenes in the foundation of empires; always the first sovereignty, at least, is a favourite of heaven: he receives the sceptre from the hands of divinity. Divinity communicates with him, it inspires him; it engraves on his forehead the sign of its power; and the laws that he dictates to his fellows are only the fruit of his celestial communications." *Against Rousseau,* trans. Richard Lebrun (Montreal: McGill-Queen's University Press, 1996), 58.

effects of violence. According to Maistre, when humans employ violence to alter their political world, that bloodshed, intentionally or not, conserves the status quo. The problem, however, is that Maistrian violence retains the same capacity to regenerate morals, redeem collectivities, and foster communal bonds as sacrificial forms of revolutionary bloodshed. If the French revolutionaries wanted to harness the peculiar characteristics of violence for the sake of political foundation, Maistre wants that same violence to inhibit such instauration. Thus, Maistre must explain how the bloodshed that appears to have founded the French Republic actually renders such a foundation impossible.

Maistre's three applications of violence—war, punishment, and sacrifice—highlight these theoretical difficulties. Each uniquely reveals the theoretical junction between antifoundational politics, violence, and conservative moral regeneration. Each also illustrates the challenge of distinguishing between regenerative and decadent violence. Furthermore, Maistre's preference for salutary applications of violence reveal that his position on blood sacrifice is more nuanced than students of Maistrian thought have previously maintained. Just as he loathes certain forms of violence, Maistre also despises particular forms of sacrifice. This distinction between different forms of sacrifice exposes an important opening in Maistrian thought: Maistre's hope that blood will no longer be necessary for human redemption. Real and symbolic martyrdom offer an exit from Maistre's dark pessimism and highlight the importance of distinguishing between Maistre's realism and violent antimaterialism.

War and the Spilling of Sacrificial Blood

Maistre's reflections on war generate some of the most chilling passages in his oeuvre. Although Maistre uses the subject of war as a platform to wax lyrical about how violence is a natural part of the human condition, these reflections offer the first indication that Maistre anticipates an end to this cyclical bloodshed. As I previously argued, Maistre believes that humans are subject to violence because their imperfection renders them incapable of upholding divine standards of justice. He conceives of war as a natural, postlapsarian activity that periodically purifies sinful human beings. War offers spiritual and political renewal by destroying heretical forms of politics and establishing Christian ones. Because everything natural has its origins in the divine, Maistre assumes that God intends war as a social remedy for the consequences of evil. But because Christ's return portends the complete elimination of the material conditions from which sin springs, Maistre also predicts a sacrificial closure of war's violent economy.

In his introduction to *Considerations on France,* Isaiah Berlin writes that Maistre was fascinated by the spectacle of war because it reinforced his fundamental belief in the primacy of irrationality. Summing up Maistre's position, Berlin claims: "Wars are not won by rational calculation but rather by moral force."[23] Nothing is particularly surprising about Maistre's argument that men win wars thanks to irrational fervor, not brilliant logic and strategy. Because Berlin is hostile to Maistre's emphasis on the role of irrationality in war, however, he misses an important Maistrian insight. Though faith may enliven men's spirits, driving them to the battlefield, Maistre believes that the *suspension* of men's moral faculties permits them to kill with abandon. It is not an irrational "moral force" that permits victory in war, but rather an amoral one. Although it is true, as Berlin argues, that Maistre's overall commitment to irrationality is emblematic of his hostility toward the Enlightenment, Maistre's views on war also illuminate the limitations of a purely rational explanation for the phenomenon of violence.

In the beginning of the third chapter of *Considerations on France,* titled "Of the Violent Destruction of the Human Species,"[24] Maistre details his position on war. He claims that when men enter battle, their irrationality permits them to dissociate from the moral and psychological consequences of their violent actions. Because this behavior strikes Maistre as enigmatic, he attributes it to divinity. If God created human beings with the capacity to suspend the very faculty that makes them human, he must have done so for a good reason. Thus, Maistre writes, "History unfortunately proves that war is in a sense the habitual state of the human species: that is to say that human blood must flow without interruption somewhere or other over the globe, and that peace, for each nation, is only a respite."[25] While Maistre's observation that war is an unfortunate reality of the human condition is hardly surprising, his assertion that human blood *must* flow uninterruptedly is more difficult to digest. This distinction between what is (war) and what ought to be (continual bloodshed) illustrates how Maistre moves from a realist position that simply laments the bloody state of human political affairs to one of antimaterialism that demands the destruction of human lives. What allows Maistre to travel between these philosophical positions is his belief, described with much rhetorical hyperbole, that war must have a beneficial function. Looking squarely into the human heart of darkness, Maistre asks how warfare ameliorates the human condition.

---

23. Joseph de Maistre, *Considerations on France,* trans. Richard Lebrun (Cambridge: Cambridge University Press, 1994), xix.

24. "De la destruction violente de l'espèce humaine."

25. "L'histoire prouve malheureusement que la guerre est l'état habituel du genre humain dans un certain sens; c'est-à-dire que le sang humain doit couler sans interruptions sur le globe, ici ou là, et que la paix, pour chaque nation, n'est qu'un répit." Maistre, *Écrits sur la Révolution,* 114.

Maistre undertakes an infamous defense of the salutary benefits of war in the following long passage from *Les Soirées de Saint-Pétersbourg.* The narrative format of this text complicates the interpretation and attribution of this passage. Like Plato's *Republic,* the *Soirées* contains a dialogue among three interlocutors: a knight, a senator, and a count. Many Maistre scholars, such as Berlin, have assumed that Maistre's position is articulated by the count, despite the fact that the senator actually delivers the passage.[26] Thus, it is not clear to what extent the dialogue's cruel lessons can be directly linked to Maistre's actual beliefs. At the very least, one should avoid Berlin's error of attributing the passage directly to Maistre without also indicating that it comes from a dialogue, not from a traditional philosophical text.[27] In the Platonic dialogues, it is unreasonable to claim that Socrates is uniquely representative of Platonic thought; rather, Platonic philosophy emerges from the discourse between Socrates and his interlocutors. To make such a mistake with Maistre is no less problematic.

In the vast domain of living nature, there reigns a manifest violence, a kind of prescribed rage that arms all beings in mutual destruction. Once you leave the world of insensible substances, you find the decree of violent death written on the very frontiers of life. Even in the vegetable kingdom, this law can be felt: from the immense catalpa to the most humble grasses, how many plants *die,* and how many are *killed!* But once you enter into the animal kingdom, the law suddenly becomes dreadfully obvious. A force, at once hidden and palpable, appears continually occupied with exposing this principle of life by violent means. In each great division of the animal species, it has chosen a certain number of animals and charged them with devouring the others: thus, there are insects of prey, reptiles of prey, birds of prey, fish of prey, and quadrupeds of prey. There is not an instant of time when some living thing is not being devoured by another. Above all these numerous animal species is placed man, whose destructive hand spares no living thing; he kills to nourish himself, he kills to clothe himself, he kills to show off, he kills to attack, he kills to defend himself, he kills to instruct himself, he kills to amuse himself, he

26. Excellent discussions of Maistre's use of dialogue can be found in Bradley, *A Modern Maistre,* 62; and Jean-Louis Darcel, "Genèse et publication des *Soirées de Saint-Pétersbourg,*" in *Les Soirées de Saint-Pétersbourg,* ed. Jean-Louis Darcel (Geneva: Editions Slatkine, 1993), 15–16. Bradley argues that each of Maistre's interlocutors represents facets of Maistrian thought. He adds, however: "The passages on executions and warfare have always been read as the direct, unmediated, unequivocal expression of Maistre's personal view. Yet the most questionable assertions are actually presented in the voice of the Senator, who represents either another person altogether or at most one tendency of Maistre's thinking, and whose questionable views are continually challenged and thus limited by the other interlocutors." *A Modern Maistre,* 62.

27. Berlin cites this passage both in his "Introduction" to Maistre, *Considerations on France,* xvii–xviii; and in "Joseph de Maistre and the Origins of Fascism." In both cases, Berlin attributes the passage to Maistre without signaling the significance of its narrative format.

kills to kill: proud and terrible king, he needs everything, and nothing can resists him. He knows how many barrels of oil he can get from the head of a shark or a sperm whale; in his museums, he mounts with his sharp pin the elegant butterfly that he caught in flight on the summit of Mount Blanc or Chimborazo; he stuffs the crocodile, he embalms the hummingbird; on his command, the rattlesnake dies in preserving fluid to keep it intact for the eyes of a long line of observers; the horse that carries his master to the tiger hunt struts about covered by the skin of the same animal. At one and the same time, man takes from the lamb its entrails in order to play a harp, from the whale its bones in order to stiffen the corset of a young girl, from the wolf its most murderous tooth in order to polish frivolous manufactures, from the elephant its tusks in order to fashion a child's toy: his tables are covered with cadavers. The philosopher can even discern how this permanent carnage is provided for and ordained in the grand scheme of things. But does this law stop with man? Undoubtedly, no. Yet, what being will exterminate the one who exterminates all else? He will. It is man who is charged with butchering man. But how will he be able to accomplish this law, he who is a moral and merciful being, who is born to love, who weeps for others as for himself, who finds pleasure in weeping, and who ends up inventing fictions in order to make himself cry; to whom finally it has been declared *that whoever sheds blood unjustly will redeem it with the very last drop of blood of his own* (Genesis 9:5)? It is war that accomplishes the *decree*. Do you not hear the *earth* demanding and crying out for blood? Animal blood does not satisfy it, nor even that of criminals spilt by the sword of the law. If human justice struck them all, there would be no war; but justice can reach only a small number of them, and often it even spares them, without itself suspecting that this cruel humanity contributes to war's necessity, especially if, at the same time, another no less stupid and deadly blindness was working to extend expiation through the world. The *earth* did not cry out in vain; war is igniting. Man, seized suddenly by a *divine* fury, foreign to both hatred and anger, advances on the battlefield without knowing what he intends or even what he is doing. What is this horrible enigma? Nothing is more contrary to his nature, yet nothing is less repugnant to him: he undertakes with enthusiasm that which horrifies him. Have you never remarked that, on the battlefield, man never disobeys? They might well massacre Nerva or Henry IV; but they will never say, even to the most abominable tyrant or the most flagrant butcher of human flesh: *We no longer want to serve you. A* revolt on the battlefield, an agreement to embrace by repudiating a tyrant, is a phenomenon that does not occur in my memory. Nothing resists, nothing can resist the force that drags man into combat; innocent murderer, passive instrument of a formidable hand, *he plunges head first into the abyss that he himself has dug; he receives death without suspecting that it is he himself who has brought about his death* (Psalms 9:[15]).

Thus is endlessly worked out, from the mite up to man, the universal law of the violent destruction of living beings. The entire earth, continually steeped in blood, is nothing but a immense altar on which every living thing must be sacrificed without end, without measure, without restraint, until the consummation of things, until the extinction of evil, until the death of death (*for the last enemy to be destroyed is death* [1 Corinthians 15:26]).

Dans le vaste domaine de la nature vivante, il règne une violence manifeste, une espèce de rage prescrite qui arme tous les êtres *in mutua funera:* dès que vous sortez du règne insensible, vous trouvez le décret de la mort violente écrit sur les frontières mêmes de la vie. Déjà, dans le règne végétal, on commence à sentir la loi: depuis l'immense catalpa jusqu'au plus humble graminée, combien de plantes *meurent,* et combien sont *tuées!* Mais, dès que vous entrez dans le règne animal, la loi prend tout à coup une épouvantable évidence. Une force, à la fois cachée et palpable, se montre continuellement occupée à mettre à découvert le principe de la vie par des moyens violents. Dans chaque grande division de l'espèce animale, elle a choisi un certain nombre d'animaux qu'elle a chargés de dévorer les autres: ainsi, il y a des insectes de proie, des reptiles de proie, des oiseaux de proie, des poissons de proie, et des quadrupèdes de proie. Il n'y a pas un instant de la durée où l'être vivant ne soit dévoré par un autre. Au-dessus de ces nombreuses races d'animaux est placé l'homme, dont la main destructrice n'épargne rien de ce qui vit; il tue pour se nourrir, il tue pour se vêtir, il tue pour se parer, il tue pour attaquer, il tue pour se défendre, il tue pour s'instruire, il tue pour s'amuser, il tue pour tuer: roi superbe et terrible, il a besoin de tout, et rien ne lui résiste. Il sait combien la tête du requin ou du cachalot lui fournira de barriques d'huile; son épingle déliée pique sur le carton des musées l'élégant papillon qu'il a saisi au vol sur le sommet du Mont-Blanc ou du Chimboraço; il empaille le crocodile, il embaume le colibri; à son ordre, le serpent à sonnettes vient mourir dans la liqueur conservatrice qui doit le montrer intact aux yeux d'une longue suite d'observateurs; le cheval qui porte son maître à la chasse du tigre, se pavane sous la peau de ce même animal. L'homme demande tout à la fois, à l'agneau ses entrailles pour faire résonner une harpe, à la baleine ses fanons pour soutenir le corset de la jeune vierge, au loup, sa dent la plus meurtrière pour polir les ouvrages légers de l'art, à l'éléphant ses défenses pour façonner le jouet d'un enfant: ses tables sont couvertes de cadavres. Le philosophe peut même découvrir comment le carnage permanent est prévu et ordonné dans le grand tout. Mais cette loi s'arrête-t-elle à l'homme? non sans doute. Cependant quel être exterminera celui qui les exterminera tous? Lui. C'est l'homme qui est chargé d'égorger l'homme. Mais comment pourra-t-il accomplir la loi, lui qui est un être moral et miséricordieux, lui qui est né pour aimer, lui qui pleure sur les autres comme sur lui-même, qui trouve du plaisir à pleurer, et qui finit par inventer des fictions pour se faire pleurer; lui enfin à qui il a été déclaré *qu'on redemandera jusqu'à la dernière goutte de sang qu'il aura versé injustement* (Gen., IX, 5)? C'est la guerre qui accomplira le *décret.* N'entendez-vous pas la *terre* qui crie et demande du sang? Le sang des animaux ne lui suffit pas, ni même celui des coupables versé par le glaive des lois. Si la justice humaine les frappait tous, il n'y aurait point de guerre; mais elle ne saurait en atteindre qu'un petit nombre, et souvent même elle les épargne, sans se douter que sa féroce humanité contribue à nécessiter la guerre, si, dans le même temps surtout, un autre aveuglement, non moins stupide et non moins funeste, travaillait à étendre l'expiation dans le monde. La *terre* n'a pas crié en vain; la guerre s'allume. L'homme, saisi tout à coup d'une fureur *divine,* étrangère à la haine et à la colère, s'avance sur le champ de bataille sans savoir ce qu'il veut ni même ce qu'il fait. Qu'est-ce donc que cette terrible énigme? Rien n'est plus contraire à sa nature; et rien ne lui répugne moins: il fait avec enthousiasme ce qu'il a en horreur. N'avez-vous jamais remarqué que, sur le champ de bataille, l'homme ne désobéit jamais? il pourra bien massacrer Nerva ou Henri IV; mais le plus abominable tyran, le plus insolent boucher de chair humaine n'entendra jamais là: *Nous ne voulons plus vous servir.* Une révolte sur le champ de bataille, un accord pour s'embrasser en reniant un tyran, est un phénomène qui ne se présente pas à ma mémoire. Rien ne résiste, rien ne peut résister à la force qui traîne l'homme au combat; innocent meurtrier, instrument passif d'une main redoutable, *il se plonge tête baissée dans l'abîme qu'il a creusé lui-même; il reçoit la mort sans ce douter que c'est lui qui a fait la mort (Et infixae sunt gentes in interitu quem fecerunt).* (Ps. IX, 16.) Ainsi s'accomplit sans cesse, depuis le ciron jusqu'à l'homme, la grande loi de la destruction violente des êtres vivants. La terre entière, continuellement imbibée de sang, n'est qu'un autel immense où tout ce qui vit doit être immolé sans fin, sans mesure, sans relâche, jusqu'à la consommation des choses, jusqu'à l'extinction du mal, jusqu'à la mort de la mort. (*Car le dernier ennemi qui doit être détruit, c'est la mort* [S. Paul aux Cor., I, 15, 26])[28]

In this oft-quoted passage, Maistre's senator claims that the earth is a great altar for the perpetual sacrifice of all living things, until the arrival of the extinction of all evil, what Maistre calls "the death of death." At first, this enigmatic assertion seems to suggest that Maistre considers all divinely inspired violence to be sacrificial. As the principal means by which human beings slaughter other human beings, war appears to be nothing but blood sacrifice on a vast scale, appeasing a thirsty earth. Such rhetoric, however, is potentially misleading, depending upon whose voice is attributed to the passage. In *Eclaircissement sur les sacrifices,* Maistre is reticent to collapse the distinction between divine violence and sacrifice because he accepts as legitimate only self-sacrifice. What is more, with the exception of this passage, Maistre rarely describes war in sacrificial terms. By blurring the distinction between sacrifice and war, the senator creates an uncompromising image of human beings at the mercy of the divine.

28. Maistre, *Soirées,* vol. 2, 22–25.

Such a description highlights Maistre's conviction that war is natural, moral, divine, and redemptive. It also pointedly emphasizes Maistre's belief that Christian eschatology holds the promise of ending war as well as the necessity for all regenerative violence.

Even though he conflates Maistre and the senator, Berlin is correct to claim that Maistre's view of nature is "red in tooth and claw . . . a vast scene of carnage and destruction."[29] This conflation, however, leads Berlin to overlook the moral significance that Maistre attributes to natural violence. Since nature reflects divine intention, which by definition is good, there must be a reason for the vast destruction of living things. Nature's violence manifests a natural, hierarchical order of creatures maintained through bloodshed. The senator believes that human beings reside at the very top of that hierarchy but remain subject to the violence dictated by natural law. Like animals and plants, they must fulfill what the senator calls nature's "decree," a task achieved specifically through war. In the natural world, violence serves the unique purpose of maintaining a divine hierarchy; in the human world—a hybrid of nature and culture—violence fosters moral perfectibility. Finally, as the senator remarks at the end of his dialogue, only humans have the opportunity to escape their violent, warlike condition.

By conceptualizing violence in moral terms, the senator voices two related Maistrian ideas of human perfectibility. First, Maistre argues that violence activates culture: "Now the real fruits of human nature—the arts, sciences, great enterprises, lofty ideas, manly virtues—belong above all to the state of war."[30] The blood spilled during war tills the human species, allowing creativity, even genius, to sprout from previously infertile ground.[31] All the arts and sciences, from architecture to gastronomy to zoology, depend on the destruction of living things. Indeed, neither economics nor politics nor religion can claim exemption from Maistre's view that violence engenders culture. Not only are wealth, political power, and faith achieved at great cost to human life; they are often born in blood.

Maistre's claim that violence fertilizes culture is not, however, an argument in support of unfettered human creativity. In Maistre's view, a wide range of activities, such as political foundation, are simply beyond the capacity of human beings. Culture is the product of God-given faculties such as reason and imagination. During wars, violence renews those faculties and their cultural fruits by

29. Maistre, *Considerations on France*, xvii.

30. "Or les véritables fruits de la nature humaine, les arts, les sciences, les grandes entreprises, les hautes conceptions, les vertus mâles, tiennent surtout à l'état de guerre." Maistre, *Écrits sur la Révolution*, 119.

31. Consider, for example, this explicit statement on the subject of blood and genius: "In a word, it could be said that blood is the fertilizer of that plant we call *genius*." ("En un mot, on dirait que le sang est l'engrais de cette plante qu'on appelle *génie*.") Ibid.

fostering moral cleansing.[32] Thus, Maistre does not believe that culture itself is born in blood; rather, culture is regenerated by it. Nature's inherent violence cultivates culture. Furthermore, Maistre argues, the production of culture mystifies the seminal role of war (violence). While many celebrate the arts and sciences produced during World War II, few honor the Third Reich for initiating the violence that inspired them. Maistre's point is that the violence that supports cultural achievement is displaced, forgotten, mystified. By arguing that violence plays an essential role in the arts and sciences, Maistre suggests that the greatest human achievements depend upon the vilest.

Maistre also offers a second argument to explain how war's violence contributes to moral perfectibility. On the basis of his belief that both the soul and original sin reside in the blood, Maistre claims that bloodshed is necessary for redemption. In *Eclaircissement sur les sacrifices*, Maistre describes how war redeems nations by paying a bloody debt for collective crimes: "And war, inexhaustible subject of reflections, would again demonstrate the same truth from a different perspective; the annals of all the peoples having only a cry to show us how this terrible scourge always rages with a violence rigorously proportional to the vices of nations, in such a way that, when *crime overflows,* there is always an *overflow of blood—Without blood there is no remission.*"[33] For Maistre, the essential moral function of war is the purgation of sin. He quotes Paul's Epistle to the Hebrews: "Sine sanguine no fit remissio."[34] War's necessity is grounded in the Fall. War, like violence itself, is a sacred activity that knows no bounds because it stems the equally unending flow of evil from the human race. War is thus the quintessential implement for the pruning of the human species, removing the morally "diseased" branches so that the "tree" may continue to survive despite its intrinsic moral frailty.

The senator's position that war is a terrible but necessary remedy fits easily into Maistre's eschatology. The universal law of violent destruction is part of a recurring, distinctively Christian cycle of crime, punishment, and redemption. Maistre believes that this tripartite structure of existence is violent and well suited to sinful human beings, who periodically suffer from self-generated

32. Maistre consistently views war in terms of purification: "There is only one way of minimizing the scourge of war, and that is to minimize the disorders that lead to this terrible purification." ("Il n'y a qu'un moyen de comprimer le fléau de la guerre, c'est de comprimer les désordres qui amènent cette terrible purification.") *Ecrits sur la Révolution,* 120.

33. "Et la guerre, sujet inépuisable de réflexions, montrerait encore la même vérité, sous une autre face; les annales de tous les peuples n'ayant qu'un cri pour nous montrer comment ce fléau terrible sévit toujours avec une violence rigoureusement proportionnelle aux vices des nations, de manière que, lorsqu'il y a *débordement de crimes,* il y a toujours *débordement de sang.—Sine sanguine non fit remissio.*" Maistre, *Sur les sacrifices,* 60.

34. Hebrews 9:22 (Revised Standard Version).

degradation. So long as humans remain imperfect, domineering creatures with a natural capacity to commit evil, they must participate in this salutary cycle of moral degradation and health. For this reason, the senator argues, as quoted above, that the "violent destruction of living things" will continue unabated until "the consummation of things . . . the extinction of evil . . . [and] the death of death." By imagining an eschatological end to a world "steeped in blood," the senator suggests that Maistre's theodicy is not quite as prescriptive and sadistic as it appears. The senator's messianic imagery indicates that he laments living in a world that necessitates unending bloodshed. With his emphasis on the relationship between violence and moral perfectibility, Maistre clearly shares the senator's pessimism, but does not extend it to the point where the earth is "steeped in blood." Instead, Maistre believes that violence maintains a delicate natural and social balance within the universe until God returns to liberate human beings from their degradation.

Maistre's violent eschatology emerges from his reading of First Corinthians (15:26), in which Paul characterizes Christ's dominion before returning to release humans from their earthly existence. No doubt with the Romans in mind, Paul claims that Christ must suppress all rule, authority, and power, as well as all enemies, in order to secure his sovereignty. According to Maistre's version of the biblical text, Paul says: "For the last enemy that shall be destroyed is death."[35] This cryptic sentence, clearly inspired by the thought of Christ's return, describes the liberation of the human soul from its temporary material home in the body. In calling for the "death of death," to use the senator's phrase, Paul hopes that all Christian souls will be reunited with God at the end of time, an event that will eradicate the materiality of death. The "death of death" is thus a classic sacrificial concept, describing a state of transcendent union achieved through violent destruction. Yet, insofar as the "death of death" is an eschatological idea, it is beyond the reach of mere mortals. It describes the very last redemptive sacrifice by *God,* not a cataclysmic slaughter of humans by humans. Rooted in Catholicism, Maistre's eschatology highlights the singular importance of self-sacrifice or martyrdom. Thus, when Maistre's senator describes the earth as an immense altar for the perpetual sacrifice of all living things, he pessimistically articulates Maistrian realism. So long as humans remain embodied and guilty, existence will be structured by an unending cycle of depraved and salutary violence. Most importantly, Maistre and his senator seek an end to the violence that makes the earth appear as a great sacrificial altar. Such a cessation of violence requires a final, redemptive self-sacrifice.

Despite what many of his critics have maintained, Maistre's work reflects less

---

35. "Car le dernier ennemi qui doit être détruit, c'est la mort." Maistre, *Soirées,* vol. 2, 26.

an ideological relish for bloodshed than a rhetorically exaggerated attempt to understand its moral implications. Maistre's providential reading of the French Revolution may lead him to glorify the redemptive value of the Terror; however, it also never stops him from repeatedly calling the Terror a "horrible effusion of human blood." When the senator describes the earth's crying for blood, he misrepresents Maistre's fascination with violence. Rather than an expression of exuberant bloodlust, Maistre's reflections on war suggest a profound pessimism about the human condition. He claims that only a martyred god can save human beings from their degraded natures. Because blood houses guilt, Maistre, following scripture, argues that bloodshed is the only form of redemption available to human beings given the nature of their embodiment. Upon Christ's return, embodiment—the root of human imperfection—will no longer matter. This claim illustrates the depth of Maistre's strident antimaterialism, a philosophical position that will later prove useful in Sorel's and Bataille's critiques of Marx. It also explains why the "death of death" is a strictly apocalyptic idea: the sacrificial negation of all violent negation. Maistre does not anticipate a surplus of human violence; instead, his strong religious beliefs lead him simultaneously to lament the cyclical violence of the human condition and to await the collapse or closure of the sacrificial economy that has demanded such bloodshed. For Maistre, the "death of death" describes the achievement of final redemption. Despite their wish that the regicide would bring a sacrificial closure to the French Revolution, the revolutionaries simply added tremendous grist to Maistre's sacrificial mill.

Executioners, Punishment, and the Maintenance of the Status Quo

Punishment is Maistre's second important application of violence. Like war, it is dependent upon the remedial effects of bloodshed. In many cases, Maistre uses similar language to describe war and punishment; he collapses these concepts because he considers war to be a form of punishment, and punishment the most basic form of redemptive, salutary violence. While Maistre raises the issue of war in *Considérations sur la France,* he is primarily concerned with explaining the significance of the Revolution's worst punitive excess: the Terror. Drawing on the gruesome, public role played by the revolutionary executioner, Maistre famously argues that the executioner is the cornerstone of society and, thus, the principal link between punishment, authority, and social unity. This trinity, however, proves difficult for Maistre to hold together, because it requires a narrow scope and definition of punitive violence. For instance, in arguing that the Terror was divine punishment, Maistre again seeks to transform revolutionary violence into a bulwark of monarchism, illustrating his belief that punitive violence serves only one master. Furthermore, he studiously avoids using sacrificial concepts to describe the executioner's work so that Maistre can distinguish between the legitimacy of state violence and the illegitimacy of human sacrifice.[36] Mindful of these caveats, Maistre declares that punishment in the absence of any sacrificial motif is the most important form of socially unifying, regenerative violence of which humans are capable.

Maistrian punishment is an expression of divine justice and a mechanism of moral regeneration. For him, when the revolutionaries used violence to overturn the French throne, they unleashed a maelstrom of divinely inspired, morally regenerative, punitive violence. In August 1794 Maistre captured this view in a letter to his friend, Louis Vignet des Etoles: "The present situation, as abominable as it is, is necessary for the accomplishment of justice in the world . . . you would have told me that all the governments are old. I will add in your ear that they are rotten. The most corrupt of all has fallen with a crash, and those that remain will be slowly regenerated with that of France when it regenerates itself."[37]

By succumbing to the revolutionary spirit, the French people have demonstrated an unprecedented cultural decadence that Maistre believes will ultimately lead to the collapse of the French Republic. Above all, Maistre holds that Enlightenment ideas have engendered this all-encompassing corruption and decadence.[38] Philosophy's emphasis on reason fostered attacks against sovereignty, an insidious form of rebellion that separated human beings from God and his sacred earthly representatives. The historian Jean-Louis Darcel encapsulates Maistre's position: "The Revolution is the political manifestation of man's rebellion against God in his will to substitute, for the natural order willed by the creator (a theocentric order), an order founded on human reason alone (an an-

36. For example, Bradley collapses the distinction between sacrifice and execution when he writes: "In fact, Maistre will present his notorious theme of the executioner and his victims within a thoroughly sacrificial framework." "Logics of Violence," vol. 1, 172. In *A Modern Maistre* (63), Bradley extends his argument: "Maistre finds the meaning of capital punishment precisely within the sacrificial economy of debts and satisfactions, of substitution and reversibility." One can certainly interpret Maistre's discussion of punishment and executioners as sacrificial. Maistre, however, avoids that interpretation because, in his view, executioners kill guilty criminals. In contrast, sacrificial victims must be innocent. In *Considérations sur la France,* Maistre defends his argument that the Terror was divine punishment and not a form of sacrifice when he writes: "For a long time no one has seen punishment so dreadful, inflicted on such a great number of sinners. No doubt there are innocents among the unfortunates, but they are far fewer than one commonly imagines." ("Depuis longtemps on n'avoit vu une punition aussi effrayante, infligée à un aussi grand nombre de coupables. Il y a des innocens, sans doute, parmi les malheureux, mais il y en a bien moins qu'on ne l'imagine communément.") Maistre, *Considérations sur la France,* in *Ecrits sur la Révolution, 99.*

37. Jean-Louis Darcel, "Maistre and the French Revolution," in Lebrun, *Maistre Studies,* 187.

38. For a discussion of Maistre's reaction to the Enlightenment, see Berlin, "Joseph de Maistre and the Origins of Fascism."

thropocentric order)."[39] Although Darcel overstates the revolutionary impulse to create an anthropocentric order founded "on human reason alone," he also captures the principal reason for Maistre's hatred of the Revolution.

According to Maistre, nothing positive can come from a revolution mounted by political and religious heretics. The fundamental error committed by the revolutionaries was their allowing themselves to undertake the task of political foundation. Such voluntaristic and positivistic thinking is wholly incompatible with Maistre's belief that human beings are incapable of creating political or religious institutions.[40] For Maistre, all great and lasting institutions emerge shrouded in mystery because they are divine miracles. Although Maistre is not entirely hostile to the idea of republicanism, he believes that the absence of large republics in Western history confirms the futility of trying to construct a great French republic.[41] Maistre believes that human beings cannot create a form of politics that has never previously existed:

> Man can modify anything in the sphere of his activity, but he creates nothing: such is his law, in the physical as in the moral realm.
>
> Man can without a doubt plant a seed, grow a tree, perfect it through grafting, and prune it in a hundred ways; but never has he imagined that he had the power to make a tree.

> L'homme peut tout modifier dans la sphère de son activité, mais il ne crée rien: telle est sa loi, au physique comme au moral.
>
> L'homme peut sans doute planter un pépin, élever un arbre, le perfectionner par la greffe, et le tailler en cent manières; mais jamais il ne s'est figuré qu'il avait le pouvoir de faire un arbre.[42]

Reflecting on freedom and necessity in a monotheistic world, Maistre argues that humans can modify the physical and moral orders, but that creation is beyond their reach. Trees, like governments or religions, can be altered in a variety of different ways—some good, some evil—but they cannot be created from

---

39. "La Révolution est la manifestation politique de la rébellion de l'homme contre Dieu dans sa volonté de substituer à l'ordre naturel voulu par le créateur (ordre théocentrique) un ordre fondé sur la seule raison humaine (ordre anthropocentrique)." Jean-Louis Darcel, "Joseph de Maistre et la Révolution française," *Revue des études maistriennes*, no. 3 (1977), 41.

40. Maistre's most powerful discussion of his antifoundational views can be found in Joseph de Maistre, *On God and Society*, trans. Laurence M. Porter (Chicago: Henry Regnery, 1959). See especially 39–42, where, among other reflections on the impossibility of political foundation, Maistre writes: "*Man cannot create a constitution, and no legitimate constitution can be written.*"

41. Maistre, *Ecrits sur la Révolution*, 122–123. Maistre, however, was willing to concede the existence of small republics, such as Rome.

42. Ibid., 141.

scratch. That the *lumières* believed it possible to create a French republic is, for Maistre, an illustration of the pure hubris of rational thought. The supreme example of this view is Robespierre's claim that "everything has changed in the physical order; everything must change in the moral and political order."[43] Such materialist ideology coupled with intense voluntarism led the revolutionaries to doubt and then to deny what Maistre considers to be the most elemental organizing and limiting principle: natural law circumscribes the political creations that human reason may entertain. When the French revolutionaries killed Louis XVI in order to establish a republic, they violated natural law, drawing God's wrath for having manipulated the political realm in ways reserved exclusively for the divine.

Maistre characterizes punishment in three ways. It is first a mode of regenerative purification. With the Revolution in mind, Maistre claims: "There is no punishment that does not purify; there is no disorder that the ETERNAL LOVE does not turn against the principle of evil."[44] God commandeers all disorders, all efforts to depart from his will, and transforms them into punishment. Thus, Maistre viewed the revolutionaries' effort to found the Republic as the work of God: "Never did Robespierre, Collot, or Barère think to establish the revolutionary government and the Reign of Terror. They were insensibly driven there by circumstances, and never will we see anything similar."[45] Evil becomes a violent juggernaut for goodness. Second, punishment that does not kill fosters moral correction. With surgical precision, punishment removes the evil that originally provoked the crime. When evil is so deeply ingrained that punishment cannot regenerate the individual, however, death is the only appropriate consequence.[46] Finally, deadly punishment applied collectively is a form of erasure. In claiming that "if Providence erases, no doubt it is to write," Maistre explains how the Terror simultaneously disintegrated French society and exhibited a divine teleology from which traditional political order was certain to emerge.[47]

Punishment's capacity for moral regeneration is not a foundational power. Rather, legitimate punishment—violence sanctioned by a divine, sovereign power—operates regeneratively. By acting against those who seek political

43. "Tout a changé dans l'ordre physique; tout doit changer dans l'ordre moral et politique." Robespierre, *Œuvres,* vol. 10, 444.

44. "Il n'y a point de châtiment qui ne purifie; il n'y a point de désordre que l'AMOUR ETERNEL ne tourne contre le principe du mal." Maistre, *Ecrits sur la Révolution,* 122.

45. "Jamais Robespierre, Collot ou Barère, ne pensèrent à établir le gouvernement révolutionnaire et le régime de la Terreur. Ils y furent conduits insensiblement par les circonstances, et jamais on ne reverra rien de pareil." Ibid., 96.

46. Maistre discusses this function of punishment at the end of the fifth dialogue in his *Soirées,* vol. 1, 291–292.

47. "Si la Providence *efface,* sans doute c'est pour écrire." Maistre, *Ecrits sur la Révolution,* 111.

change, punishment restores the moral fabric that supports royal and ecclesiastic authority.[48] More generally, since crimes against sovereignty result only in political disorder, punishment is the mechanism through which sovereignty and order are reestablished. As Maistre explains, punishment restores the social and political equilibrium disturbed by criminality:

> Therefore, there is, in the temporal circle, a divine and visible law for the punishment of crime; and that law, as stable as the society that it sustains, has been invariably executed since the origin of things: evil being on the earth, it acts constantly, and, by a necessary consequence, it must be constantly repressed through punishment; and in effect, we see on the surface of the globe a constant action on the part of all governments to arrest or to punish attempts at crime: the sword of justice has no sheath; always it must menace or strike.

> Il y a donc, dans le cercle temporel, une loi divine et visible pour la punition du crime; et cette loi, aussi stable que la société qu'elle fait subsister, est exécutée invariablement depuis l'origine des choses: le mal étant sur la terre, il agit constamment, et, par une conséquence nécessaire, il doit être constamment réprimé par le châtiment; et en effet, nous voyons sur la surface du globe une action constante de tous les gouvernements pour arrêter ou punir les attentats du crime: le glaive de la justice n'a point de fourreau; toujours il doit menacer ou frapper.[49]

Because crime causes social and political instability, divine law requires that punishment guarantee society's return to the rule of crown and scepter. Although temporal authority often takes responsibility for the punishment of crime, human justice is as imperfect as its administrators. The ceaseless task of punishment is therefore shared by monarchs and God, who use punitive violence to maintain their power. Berlin accurately describes this Maistrian view of punishment as "the expression of a genuine conviction . . . that men can only be saved by being hemmed in by the terror of authority."[50] In other words, brutal, salutary justice is a central feature of Maistre's worldview. Violent punishment is the sine qua non for obedience and order.

The solitary and foreboding executioner, the most interesting, violent figure

---

48. Michel Foucault writes: "The public execution, however hasty and everyday, belongs to a whole series of great rituals in which power is eclipsed and restored . . . over and above the crime that has placed the sovereign in contempt, it [public execution] deploys before all eyes an invincible force. Its aim is not so much to re-establish a balance as to bring into play, as its extreme point, the dissymmetry between the subject who has dared to violate the law and the all-powerful sovereign who displays his strength." *Discipline and Punish*, trans. Alan Sheridan (New York: Vintage, 1979), 48–49.

49. Maistre, *Soirées*, vol. 1, 34.

50. Maistre, *Considerations on France*, xxix.

in Maistre's political imagination, superbly illustrates the theoretical importance of punishment. Called the *bourreau* in French, the executioner is responsible for enforcing justice on behalf of earthly sovereigns. He symbolizes the intimate connection between sacred violence and the maintenance of sovereignty. Wielding the "sword of the law," the executioner serves Maistre as a concrete example of conservative violence. Here is Maistre's long description of the executioner, which powerfully communicates why Maistre labels him the cornerstone of society:

> Who is this inexplicable being, who, when there are so many agreeable, lucrative, honest and even honourable professions to choose among, in which a man can exercise his skill or his powers, has chosen that of torturing or killing his own kind? This head, this heart, are they made like our own? Is there not something in them that is peculiar, and alien to our nature? Myself, I have no doubt about this. He is made like us externally. He is born like all of us. But he is an extraordinary being, and it needs a special decree to bring him into existence as a member of the human family—a *fiat* of the creative power. He is created like a law unto himself. Consider what he is in the opinion of mankind, and try to conceive, if you can, how he can manage to ignore or defy this opinion. Hardly has he been assigned to his proper dwelling-place, hardly has he taken possession of it, when others remove their homes elsewhere whence they can no longer see him. In the midst of this desolation, in this sort of vacuum formed around him, he lives along with his mate and his young, who acquaint him with the sound of the human voice: without them he would hear nothing but groans . . . The gloomy signal is given; an abject servitor of justice knocks on his door to tell him that he is wanted; he goes; he arrives in a public square covered by a dense, trembling mob. A poisoner, a parricide, a man who has committed sacrilege is tossed to him: he seizes him, stretches him, ties him to a horizontal cross, he raises his arm; there is a horrible silence; there is no sound but that of bones cracking under the bars, and the shrieks of the victim. He unties him. He puts him on the wheel; the shattered limbs are entangled in the spokes; the head hangs down; the hair stands up, and the mouth gaping open like a furnace from time to time emits only a few bloodstained words to beg for death. He has finished. His heart is beating, but it is with joy: he congratulates himself, he says in his heart "Nobody quarters as well as I." He steps down. He holds out his bloodstained hand, the justice throws him—from a distance—a few pieces of gold, which he catches through a double row of human beings standing back in horror. He sits down to table, and he eats. Then he goes to bed and sleeps. And on the next day, when he wakes, he thinks of something totally different from what he did the day before. Is he a man? Yes. God receives him in his shrines, and allows him to pray. He is not a criminal. Nevertheless no tongue dares declare that he is virtuous, that he is an honest man, that he is estimable. No moral

praise seems appropriate to him, for everyone else is assumed to have relations with human beings: he has none. And yet all greatness, all power, all subordination rest on the executioner. He is the terror and the bond of human association. Remove this mysterious agent from the world, and in an instant order yields to chaos: thrones fall, society disappears. God, who has created sovereignty, has also made punishment; he has fixed the earth upon these two poles: "for Jehovah is master of the twin poles and upon them he maketh turn the world" ([1 Samuel] 2:8).[51]

Qu'est-ce donc que cet être inexplicable qui a préféré à tous les métiers agréables, lucratifs, honnêtes et même honorables qui se présentent en foule à la force ou à la dextérité humaine, celui de tourmenter et de mettre à mort ses semblables? Cette tête, ce coeur sont-ils faits comme les nôtres? ne contiennent-ils rien de particulier et d'étranger à notre nature? Pour moi, je n'en sais pas douter. Il est fait comme nous extérieurement; il naît comme nous; mais c'est un être extraordinaire, et pour qu'il existe dans la famille humaine il faut un décret particulier, un FIAT de la puissance créatrice. Il est créé comme un monde. Voyez ce qu'il est dans l'opinion des hommes, et comprenez, si vous pouvez, comment il peut ignorer cette opinion ou l'affronter! A peine l'autorité a-t-elle désigné sa demeure, à peine en a-t-il pris possession que les autres habitations reculent jusqu'à ce qu'elles ne voient plus la sienne. C'est au milieu de cette solitude et de cette espèce de vide formé autour de lui qu'il vit seul avec sa femelle et ses petits, qui lui font connaître la voix de l'homme: sans eux il ne connaîtrait que les gémissements . . . Un signal lugubre est donné; un ministre abject de la justice vient frapper à sa porte et l'avertir qu'on a besoin de lui: il part; il arrive sur une place publique couverte d'une foule pressée et palpitante. On lui jette un empoisonneur, un parricide, un sacrilège: il le saisit, il l'étend, il le lie sur une croix horizontale, il lève le bras: alors il se fait un silence horrible, et l'on n'entend plus que le cri des os qui éclatent sous la barre, et les hurlements de la victime. Il la détache; il la porte sur une roue: les membres fracassés s'enlacent dans les rayons; la tête pend; les cheveux se hérissent, et la bouche, ouverte comme une fournaise, n'envoie plus par intervalle qu'un petit nombre de paroles sanglantes qui appellent la mort. Il a fini: le coeur lui bat, mais c'est de joie; il s'applaudit; il dit dans son coeur: *Nul ne roue mieux que moi.* Il descend: il tend sa main souillée de sang, et la justice y jette de loin quelques pièces d'or qu'il emporte à travers une double haie d'hommes écartés par l'horreur. Il se met à table, et il mange; au lit ensuite, et il dort. Et le lendemain, en s'éveillant, il songe à tout autre chose qu'à ce qu'il a fait la veille. Est-ce un homme? Oui: Dieu le reçoit dans ses temples et lui permet de prier. Il n'est pas criminel; cependant aucune langue ne consent à dire, par exemple, *qu'il est vertueux, qu'il est honnête homme, qu'il est estimable, etc.* Nul éloge moral ne peut lui convenir; car tous supposent des rapports avec les hommes, et il n'en a point.

51. This translation is from Berlin, *Crooked Timber of Humanity,* 116–117.

Et cependant toute grandeur, toute puissance, toute subordination repose sur l'exécuteur: il est l'horreur et le lien de l'association humaine. Otez du monde cet agent incompréhensible; dans l'instant même l'ordre fait place au chaos, les trônes s'abîment et la société disparaît. Dieu qui est l'auteur de la souveraineté, l'est donc aussi du châtiment: il a jeté notre terre sur ces deux pôles; car Jéhovah est le maître des deux pôles, et sur eux il fait tourner le monde.[52]

Maistre's description of the executioner is chillingly detached. He marries, has children, prays; and yet, because he takes pride in the brutal artfulness of his craft, the executioner seems barely human. Despite appearing barbaric and antimodern, this portrait of the executioner illustrates an important facet of Maistre's critique of modernity. Isolated, instrumental, and obedient, Maistre's executioner is a professional whose humanity has been debased by the peculiar circumstances of his work. Under the Old Regime, the executioner was an extraordinary, exceptional figure; he singularly defied natural law in order to prevent its corruption. In contrast, the French revolutionaries universalized this modern executioner. Rather than relying upon one man to exercise the otherwise forbidden violence required to legitimize pure sovereignty, the revolutionaries disseminated that hideous power to society as a whole and thereby demonstrated human action shorn of divine limitation. In making this critique, Maistre anticipates twentieth-century thinkers, such as Max Horkheimer and Theodore Adorno, who recognize the terrible dangers of applying instrumental rationality to violence.

In contrast to Maistre's modern, dehumanized executioner, Henri Sanson, the last of France's dynastic family of executioners, communicates overwhelming humanism in his memoirs.[53] Like his forefathers, Sanson is a reluctant executioner, resentful that his terrible professional inheritance has separated him from society. Sanson, who read Maistre's *Soirées*, was fascinated by Maistre's claim that executioners are the keystones of society, but somewhat revolted by the Maistrian idea that human blood must continually flow on earth.[54] Whereas Sanson laments his worldly detachment, Maistre's executioner appears to relish his extraordinary status. Brutish and mechanistic, "a law unto himself," Maistre's executioner exists beyond good and evil. It is ironic that Maistre attributes such *inhuman* traits to a man whose duty is to torture and kill. Maistre constantly reminds his readers that human beings are evil, bloodthirsty creatures who take pride and joy in harming other living things. Compared with the all-too-human Sanson, Maistre's executioner is a superman and unnecessarily sepa-

---

52. Maistre, *Soirées*, vol. 1, 32–34.
53. Henri Sanson, *Sept générations d'exécuteurs, 1688–1857*, 6 vols. (Paris: Dupray de la Mahérie, 1862).
54. Ibid., vol. 1, 22–23; vol. 6, 272–273.

rated from his fellow human beings, who ultimately have few qualms about bloodshed.

In contending that the executioner is "the terror and bond of human association," Maistre raises the important political question of why people form societies. Blending Christian and Aristotelian views of human nature, Maistre reasons that man is a naturally social creature. On the basis of historical observation, he concludes that "man is a social being who has always been observed in society."[55] Humans naturally gravitate toward each other because they possess divine faculties that foster sociability. Reason and language, or "manifest reason," "prove that man is made for society, because a creature cannot have received faculties in order not to use them." By exercising reason and language in a social context, humans fulfill God's desire that they achieve collective strength and natural dominion over the earth. Thus, the God-given fruit of social life is the capacity to dominate other creatures and to manipulate nature for the benefit of human existence. In Maistre's estimation, humans would never choose a state of isolation, which would prevent them from using their natural faculties and cause them to suffer from nature's vicissitudes. Maistre categorically rejects the view of Enlightenment thinkers, such as Jean-Jacques Rousseau, who maintain that human beings originated in a presocial, prepolitical, prelapsarian state of nature. Instead, Maistre argues that human beings are subhuman in a natural state: "for *man* there has never been a time prior to society, because before the formation of political societies, man was not quite man."[56]

Although humans are naturally social, they also possess the capacity to provoke social entropy. Decadence, degradation, decline, corruption, dissolution, and disorder—these words characterize the human proclivity for antisocial behavior. The executioner's role is to check these entropic forces, thereby regenerating society. The executioner can fulfill this sacred role because sovereignty and punishment are divine creations that occupy opposite ends of the axis of political power. The positive sacred power of the king and negative sacred power of the executioner are mutually dependent and reinforcing. By enforcing obedience to the law, understood in its broadest religious, cultural, and political sense, the executioner serves as the bond of human association. In this world, social and political life must occur within a limited sphere of activity whose boundaries are policed by the executioner. Through punishment, the executioner stabilizes society by reinscribing the matrixes of terrestrial power authorized by God.[57]

55. Maistre, *Against Rousseau,* 23.

56. Ibid., 31, 49.

57. For a discussion of violent punishment as the "force of law," see Jacques Derrida, "Force of Law: The 'Mystical Foundation of Authority,'" *Cardozo Law Review* 11, nos. 5–6 (July–August 1990).

Because Maistre's analysis of the executioner's social and political roles depends upon divine authorization, his theory of punishment is easily co-opted. Maistre may be adamant that divine punishment is not sacrificial, but, from the perspective of the French revolutionaries, their sacrificial acts exhibited both sacred and punitive qualities. Similarly, Maistre claims that the revolutionary executioner was an agent of divine retribution, working toward the conservative regeneration of French society. In the revolutionary imagination, however, the executioner used sacred, regenerative violence to mold the moral foundation of a new republic. Only the existence and role of God separate the revolutionaries' view of punishment from Maistre's. Indeed, without the centrality of Maistre's Catholic God, Maistre's position that the executioner is the "terror and bond of human association" would have strongly appealed to the authors of the French Revolution. It was always their belief that sacrifice generated sublime violence around which a new, republican nation would form. Despite the fact that Maistre abhorred this outcome, he unintentionally lends theoretical support to it by embracing the socially unifying power of violent regeneration.

Maistre's Conservative Theory of Sacrifice

Sacrifice is the most complicated of Maistre's applications of violence. Although both punishment and sacrifice operate regeneratively in his work, Maistre goes to great lengths to distinguish the two forms of bloodshed. He explores the theoretical significance of sacrifice in *Eclaircissement sur les sacrifices,* posthumously published along with his most ambitious work, *Les Soirées de Saint-Pétersbourg* (1821). In *Eclaircissement,* Maistre studies the religious function of sacrifice and makes an essential distinction between its Christian and pagan forms. Although Maistre argues that all sacrificial rites have the same origin, he considers only Christian sacrifice, or martyrdom, to be morally legitimate. Maistre celebrates Christian martyrs who reenact Christ's crucifixion by choosing to suffer and die in order to give life to the *corpus mysticum.* Maistre also highlights the Eucharist, a symbolic Christian sacrifice that achieves the same effect as martyrdom but without actual bloodshed. For Maistre, however, all non-Christian human sacrifice or scapegoating is corrupt. Maistre's contempt for pagan sacrifice is rooted in his belief that sacrificial practices cannot create a relationship of obligation between a people and their god(s). To sacrifice friend or foe for the sake of healthy crops or victorious battles strikes Maistre as an egregious misinterpretation of the "dogma of reversibility," Maistre's phrase for the basic principle underlying all sacrificial rites. Although Maistre sympathizes with the impulse of pre-Christian peoples to expiate their collective sins through human sacrifice, he never condones the practice itself.

Maistre argues that the practice of human sacrifice is deduced from the dogma of reversibility, which holds that the destruction of innocence remedies guilt. Thanks to this dogma, Maistre can avoid labeling the executioner's craft sacrificial because he directs violence against the guilty, not the innocent. Punishment does not entail a sacrificial metamorphosis, a substitution of innocence for guilt; rather, punishment is a rite of purification through which the victim's sin or guilt is expiated, thus eliminating the threat of contamination. Although Maistre firmly believes that redemption results from the destruction of innocence, he also explains that this dogma has historically inspired terrible misinterpretations, the most important of which is human sacrifice. The dogma of reversibility achieves legitimate expression only when it becomes codified by Christianity and expressed through practices that involve the destruction of innocence, such as self-sacrifice or martyrdom. In his discussion of the suffering of innocents for the benefit of the guilty in *Considérations sur la France,* Maistre notes that martyrs are the only victims capable of achieving this sacrificial effect: "Decius had faith that the sacrifice of his life would be accepted by Divinity, and that he could balance all the evils that were menacing his country. Christianity came to consecrate this dogma, which is infinitely natural to man, although it appears difficult to achieve it through reason."[58]

Maistre maintains that sacrifice is an ancient, widely performed ritual practice that originated in ideas consistent with Christian beliefs. He argues that pre-Christian peoples accepted the basic truth of original sin, which they demonstrated when, in comparing themselves to their gods, they became aware of their distinctively human flaws.[59] In describing this ancient belief, Maistre offers the original rationale for sacrifice: "The gods are good, and we take from them all the benefits that we enjoy: we owe them praise and thanksgiving. But the gods are just, and we are guilty: we must appease them, we must expiate our crimes; and, in order to do that, the most powerful means is *sacrifice.*"[60] Maistre considers the ancient syllogism that led the ancients to initiate the practice of sacrifice. This logic is familiar because it begins with the basic Christian principle that all are born guilty in need of redemption. While Maistre can take com-

---

58. "Decius avait la foi que le sacrifice de sa vie serait accepté par la Divinité, et qu'il pouvait faire équilibre à tous les maux qui menaçaient sa patrie. Le Christianisme est venu consacrer ce dogme qui est infiniment naturel à l'homme, quoiqu'il paroisse difficile d'y arriver par le raisonnement." Maistre, *Ecrits sur la Révolution,* 121.

59. See Maistre, *Sur les sacrifices,* 21–22.

60. "Les dieux sont bons, et nous tenons d'eux tous les biens dont nous jouissons: nous leur devons la louange et l'action de grâce. Mais les dieux sont justes, et nous sommes coupables: il faut les apaiser, il faut expier nos crimes; et, pour y parvenir, le moyen le plus puissant est le *sacrifice.*" Ibid., 22.

fort in his belief that all human beings have the same spiritual needs, he cannot, as a good Christian, praise those whose guilty impulses drive them to spill human blood. Because they were not Christians, the ancients misunderstood how to expiate their sins properly and thus engaged in what Maistre viewed as corrupt sacrificial practices.[61]

Maistre holds that the ancients reasoned correctly about the universality of human guilt, but were deeply mistaken about how to expiate it. Following the "incontestable truth" of the dogma of reversibility, the ancients engaged in animal and human sacrifice. What the ancients misunderstood, however, is that the reversibility of innocence and guilt cannot be achieved through simple substitution. Here Maistre describes how the misinterpretation of the dogma of reversibility led to animal sacrifice: "It was believed (as one has and always will believe) *that the innocent could pay for the guilty;* from which it was concluded that, life being guilty, a *less precious life could be offered and accepted for another.* Thus the blood of animals was offered, and this *soul,* offered for a *soul,* the ancients called *antipsychon, vicariam animam;* as one would say *soul for soul* or *substituted soul.*"[62]

Maistre recognizes in animal sacrifice a principle of substitution that has important implications for the redemption of guilt. The ancients practiced animal sacrifice because they thought that an innocent soul, less precious to God (or to the gods), could redeem the guilt of a more precious, sinful human one. Well before the advent of anthropology, Maistre insightfully recognizes that only useful, gentle, and docile animals—anthropomorphically innocent—were selected for sacrifice. He also perceptively remarks that bloodshed is essential to animal sacrifice, reinforcing his belief that blood must house the soul. Finally, and most importantly for his theory of sacrifice, Maistre suggests that the dogma of reversibility has two related components: it describes the capacity for innocence to redeem guilt, and it implies that substitution is the means to achieve that end.

The political significance of the dogma of reversibility becomes explicit when Maistre considers its extension to human sacrifice. Soon after humans decided that killing an animal could expiate their guilt, Maistre contends that humans extended the logic of reversibility to the belief that the life of one human being could redeem a whole collectivity. This logic is precisely that of the scapegoat. While Maistre's judgment of animal sacrifice may be equivocal, he unabashedly condemns human sacrifice, calling it a "horrible superstition," an "abominable custom," and a "frightful error." Maistre argues that this cruel ex-

---

61. Ibid., 47.
62. "On croyait (comme on a cru, comme on croira toujours) *que l'innocent pouvait payer pour le coupable;* d'où l'on concluait que la vie étant coupable, *une vie moins précieuse pouvait être offerte et acceptée pour une autre.* On offrit donc le sang des animaux, et cette âme, offerte pour une âme, les anciens l'appelèrent *antipsychon, vicariam animam;* comme qui dirait âme pour âme ou âme substituée." Ibid., 31–32.

tension of the dogma of reversibility was based on the following two sophisms, which he poses as interrogatives: (1) *"To save an army, a town, even a great sovereign, what is one man?"* and (2) *"What is the life of a culprit or an enemy?"*[63] Both questions reveal how the extrapolation of the dogma of reversibility to scapegoating departs from Maistre's Christian view of ritual destruction. No longer is sacrifice concerned with sin, redemption, and reversibility; religious language is entirely absent from these interrogatives. Instead, Maistre suggests that the practitioners of human sacrifice began to view their rites in terms of politics and obligation. They erroneously believed that they could sacrifice a human being to God or the gods in exchange for a divine guarantee of terrestrial benefits, such as success in a war, the health of a sovereign, or the safety of a collectivity. Maistre's claim is weak because it is only the nature of Christian obligation that allows him to distinguish between "good" violence, such as punishment and war, and "bad" violence, such as scapegoating. In a Christian world, punishment expiates criminals, and war redeems collectivities. Human sacrifice, however, reflects only the debasement of its practitioners and occurs only where Christianity is not practiced. Thus, Maistre maintains that bloodshed's salutary effects do not extend beyond the Christian realm, illustrating once again how Maistre problematically links the properties of violence to the context in which it occurs.

Despite his condemnation of human sacrifice, Maistre paradoxically acknowledges that it fulfills important social functions. For instance, he observes that the Indian practice of suttee is designed to maintain patriarchal control of women. Praising a similar impulse to control women in Catholicism, Maistre concludes that the sacrifice of women is just one of the many ways in which non-Christian men have taken precautions against the social dangers posed by women. Although Maistre acknowledges that the Gospel elevates women to the level of men in Christian societies by giving them certain "rights," he celebrates the strict limits to women's freedom imposed by natural law. In Maistre's view, all societies have cultural boundaries and social hierarchies that hem individuals into particular roles and support a distinct status quo. Violent sacrifice performs the same function in India as divine law does in Christian countries: it maintains social order by rigidly defining gender roles. This is precisely Maistre's point when he writes: "Finally, no legislator should forget this maxim: *Before erasing the Gospel, one has to lock up the women,* or crush them by terrible laws, such as those in India."[64]

---

63. *"Pour sauver une armée, une ville, un grand souverain même, qu'est-ce qu'un homme?"* and *"Qu'est-ce que la vie d'un coupable ou d'un ennemi?"* Ibid., 34–35.

64. "Enfin aucun législateur ne doit oublier cette maxime: *Avant d'effacer l'Evangile, il faut enfermer les femmes,* ou les accabler par des lois épouvantables, telles que celles de l'Inde." Ibid., 45–46.

Maistre's explanation of suttee and his reflections on ancient Greek and Roman sacrificial practices illustrate his development of a social theory of sacrifice. Years before Marcel Mauss and Emile Durkheim, Maistre peered into the murky symbolism of blood sacrifice and discovered its capacity to forge cultural distinctions and foster social unification. This discovery supports Maistre's view that sacrificial practices are a mechanism of social maintenance, initiation, discipline, and control. More importantly, it lays the groundwork for the conservative view of sacrifice that dominates the French discourse. Although the French revolutionaries hoped that sacrifice would inspire novelty in politics, Maistre's theoretical critique of their practices pushes the French intellectual debate about sacrifice and politics in an antirevolutionary direction, the co-optive efforts of Sorel and Bataille notwithstanding.

Girard's notion of sacrificial substitution, which secularizes Maistre's dogma of reversibility, offers one contemporary illustration of this conservative trend. In *Violence and the Sacred,* Girard argues that sacrificial substitution is a mechanism for preventing and quelling intracommunal violence.[65] The sacrificial substitute or scapegoat fulfills this explicitly politically conservative function by allowing communities to direct violence outward toward socially marginal victims. In this way, communities without functional judicial institutions can dissipate the violence that would otherwise destabilize or destroy them. In Girard's view, reliance on stabilizing sacrificial rites reestablishes the cultural boundaries, social hierarchies, and customary rules of a particular status quo. Girard's conservative theory of sacrifice is thoroughly Maistrian in political orientation.

Although Maistre appreciates both non-Christian and Christian sacrifice because it is socially and politically conservative, he is loath to believe that human sacrifice achieves the same redemptive effects as Christ's crucifixion. Through a process of exchange—death for redemption—Christ destroys his own innocence in order to bring salvation to the abject. Maistre admires how those who practiced human sacrifice rightly sought the same morally regenerative effect, despite their being mistaken about the proper sacrificial mechanism to achieve it. By offering the Crucifixion, martyrs, and the Eucharist, Christianity has perfected these ancient, decadent sacrificial practices. By providing universal redemption, a single Christian sacrifice and mimetic versions of it obviate the need for human scapegoats. Furthermore, Maistre conceives of Christian sacrifices—real and symbolic—as providing communities with the ability to stabilize ritually their cultural distinctions. When, for example, the customary rules that circumscribe the relationship between men and women

65. René Girard, *Violence and the Sacred,* trans. Patrick Gregory (Baltimore: Johns Hopkins University Press, 1992).

break down, how does society reestablish them? In Maistre's view, Christianity solves this and other forms of cultural ambiguity through punishment, war, and, most important, sacrifice. By touting its morally regenerative and culturally restrictive powers, Maistre demonstrates that sacrifice is a political device for the maintenance of a particular type of authority. The regeneration of a morality that affirms "natural" social distinctions allows Christian sacrificial rites to legitimate the sovereign power of the monarch, whose rule depends upon those inequalities.

Maistre also argues that human sacrifice has ontological implications for the human soul. To make this point, he weds Christianity's Manichaean view of guilt and innocence with his antimaterialism: guilt is associated with the body and blood, which act as fetters upon the soul. In describing how ancient people understood this aspect of their nature, Maistre writes: "But the root of this debasement, or the *reification* of man, if I am permitted to make up this word, resided in the *sensuous principle, in life,* in short *in the soul,* so carefully distinguished by the ancients from *the mind* or intelligence."[66] Animals and humans are embodied creatures, a condition that Maistre presciently labels *réité,* or "reified."[67] It is the "thingness" of human beings, their materiality, from which guilt springs. *Réité* thus describes the materiality of original sin, the aspect of the human dualism shared by the sensible world. If, as Maistre suggests, the ancients viewed themselves as degraded because of their reification, then animal and human sacrifice must serve to alleviate that condition. Sacrifice thus permits a guilty community to participate collectively in the destruction of some*thing* deemed innocent. By spilling blood—Maistre's fetish for guilt—the community vicariously experiences the destruction of materiality and achieves collective self-transcendence, a profoundly anti-individualistic sentiment that fosters social union.

Sacrifice is thus a Maistrian weapon against materialism and materiality. In its non-Christian forms, ritual bloodshed is antiutilitarian because it involves the destruction of a useful thing in order to create a bond between a people and their god(s). In its Christian form, sacrifice becomes a mimetic expression of the founding moment when Jesus, a theandric being, martyrs himself, destroys his physical body, and breathes life into his *corpus mysticum.* Maistre extends this mimetic view of sacrifice when he suggests that the Eucharist perfects Chris-

---

66. "Mais la racine de cette dégradation, ou la *réité* de l'homme, s'il est permis de fabriquer ce mot, résidait dans le *principe sensible, dans la vie, dans l'âme* enfin, si soigneusement distinguée par les anciens, de *l'esprit* ou de l'intelligence." Maistre, *Sur les sacrifices,* 22.

67. The word *réifié,* which translates as "reified," entered the French language only in the mid-nineteenth century. Given the context in which Maistre uses the word *réité,* I believe he meant it to signify the same idea, namely, the congealing of a living process or concept, such as the human soul, into a thing.

tian sacrifice by achieving the same function as martyrdom but without actual violence.[68] In generating a state of immanence from the loss or destruction of materiality, each of these forms of sacrifice emphasizes ideal collective identity over more embodied, concrete individual ones. Sacrifice also graphically illustrates how a unified, social, abstract whole is constructed by "wasting" a singular, differentiated, corporeal part.

Although one might expect Maistre to expand his critique of human sacrifice to the French Revolution, he does so in only a limited fashion. Maistre sees no explanation for the bloody horrors of the Revolution other than revolutionary contempt for Christianity. Four centuries of experience, he writes, have established the following truth: *"That wherever the true God is not known and served by virtue of an explicit revelation, man will always sacrifice man and often will eat him."*[69] By claiming that sacrifice and cannibalism occur among pre- and non-Christian peoples, Maistre recalls the language used by the *sans-culottes* to describe their excessive preregicidal violence. Maistre says little about revolutionary sacrificial practices, choosing instead to characterize the Terror almost exclusively in terms of human crime and divine punishment. Only the regicide of Louis XVI elicits sacrificial language from Maistre: "The august martyr seems to fear escaping his sacrifice, or rendering his victimization less perfect: what acceptance!"[70] Maistre describes Louis XVI's willingness to become the "perfect" sacrificial victim. The sacrifice to which Maistre refers, however, is not akin to those practiced by the ancients. Maistre extols Louis XVI for choosing his death, transforming regicide into martyrdom, the only form of sacrifice consistent with Christian principles.

Martyrdom is the only form of blood sacrifice Maistre lauds because it repeats Christianity's founding act and offers collective benefits. Martyrs, whom Maistre deems innocent, ideally express the dogma of reversibility because they choose to give their lives in order to redeem collective guilt. This religious function is accompanied by a similar and equally important political one. Just like individuals, families, and sovereigns, nations benefit from the blood of martyrs: "We especially find all nations in agreement on the marvelous efficacy of the voluntary sacrifice of innocence that is devoted to divinity like a propitiatory victim."[71] Maistre signals the martyr's value for the health of the nation. With

---

68. Maistre, *Sur les sacrifices*, 66–67.

69. *"Que partout où le vrai Dieu ne sera pas connu et servi, en vertu d'une révélation expresse, l'homme immolera toujours l'homme, et souvent le dévorera."* Ibid., 47.

70. "L'auguste martyr semble craindre d'échapper au sacrifice, ou de rendre la victime moins parfaite: quelle acceptation!" Ibid., 59.

71. "On trouve spécialement toutes les nations d'accord sur l'efficacité merveilleuse du sacrifice volontaire de l'innocence qui se dévoue elle-même à la divinité comme une victime propitiatoire." Ibid., 58.

the French Revolution in mind, he continues: "When two parties clash in a revolution, if one sees precious victims fall on one side, one can wager that that party will finish the victor, despite all appearances to the contrary."[72] Although Maistre's "precious victim" is the king of France, his description of martyrdom's political function applies to the Revolution. Maistre contends that the expiatory power of the martyr serves only the party of order during periods of instability. In his view, the sublime attraction of sacrificed innocence fosters the social union of a newly purified, energized people. Maistrian martyrs, however, renew and regenerate nations; they do not found them. It is unimaginable to Maistre that partisans of the French Revolution could themselves successfully harness martyrdom's unique, salutary power.

Maistre's reflections on sacrifice culminate in the Eucharist, an abstract Catholic symbol of martyrdom. By thoroughly ritualizing self-sacrifice, the Eucharist allows the church to reenact perpetually its founding gesture. As Maistre writes, "This flesh made divine and perpetually sacrificed is presented to man under the exterior form of his privileged food: *and he who refuses to eat it will not live.*"[73] The Eucharist offers the possibility of purification to human beings born into sin. Furthermore, life in the *corpus mysticum,* like that in *corpus politicum,* is denied to those unwilling to participate in this rite. Thus, Catholic symbolic sacrifice is the perfect expression of the dogma of reversibility and humanity's escape from an earth "thirsting for blood." The Eucharist, which represents the flesh and blood of the original theandric sacrificial surrogate, obviates the need for an actual communal repetition of the bloody sacrifice, a significant advance in the perpetual human search for redemption.

A symbol of self-sacrifice and cannibalism, the Eucharist is a simulacrum of the sacrificial rites that Maistre deems degenerate. Indeed, it performs an identical function: "More rapid than a flash of lightning, more active than a thunderbolt, the theandric blood penetrates the guilty entrails in order to devour the pollution."[74] Maistre describes how the symbolic blood of Christ purifies the interior of the corrupt human body, cleansing it of sin. Here, for the first time, Maistre's blood fetish culminates in the consecration of a nonviolent religious practice. In celebrating the Eucharist, however, Maistre also reveals the flimsiness of his Manichaean view of sacrifice. What, ultimately, is the difference between the forms of sacrifice discussed by Maistre—animal, human, martyr, and

---

72. "Lorsque deux partis se heurtent dans une révolution, si l'on voit tomber d'un côté des victimes précieuses, on peut gager que ce parti finira par l'emporter, malgré toutes les apparences contraires." Ibid., 59.

73. "Cette chair divinisée et perpétuellement immolée est présentée à l'homme sous la forme extérieure de sa nourriture privilégiée: *et celui qui refusera d'en manger ne vivra point.*" Ibid., 66.

74. "Plus rapide que l'éclair, plus actif que la foudre, le sang théandrique pénètre les entrailles coupables pour en dévorer les souillures." Ibid.

Eucharist—when each derives from the dogma of reversibility and performs the same function? Maistre clearly celebrates the Eucharist because it is purely symbolic, a position that contrasts sharply with the hyperviolent characterizations of Maistre drawn by some of his most vociferous critics. Yet Maistre's lasting contribution to the French discourse on sacrificial violence is his discussion of the function, not the form, of sacrifice. For centuries, political thinkers have underscored the importance of dying for one's country. Maistre is the first to explain the social, cultural, and political effects of sacrifice. He is also the first to join these effects to a particular sacrificial economy upon whose balance humanity depends for earthly peace and heavenly rewards.

Although Maistre expects this sacrificial economy to support his politics, there is an unavoidable slippage between theocratic and republican sacrifice. Functionally, Maistrian sacrifice can just as easily support faith and a *corpus mysticum* as it can patriotism and a *corpus politicum*. It is mainly through the practice of sacrifice that Maistre attempts to part ways with the revolutionaries: he demonizes scapegoating, limiting sacrifice to martyrdom and symbolic self-sacrifice, such as the Eucharist. Though the revolutionaries tried to weave revolutionary martyrs into the fabric of republican identity, they relied more heavily on scapegoats to found their republic. Their troubles in applying sacrifice to political foundation, coupled with Maistre's difficulties in finding theoretical limits for the functions of sacrifice, illustrate why the revolutionary and Maistrian sacrificial economies are similarly unstable. The fact that the Terror generated such visceral, antirevolutionary sentiments among the Republic's greatest defenders demonstrates the instability of the revolutionary sacrificial economy. Rather than lending pure, sacred support to the legitimacy of the republic, the Terror disseminated sacrificial impurity, calling the sovereignty of the people into question. In other words, once placed in the service of politics, sacrificial violence exceeded revolutionary control. Despite the fact that Maistre distinguishes between Christian and non-Christian sacrificial economies, he faces the same problem as the French revolutionaries, only theoretically. Maistre's claim that "good" sacrifice is morally regenerative and "bad" degrading is based on a monotheistic sacrificial economy. Without that anchor, the functions of sacrifice, which Maistre places in the service of crown and scepter, would extend beyond Maistre's limits. Thus, as a model of sacrifice, the Crucifixion would become available to anyone who wished to harness the power of sacrifice for the sake of moral and political change. In the work of Georges Sorel and Georges Bataille, Maistrian sacrificial ideas become the basis for dynamic sacrificial economies that serve profoundly insurgent politics.

CHAPTER 3

Proletarian Redemption

Martyrdom and the Myth of Class Violence in the Work of Georges Sorel

With the possible exception of Karl Marx, who has so often been mis-interpreted as a theorist of violence, no thinker has been more closely identi-fied with socialist revolutionary bloodshed than Georges Sorel (1847–1922).[1] Marx theorized class conflict, a workingman's revolution, and the dictatorship of the proletariat. In all of Marx's massive oeuvre, however, he never develops a theory of violence. When Sorel entered socialist debates around the turn of the twentieth century, he significantly revised Marx's approach to the revolu-tionary role of violence. Whereas Marx emphasized a rational, scientific ex-amination of social phenomena, Sorel stressed the roles of myth and irrational drives. Marx devoted volumes to explaining how objective economic forces would propel the socialist revolution. In contrast, Sorel defended proletarian violence on moral grounds, arguing that class bloodshed could pry loose Marx's stubbornly uncooperative, objective economic forces. With the publi-cation of *Réflexions sur la violence* in 1906, Sorel immediately secured his place in the history of political thought by appearing to provide a theoretical voice to the class violence that was increasingly disrupting industrialized European countries.[2] Despite the longevity of this interpretation of his work, Sorel's reflections on violence reveal a radical intellectual whose deep reservations about the utility of bloodshed led him to celebrate the power of symbolic vi-olence. It is a concept of martyrdom that forms the core of Sorel's theory of

---

1. For a thoughtful discussion of the secondary importance of violence for Marx, see Hannah Arendt, *On Violence* (New York: Harcourt, Brace, 1970), 10–31.
2. Sorel originally published *Réflexions sur la violence* in 1906 as a series of articles in the journal *Le Mouvement socialiste*. These articles first appeared in book form in 1908 with an introduction titled "Let-tre à Daniel Halévy."

violence and that certifies his affinity to the sacrificial legacy of the French Revolution.[3]

The theoretical concept of violence that Sorel developed during his anarcho-syndicalist phase is a dynamic form of self-sacrificial bloodshed whose nature is principally symbolic and restrictive, whose function is morally regenerative, and whose goal is ultimately socialist revolution.[4] Although class conflict drives Sorel's anarcho-syndicalism, *Reflections on Violence*—his most infamous work—neither equates class conflict and violence, nor celebrates bloodshed, nor glorifies the experience of violence. Historically, class conflict has been bloody because, more often than not, states and employers have used force to compel workers to be productive, and because workers have sometimes resisted. Sorel links worker resistance, which he calls "proletarian violence," to strike activity, but does not assume that such militant collective action is necessarily violent. When strike violence does occur, Sorel anticipates the death of workers, not of bourgeois.

In lieu of strike violence or some other form of revolutionary bloodshed, Sorel develops an elaborate concept of worker self-sacrifice modeled on early Christian martyrs. He argues that proletarian martyrdom is the only effective form of revolutionary violence because it inspires—through an explicit sacrificial logic—the birth of a new community of producers based on socialist morals. Proletarian self-sacrificial violence inspires that morality, however, only when it is mediated by the "myth of the general strike," Sorel's name for the totality of feelings and images conjured by the expectation of a widespread and total cessation of productive activity. The myth of the general strike conveys a transcendent, redemptive meaning to martyrdom; martyrdom, in turn, gives the myth of the general strike an affective capacity to inspire revolutionary action. Remarkably, Sorel envisions no conclusion to class conflict, because the anarcho-syndicalist revolution is principally moral and its realization paradoxically creates the conditions of its own demise. For Sorel, self-sacrificial proletarian violence and the myth of the general strike participate in a process of socialist moral creation that has no concrete, revolutionary end.

3. I am mainly concerned with the development of Sorel's thought from 1889, the year of his first publication, to 1909, when he declared a break with the anarcho-syndicalist movement. This time span covers the period when Sorel produced his most mature theory of violence and, more importantly, when Sorel's work exhibited the closest affinity to the French discourse of sacrificial violence. Although Sorel's intellectual peregrinations after 1909 generated substantial contributions to his oeuvre and must form part of any global assessment of Sorel's work, he developed his concepts of myth and violence so little during this period that it does not warrant consideration here.

4. Sorel's hope for the development of socialist morals or the pursuit of a socialist revolution is perfectly consistent with his anarcho-syndicalist ideology. Turn-of-the-century French anarcho-syndicalists typically referred to revolution in socialist terms, even though they disagreed with a variety of socialist and Marxist organizations over issues such as revolutionary means, ends, and strategies.

At first glance, Sorel's intellectual background appears to have little in common with the French discourse on sacrificial violence. Primarily influenced by Marx, Proudhon, Nietzsche, and Bergson, Sorel was a French anarcho-syndicalist who embraced *Lebensphilosophie*. These intellectual credentials, however, belie a more fundamental truth about the man whom G. D. H. Cole once called a pessimist "moaning for blood."[5] While Marx and Proudhon strongly influenced Sorel's "conversion" to anarcho-syndicalism, and while Nietzsche and Bergson profoundly shaped Sorel's understanding of morality and will, it was Sorel's exploration of ancient Greek and early Christian sacrificial themes that shaped his concept of violence. Sorel repeatedly emphasized the historical connection between Christian martyrdom and his notion of proletarian violence, a parallel that was perfectly in keeping with the traditions of thought that animated both Joseph de Maistre and the authors of the French Revolution. Sorel was also attracted to secular ideas of sacrifice, which he acquired from his study of ancient Greece. It is true that the French revolutionaries extracted their notions of patriotism, heroism, and self-sacrifice from Roman republicanism. Sorel, however, found that these ancient virtues were best exemplified by the demos in pre-Socratic Athens. Despite the fact that he is now famous for his anarcho-syndicalist work on violence, Sorel gathered the seeds of what would later become his *Reflections on Violence* during the first fifteen years of his intellectual life—years devoted to the study of Hellenistic and biblical topics.[6]

Sorel belongs to the French discourse on sacrificial violence because he argues that self-sacrifice and myth collaborate in the regeneration of proletarian morality. His approach to the politics of sacrifice reflects, above all, his criticism of French revolutionary bloodshed and its role in the instauration of the French Republic. Yet, like Maistre's providential rereading of the French Revolution, Sorel's attempt to critique and correct the revolutionaries' mistakes ultimately belies itself. In Sorel's estimation, the revolutionary project was bound to fail because it relied on state terror, a form of violence that Sorel deemed counter-revolutionary and psychopathological. State violence not only supported the very institutions that Sorel, as an anarchist, wished to dismantle; it was also morally pernicious. Yet Sorel's concerns about the use and abuse of French revolutionary bloodshed did not prevent him from seeking to identify a truly revolutionary form of proletarian violence. Ironically, an analysis of this theoretical

5. G. D. H. Cole, *The Second International, 1889–1914*, vol. 3, part 1 of *A History of Socialist Thought* (London: Macmillan, 1956), 387.

6. The major works produced by Sorel during this period include *Le Procès de Socrate* (1889), a condemnation of Socrates for corrupting democratic Athens; *Etude sur Vico* (1896), in which Sorel adapts Vico's historicism to a Marxist framework; and *Contribution à l'étude profane de la Bible* (1889) and *Le Système historique de Renan* (1905), in which Sorel grapples with Ernest Renan, a towering nineteenth-century French historian of religion.

endeavor reveals that Sorel constructs proletarian violence with characteristics borrowed directly from the bloodshed that he despises.

Seeking an alternative to bloody, state-sponsored revolution, Sorel became dedicated to the idea that a few martyred workers could animate a world-historical, anarcho-syndicalist movement capable of regenerating, but not founding, politics. Although Sorel hoped that his version of socialism would triumph over capitalism, his writings emphasize a developmental path toward a socialist future, not the specific details of its achievement. With his refusal to embrace mass bloodshed as well as his process-oriented approach to revolution, Sorel departs from the revolutionaries' political and sacrificial ideas, which emphasize ends over means and experiential bloodshed over symbolic substitution. Instead, Sorel radicalizes and secularizes Maistre's hope that Christ's sacrifice and return will obviate the need for endless cycles of accumulated guilt and purifying bloodshed. Sorel transforms Maistre's eschatology by imagining that final human redemption will be achieved through the proletariat and socialism, not Christ and his Second Coming.

Read in concert with his earlier works, Sorel's *Reflections* reveals a synthesis of revolutionary and Maistrian ideas that leads to a fundamental shift in the French discourse on sacrificial violence. The revolutionaries optimistically employed violence as an aggressive tool for the creation and destruction of states and sovereign power. They engaged in a variety of sacrificial practices under the assumption that they would broadly support revolutionary goals. In contrast, Sorel distinguishes between revolutionary and reactionary forms of bloodshed, claiming that "force" is always conservative and "violence" liberating when used to resist state power. Agreeing with Maistre's critique of revolutionary violence but without embracing his providential views, Sorel rejects the revolutionaries' use of terror and targeting of scapegoats. Yet, like Maistre, Sorel also approves of certain forms of violence, such as war and martyrdom. Indebted to the Christian sacrificial tradition, Sorel's reflections highlight the symbolic value of bloodshed and its communication by redemptive myths. Sorel is not hostile to the exercise of violence; he simply rejects the moral and political value of committing it. In this respect, Sorel breaks with the revolutionary and Maistrian celebrations of the experience of violence, which Sorel criticizes as harmful to proletarian moral development and political action.

By rejecting French revolutionary violence and reconfiguring Maistre's response to it, Sorel finds a theoretically creative way to adapt sacrifice to modern political change without extreme bloodshed or religious dogmatism. However, Sorel's effort is significantly flawed by the fact that he refuses to dispense with the notion that sacrificial violence is regenerative. Like his predecessors, Sorel contends that even limited, symbolic sacrifices have the power to regenerate morality and, thus, change politics. Insofar as his understanding of sacrifice remains similar to that of the revolutionaries and Maistre, Sorel also faces their theoretical dilemmas. How does one determine the function of an ambiguous, unstable form of violence, such as sacrifice? How can one know that sacrifice will support a particular form of politics to the exclusion of all others? Though Sorel is critical of the revolutionary violence used to crush the monarchy and establish a French Republic, he nonetheless posits that limited sacrifices will morally regenerate the proletariat, helping it to achieve a socialist revolution.

By conceptualizing proletarian violence in terms of martyrdom and restricting its revolutionary role, Sorel redefines how violence participates in the task of political foundation. Scholars who maintain that Sorel advocates cataclysmic violence mistakenly imagine that Sorel's myth of the general strike involves bloody strikes. There is little evidence to support this conclusion. Nowhere does Sorel call upon the workers to turn their factories into slaughterhouses. Rather, Sorel's reflections on Christian martyrdom suggest that he wants self-sacrifice to be the form of proletarian violence par excellence. What is more, he indicates in *Reflections* that martyred workers would be few and would die relatively unnoticed. In his discussion of the morality of violence, Sorel addresses the common objection to revolutionary socialism that it would be too bloody: "There is no danger of civilization's succumbing to the consequences of a development of brutality, since the idea of the general strike may foster the notion of the class war by means of incidents which would appear to middle-class historians as of small importance."[7] Just as the Romans failed to recognize the symbolic importance of Christian martyrdom, the bourgeoisie would pay little heed to the incidences of workers giving their lives during violent strikes. Yet, in the same way that each Christian martyr magnified the revolutionary effect of Christian ideology, each martyred worker would dramatically enhance both the appeal and revolutionary potential of socialist ideals. Ultimately, myth radically amplifies the impact of proletarian violence, preventing the need for widespread incidences of bloodshed. Thus, violence contributes to the formation of a socialist future, but without death on a revolutionary scale.

In reflecting upon Sorel's concept of proletarian violence, it is crucial to remember that his revolutionary project is fundamentally a moral one: "the moral education of the working classes through personal experience with a view to

---

7. "La civilisation n'est point menacée de succomber sous les conséquences d'un développement de la brutalité, puisque l'idée de grève générale permet d'alimenter la notion de lutte de classe au moyen d'incidents qui paraîtraient médiocres aux historiens bourgeois." Georges Sorel, *Réflexions sur la violence* (Paris: Editions de Seuil, 1990), 184. Here I am using the English translation by T. E. Hulme and Jack Roth, *Reflections on Violence* (London: Collier, 1969), 186.

self-government is the great modern social problem."[8] Autonomous workers' syndicates, heightened class conflict, as well as certain forms of symbolic violence all contribute to the moral development of the working class. As early as 1898, Sorel argued in *L'Avenir socialiste des syndicats* that the development of the proletariat as a class requires what he calls an immense labor of decomposition and recomposition.[9] Anticipating arguments that the Italian Communist Antonio Gramsci would later develop, Sorel declares that the moral development of the proletariat occurs within capitalist society, but nonetheless carefully isolated from it. Sorel expresses what he labels "the morality of the producers" in conservative terms: hard work, personal responsibility, patriarchal family relations, heroism, and discipline. Syndicates function as pedagogical institutions, offering workers moral instruction in new forms of social organization, economic production, and political action. Sorel underscores this regenerative function when he writes: "At the heart of the capitalist society there must develop not only new productive forces, but the relations of a new social order as well, which one can call the moral forces of the future."[10] In seeking the moral renewal of the proletariat, Sorel departs from the purely materialist understanding of historical change so commonly associated with Marxist thought.

Unlike the French revolutionaries, who viewed foundational violence as constructive of massive moral and institutional transformation, Sorel conceives of proletarian martyrdom as engendering only moral change. Worker self-sacrifice inspires a myth that draws together a community of producers around a set of sacred, revolutionary socialist ideals. Only one Christ had to die in order to breathe life into the *corpus mysticum*. Each subsequent Christian martyr invoked the significance of that original sacrifice, thus allowing a death that might have otherwise passed entirely unnoticed to assume transcendent importance. This mythic power of the martyr concerns Sorel when he writes:

> Every case of persecution borrowed from the mythology of the Antichrist something of its dread dramatic character; instead of being valued on its actual importance as a misfortune befalling a few individuals, a lesson for the community, or a temporary check on propaganda, it became an incident in the war carried on by *Satan, prince of this world,* who was soon to reveal his Antichrist. Thus, the schism resulted from both persecutions and the feverish expectation of a decisive battle.

8. "La formation morale des classes ouvrières par l'expérience personnelle et en vue du self-gouvernement [*sic*] est le grand problème social moderne." Quoted in Patrice Rolland, "Georges Sorel et la démocratie au XXe siècle," *Mil neuf cent,* no. 9 (1991), 133.

9. Georges Sorel, *L'Avenir socialiste des syndicats* (Paris: Librairie de l'Art Social, 1898), 17.

10. "C'est dans le sein de la société capitaliste que doivent se développer, non seulement les forces productives nouvelles, mais encore les relations d'un nouvel ordre social, ce qu'on peut appeler les forces morales de l'avenir." Ibid., 22.

Tout incident de persécution empruntait à la mythologie de l'Antéchrist quelque
chose de son caractère effroyablement dramatique; au lieu d'être apprécié en raison de son importance matérielle, comme un malheur frappant quelques individus,
une leçon pour la communauté ou une entrave temporaire apportée à la propa-
gande, il était un élément de la guerre engagée par *Satan, prince de ce monde,* qui al-
lait bientôt révéler son Antéchrist.   Ainsi la scission découlait, à la fois, des
persécutions et d'une attente fiévreuse d'une bataille décisive.[11]

In the context of the myth of the general strike, proletarian martyrdom assumes
the same meaning and function that Christian persecutions did during the first
and second centuries when Christians viewed their sacrifices through the lens
of apocalyptic biblical fables. In the Christian milieu, martyrdom formed a new
community around its consecration of a new ideological imperative: the preparation of human souls for the Second Coming. Translated into anarcho-syndicalist terms, Christian eschatology becomes socialist, revealing Sorel's hope that
proletarian martyrdom would heighten class conflict, propagate socialist ideals,
radically alter the moral landscape, and contribute to the foundation of a new
age.

Violence, myth, and morality anchor Sorel's revolutionary thought because
they alter human behavior. To capture this dynamic interaction of different elements of revolutionary violence, Sorel uses the word "sublime," which was also
commonly invoked during the French Revolution. Indeed, the revolutionaries
often described their violent acts as sublime when they wished to draw attention to bloodshed's capacity to regenerate the decadent moral beliefs of the aristocracy. Similarly, Sorel views sublimity as a unique weapon in the war against
bourgeois decadence. In *Reflections,* Sorel argues that the bourgeoisie, in its pursuit of power and profit, is demoralizing the working class. He claims that both
the free exchange of capital and the political system founded upon the protection of private property are forcing human beings to fall back upon their worst
impulses. In order to combat the moral decadence of the bourgeoisie and to
avoid the risk of their contaminating the proletariat, the working class must develop its own moral framework, a task that Sorel links directly to the role of violence in reconstituting the sublime. In *Reflections,* for example, Sorel agrees
with Ernest Renan that the rise of the bourgeoisie and weakening of religious
sentiments fostered a precipitous decline in sublimity: "The sublime is dead in
the middle class, and so they are doomed no longer to possess any morality."[12]
For Sorel, the death of sublimity signals a life of utter banality, preoccupation

11. Sorel, *Réflexions,* 183.
12. "Le sublime est mort dans la bourgeoisie et celle-ci est donc condamnée à ne plus avoir de
morale." Ibid., 232.

with the details of capital accumulation, vague enjoyment of its material fruits, and complete lack of passionate, productive engagement. Depleted of sublimity, neither the bourgeoisie nor the proletariat could be counted on to pursue arduously its class interests and, thus, the conflict upon which the development of a new socialist morality depended. Fearful that this condition would undermine the struggle of the working class, Sorel engaged in a study of how the violence already in evidence throughout Europe might further the proletariat's revolutionary aspirations.

Cultivation of the sublime represents both the novelty and the frailty of Sorel's theoretical project. What is novel is Sorel's belief that sublime bloodshed might regenerate morality without the terror anticipated by the French revolutionaries and Maistre. For Sorel, sublimity appears only when revolutionary violence is limited to proletarian self-sacrifice. The appearance of the sublime, however, also indicates that Sorel and the other participants in the French discourse on sacrifice share a broad commitment to the catalytic properties of violence. Even though Sorel wishes to apply those properties differently from his predecessors, he relies on sacrificial violence to generate the sublimity that alters the feelings, perceptions, values, and moral beliefs of the working class. Thus, Sorel's claim that the actual experience of violence can serve neither the purpose of moral regeneration nor that of political foundation rings hollow when he tasks his own version of self-sacrifice, and the sublimity it engenders, with similar goals. Sorel, however, must also be credited as the first to develop a theoretical awareness of the political limitations of founding bloodshed in the French discourse on sacrificial violence. In rejecting the morally constitutive power of the guillotine, Sorel turns his back on Brutus in favor of Christ.

The Question of Sorel's Fascism

Most Sorel scholars have discounted the importance of his restrictive concept of violence because Sorel's ardent enthusiasm for proletarian violence has overshadowed his disdain for state violence and his concept of violence is notoriously ambiguous. Read without reference to his earlier works, *Reflections* can be easily misinterpreted as a call for unmitigated and bloody class war. Sorel, however, anticipates this confusion by devoting the first chapter of *Reflections* to the differentiation of class war and violence. Class war, or class conflict, describes a fundamental antagonism between the bourgeoisie and proletariat that transcends mere differences of interest.[13] For Sorel, class war encompasses a wide

---

13. Sorel, *Reflections,* 70–74.

range of action, taken on behalf of either capital owners or producers, which increases workers' understanding of their economic condition as well as their awareness of possessing the ability to liberate themselves from that condition.[14] Activities that fall under the rubric of class war need not be violent, but they must promote the heightening of class distinctions. Sorel considers class violence to be the most effective weapon in the arsenal of class war in the sense that it, more than any other activity, exacerbates class antagonism. The state, the bourgeoisie, and the proletariat can all engage in class violence, but in each case it takes different forms and gives rise to different consequences. The form of class violence that preoccupies Sorel in *Reflections* is uniquely proletarian. The subtle distinction between class war and violence is important for understanding Sorelian thought because it points to the multitude of activities—violent and nonviolent, bourgeois and proletarian—that characterize class relations in a capitalist society. As John Stanley contends, "By conventional terminology, the most violent thing about *Reflections on Violence* is the title."[15]

Sorel is partially responsible for the conceptual confusion surrounding his notion of violence because, as Isaiah Berlin remarked thirty years ago, the nature of proletarian violence in *Reflections* is "never made clear."[16] That ambiguity, combined with Sorel's own, often conflicting, flirtations with the twentieth century's most devastating ideologies, has often led to Sorel's being associated with fascism, Marxist-Leninism, and, strangely enough, French royalism.[17] Indeed, much of the secondary literature on Sorel—and this is especially true in the Anglo-American tradition—regards the ambiguity of Sorel's concept of violence as evidence of its political danger. For example, at the beginning of the Cold War, Edward Shils, in the introduction to an English translation, dubbed Sorel's *Reflections* "morally and politically pernicious."[18] Twenty years later, J. L. Talmon joined the anti-Sorel chorus, calling him an "apologist of violence" and linking him to fascist and Leninist totalitarianism.[19] Similarly, Isaiah Berlin placed Sorel in his pantheon of intellectuals noteworthy for their revolt against

14. Ibid., 77–79.

15. John Stanley, *The Sociology of Virtue* (Berkeley: University of California Press, 1981), 221.

16. Isaiah Berlin, "Georges Sorel," *Times Literary Supplement*, December 31, 1971, 1621.

17. Both Mussolini and the French fascists Georges Valois and Ramon Fernandez claimed Sorel as an inspiration. See J. L. Talmon, "The Legacy of Georges Sorel," *Encounter* 34 (February 1970), 47–60. For a short time Sorel took refuge in the royalist Charles Maurras's Action Française. Although Lenin famously labeled Sorel a "notorious muddle-head," Sorel's thought had some influence on Communists in the Soviet Union as well as in France and Italy. See Jack Roth, *The Cult of Violence* (Berkeley: University of California Press, 1980), 172–178.

18. Sorel, *Reflections*, 25.

19. Talmon, "The Legacy of Georges Sorel."

rationalism and Enlightenment thought as well as for their overly enthusiastic embrace of bloodshed.[20]

The attempt to make Sorel an intellectual forefather of fascism and Marxist-Leninism has led some left-leaning scholars to revise and defend Sorel's legacy. Walter Benjamin was perhaps the first to suggest that Sorel's concept of violence had been too negatively interpreted. Benjamin wrote that Sorel's "rigorous conception of the general strike as such is capable of diminishing the incidence of actual violence in revolutions."[21] Though harder to classify politically, Hannah Arendt also expressed skepticism about the violent implications of Sorelian thought when she wrote: "Yet he [Sorel] ended by proposing nothing more violent than the famous myth of the general strike, a form of action which we today would think of as belonging rather to the arsenal of non-violent politics."[22] More recently, Shlomo Sand has argued: "In effect, Sorel will celebrate violence at a certain moment, but contrary to Sartre, he does not envision terrorist acts, sabotage, or bloodshed."[23] In a note Sand elaborates upon this point, claiming: "This does not mean that Sorel's term is not ambiguous, but in general he uses it to express resistance, refusal, and threat."[24] Sand is not only correct that Sorel criticizes terrorist acts and sabotage; Sand also captures the spirit of resistance that characterizes proletarian violence. Although I disagree with Sand's claim that Sorel is uninterested in bloodshed, Sand remains one of the few contemporary Sorel scholars to recognize that Sorel imposes clear theoretical limitations on his concept of violence.[25] Recognition of these limitations is a necessary step toward understanding the distinctiveness of Sorelian thought.

Berlin may ultimately be correct that Sorel's concept of violence remains mysterious, but even a cursory reading of *Reflections* reveals Sorel's unambiguous hostility to state violence. Sorel's critics have often maintained that, during

20. Berlin, "Georges Sorel," 1617–22.

21. Quoted in Stanley, *The Sociology of Virtue*, 332. Benjamin's "Critique of Violence," written between 1916 and 1921, clearly reveals Sorel's influence. Like Sorel, who distinguishes between conservative force and redemptive violence, Benjamin argues that most human violence either constitutes or supports the law, whereas "divine" violence is both extralegal and expiatory. See Walter Benjamin, "Critique of Violence" in *Reflections*, ed. Peter Demetz and trans. Edmund Jephcott (New York: Schocken, 1986), 277–300.

22. Arendt, *On Violence*, 12.

23. "Sorel, en effet, célébrera, à un certain moment, la violence, mais, contrairement à Sartre, il n'a pas en vue des actions terroristes, de sabotages ou de sang versé." Shlomo Sand, *L'Illusion du politique* (Paris: Editions la Découverte, 1984), 8.

24. "Cela ne signifie que ce terme ne soit pas ambigu chez lui, mais en général il l'utilise pour exprimer la résistance, le refus, la menace." Ibid., 229.

25. In addition to John Stanley, many of the intellectuals who articulate this position, including Michel Charzat, Jeremy Jennings, Larry Portis, and Patrice Rolland, have published in the journal *Cahiers Georges Sorel*, which first appeared in 1982. This journal later changed its name to *Mil neuf cent.*

the twilight of his life, he reversed this position on violence by expressing un-
abashed excitement about Lenin and the Bolshevik Revolution. In his intellectual biography of Sorel, however, Jeremy Jennings argues that Sorel knew very
little about Lenin, the importance of the Bolshevik party, or their violent methods. Jennings writes: "It is necessary to recognize just how little Sorel and most
other members of the French left knew of Lenin and the events of the Russian
Revolution. Sorel's correspondence—certainly immediately after the Revolution—persistently returns to the theme of attempting to discover the identity
of Lenin and the exact events taking place in Russia."[26] Because Sorel died in
1922—before Mussolini's March on Rome, Soviet collectivization, the Gulag,
or the Final Solution—his remarks concerning Soviet communism and European fascism must be met with a good deal of skepticism.

Zeev Sternhell has made the most convincing case for a protofascistic Sorel.
In *The Birth of Fascist Ideology*, Sternhell argues that by 1910 Sorel had begun to
contemplate seriously a nationalist-socialist synthesis. Based partly on Sorel's
ideas, political affiliations, and intellectual legacy, Sternhell's critique of Sorel has
merit. Taken together, Sorel's crude expressions of anti-Semitism, heroic exal-
tation of nationalism, antimaterialist revision of Marxism, and well-known defense of violence are easily fitted into a fascist mold.[27] In the final analysis,
however, Sternhell's argument also leaves room for much doubt. First, Sorel's
flirtation with the right-wing Action Française, Charles Maurras, and Georges
Valois took place briefly and in the context of a monarchist movement that, according to Jennings, appealed primarily to Sorel's interest in aristocratic values
and his hatred of modernism.[28] It is problematic to label Sorel a fascist for his
temporary attraction to monarchist ideas, few of which were later absorbed into
fascism. Second, although Sorel reportedly praised Mussolini on several occasions, there is also documentation of Sorel's criticisms of fascism, which suggest,
as Stanley has argued in his dispute with J. L. Talmon, that there were important
ideological distinctions between Sorel and the early fascist movements in Italy
and France.[29] Third, while it is true that versions of Sorel's ideas made their way
into fascist intellectual circles, often by way of Sorel's closest disciples, that fact
only begs the question of Sorel's responsibility for the ends to which others put

26. J. R. Jennings, *Georges Sorel* (Oxford: Macmillan, 1985), 161.

27. Zeev Sternhell, *The Birth of Fascist Ideology*, trans. David Maisel (Princeton: Princeton University
Press, 1994), 36–91.

28. Jeremy Jennings, *Syndicalism in France: A Study of Ideas* (New York: St. Martin's, 1990), 100–110.

29. John Stanley, ed., *From Georges Sorel: Essays in Socialism and Philosophy*, trans. John Stanley and Char-
lotte Stanley (New Brunswick, N.J.: Transaction, 1990), 1–5; Stanley, *The Sociology of Virtue*, 297–303; Paul
Mazgaj, *The Action Française and Revolutionary Syndicalism* (Chapel Hill: University of North Carolina
Press, 1979); Michel Charzat, "Georges Sorel et le fascisme: Eléments d'explication d'une légende tenace,"
Cahier Georges Sorel 1 (1983), 37–51.

his ideas.[30] Fourth, and most important, Sorel neither incorporated nationalism, fascism's idea sine qua non, nor the concept of state violence, fascism's ultima ratio, into the fabric of his work. There is little question that Sorel deserves criticism for testing a variety of noxious ideas and for collaborating with a number of unsavory intellectuals. But whether those ideas and affiliations collectively add up to fascism, as Sternhell maintains, remains doubtful.

Sacrifice, Morality, and the Concept of Proletarian Violence

Disgust with the Terror profoundly shapes Sorel's reflections on violence and his contributions to the French discourse on sacrificial violence. Unlike Maistre, who at times exhibits an ironic admiration for the handiwork of the Committee of Public Safety, Sorel loathes the Jacobin tradition of political violence. This antipathy is fundamentally anarchistic and was shared by other prominent members of the syndicalist movement. Sorel interprets the Terror—the use of state violence to achieve radical social and political change—as a telltale sign that the revolutionaries were naïvely participating in a changing of the guard. In agreement with Alexis de Tocqueville's argument in *The Old Regime and the French Revolution,* Sorel believed that French revolutionary violence led the Jacobins to conserve unintentionally the Old Regime's institutional apparatus and structures of authority.[31] Sorel applied this same argument to turn-of-the-century French politics because he worried that his socialist contemporaries, in their own quest for state power, would make the same bloody mistakes as their Jacobin forefathers. In criticizing the forms of violence used by the authors of the French Revolution, Sorel sought to distance turn-of-the-century French socialism from the Jacobins' extraordinary emphasis on dictatorial statism. Sorel's hostility toward the Terror also underscores the importance of his anarchism for the development of his concept of violence. Jeremy Jennings argues that Sorel maintained this critique of state power throughout his career, an important point of consistency for an intellectual so often criticized for his ideological fluctuations.[32]

---

30. A debate persists concerning the authenticity of Sorel's statements in praise of fascism as reported by some of his more ideological disciples, such as Jean Variot. See James Meisel, *The Genesis of Georges Sorel* (Ann Arbor: George Wahr, 1951), 167–168; Mazgaj, *The Action Française,* 117; Charzat, "Georges Sorel et le fascisme," 42. Furthermore, although Sternhell raises some important points regarding Sorel's contributions to fascist ideology, he also makes liberal use of "guilty by association" logic. In *The Birth of Fascist Ideology* (99–118), Sternhell often collapses the distinction between Sorel and Sorelians, thus blaming the intellectual father for the sons' sins. For a more balanced view of Sorel's relationship to his disciples, see Jennings, *Syndicalism in France,* 71–113.

31. Sorel, *Reflections,* 93–95.

32. Jeremy Jennings, "Syndicalism and the French Revolution," *Journal of Contemporary History* 26

Seeking an alternative form of regenerative violence to state terror, Sorel attempts in various theoretically problematic ways to isolate a purely proletarian concept of bloodshed. In contrast to many of the intellectuals in the anarcho-syndicalist movement, Sorel rejects the use of sabotage because it is "a reactionary vestige of the *ancien régime* which society should abolish."[33] At the same time, however, he contends that proletarian violence involves acts that cause bodily harm or death. In *Reflections,* for example, Sorel writes enthusiastically about the anarchists who brought the idea of "propaganda by deed" to the syndicalist movement, thus ushering in a period of revolutionary activity in which the workers no longer had to make excuses for the bloodshed that sometimes accompanied their strikes.[34] Despite this acceptance of the quintessential form of anarchist violence, Sorel never tethers proletarian violence to "propaganda by deed." Instead, he attempts to define proletarian violence in moral terms, claiming that it is distinguished by its lack of hatred.[35] "Hatred," he writes, "can unleash upheavals, destroy social organization, and throw a country into an era of bloody revolutions; but it produces nothing."[36] A theoretically and empirically dubious claim, Sorel's association of hateful revolutionary violence with the Jacobins and the Terror is intended to steer the proletariat away from the bloodshed that had led the French revolutionaries to become just as tyrannical as their former king. Equally problematic, Sorel argues tautologically that proletarian violence is ethical because bloodshed employed by ethical agents is morally right.[37] In his view, there is a reciprocal relationship between ethics and violence: the working class is justified in its use of particular forms of bloodshed, and that violence, in turn, contributes to the workers' proper moral formation. By assigning proletarian violence a specific moral function, while also seeking to restrict its forms, Sorel illustrates his theoretical preparation for a type of violence that will best serve the working class.

(January 1991), 71–95. Jennings also indicates that Sorel's criticism of the Paris Commune stemmed directly from this critique of Jacobinism. Ibid., 80.

33. Quoted in Stanley, *The Sociology of Virtue,* 24.

34. Sorel, *Reflections,* 56. Fernand Pelloutier, the president of the Fédération des Bourses de Travail, rejected the anarchist notion of "propaganda by deed." In his study of syndicalism in France, Jennings also confirms that many of the leaders of the anarcho-syndicalist movement were men of action, not of violence per se. None of them systematically theorized about the creative or regenerative qualities of bloodshed; those who embraced violence as a revolutionary instrument did so reluctantly, aware that capitalism fostered a violent world, in which the workers would occasionally have to resist in equal measure. Jennings, *Syndicalism in France,* 49.

35. Sorel, *Reflections,* 152.

36. "La haine peut provoquer des bouleversements, ruiner une organisation sociale, jeter un pays dans l'ère des révolutions sanglantes; mais elle ne produit rien." Georges Sorel, "L'Ethique du socialisme," *Revue de métaphysique et de morale,* no. 3 (May 1899), 288.

37. Ibid., 288–290.

Although Sorel never advocates vigilante justice, his discussion of this form of violence illustrates his brief flirtation with a scapegoat mechanism. In *Reflections,* Sorel begins his argument about the ethics of violence with several examples of vigilantism. He is enthralled by Paul Bureau's description of rural Norwegians who settle personal disputes with daggers as opposed to through the formal justice system.[38] Similarly, Sorel is attracted to Paul de Rousier's account of the Vigilance Committees in mid-nineteenth-century Denver, Colorado, and their expeditious use of the Lynch Law to deal with "criminals."[39] For Sorel, both cases demonstrate the same anarchistic point: individuals can, in the absence of the state, follow their own moral impulses to achieve justice. Recognizing that the French revolutionaries adopted this principle at the beginning of the Revolution and then converted it into a justification for state terror, Sorel suggests limitations to such violence: "It is, in fact, certain that a great development of brutality accompanied by much blood-letting is quite unnecessary in order to induce the workers to look upon economic conflicts as the reduced facsimiles of the great battle which will decide the future."[40] Sorel displays his characteristic discomfort with the experience of violence. His attraction to vigilante justice paradoxically illustrates not his enthusiasm for a particular type of sacrificial violence, but his appreciation of a revolutionary imperative. Sorel understands that revolutionary violence requires a moral justification because it is illegal. Driven by popular moral outrage unmitigated by formal laws or judicial institutions, vigilantism fits this mold. Thus, anarchism drives Sorel's appreciation of both the revolutionary potential and risks of vigilantism. Yet, because vigilantism opens the door to bloodshed grounded precariously on shifting notions of popular justice, Sorel never advocates that workers embrace it as an ethical form of violence.

More than any other form of collective action, the strike is what Sorel associates with proletarian violence. The precise meaning of his use of the term "strike," however, is highly elusive. In *Reflections,* Sorel makes reference to "strikes," "political strikes," "proletarian strikes," "syndicalist strikes," "general strikes," "political general strikes," "syndicalist general strikes," and "proletarian general strikes," as well as the "idea of the general strike" and "myth of the general strike." In some instances, Sorel conceptualizes strikes with violence clearly

38. Paul Bureau, *Le Paysan des fjords de Norwège* (Paris: Bureau de la science sociale, 1906), 114–115. Quoted in Sorel, *Reflections,* 181.

39. Paul de Rousiers, *La Vie américaine: Ranches, fermes et usines* (Paris: Fermin-Didot, 1899), 224–225. Quoted in Sorel, *Reflections,* 181.

40. Sorel, *Reflections,* 182. "Il est certain, en effet, que pour amener les travailleurs à regarder les conflits économiques comme des images affaiblies de la grande bataille qui décidera de l'avenir, il n'est point nécessaire qu'il y ait un grand développement de la brutalité et que le sang soit versé à flots." Sorel, *Réflexions,* 179–180.

in mind. For instance, in the "Introduction to the First Publication" of *Reflections,* he writes: "For a long time I have been struck by the fact that the *normal development* of strikes is accompanied by an important series of acts of violence . . . Revolutionary syndicalism keeps alive in the minds of the masses the desire to strike, and only prospers when important strikes, accompanied by violence, take place."[41] Midway through *Reflections,* however, Sorel abandons the idea of violent strikes. Instead, he subsumes proletarian violence under the concept of the general strike, which he compares to "the Napoleonic battle which definitely crushes an adversary."[42] Just when it appears that the strike has metamorphosed into an instrument of total class war, Sorel delves into long discussions of the "myth" and "idea" of the general strike. Through a conceptual sleight of hand, he shifts his focus from actual strike violence and the warlike conflict of a general strike to the psychological and ideological value of the idea of those phenomena. This shift underscores Sorel's penchant for conceiving of proletarian violence in abstract as opposed to concrete terms.

The ambiguity of Sorel's concept of the strike is further underscored by the surprising dearth of analysis of actual strikes in his work. With the exception of an article and a letter, Sorel rarely wrote about actual strikes during his anarcho-syndicalist phase. In a 1901 article titled "Les Grèves de Montceau-les-Mines et leur signification," Sorel briefly explored the twenty-year history of strikes in this region, concluding that it appeared to be not so much an economic struggle ("lutte économique") as one in favor of the principles of the Revolution ("en faveur des principes de la Révolution").[43] In other words, Sorel considered strike activity in this region to be animated by relatively conservative revolutionary ideas such as workers' rights, as opposed to more radical demands, such as the transformation of the economic system. In 1904, when Sorel was thinking more specifically about strikes, proletarian violence and socialist revolution, his only mention of a widely publicized violent strike of watchmakers, known as the Cluses Affair, occurred in a letter to his friend Edouard Berth: "I don't know if you have noticed the entente that existed between Briand, the prosecutor and the president in the Cluses Affair. There is perhaps nothing more curious and more characteristic of our time."[44] Aristide Briand, a socialist

41. Sorel, *Reflections,* 57. "Depuis longtemps, j'ai été frappé de voir que le *déroulement normal* des grèves comporte un important cortège de violences . . . Le syndicalisme révolutionnaire entretient l'esprit gréviste dans les masses et ne prospère que là où se sont produites des grèves notables, menées avec violence." Sorel, *Réflexions,* 39.

42. Sorel, *Reflections,* 119. "La bataille napoléonienne qui écrase définitivement l'adversaire." Sorel, *Réflexions,* 111.

43. Georges Sorel, "Les Grèves de Montceau-les-Mines et leur signification" (Strikes in Montceau-les-Mines and Their Significance), *Pages libres* 9 (March 2, 1901), 169−173.

44. "Je ne sais si vous avez remarqué l'entente qui existait entre Briand et le Parquet et le Président

deputy to the French National Assembly, served as legal counsel for a group of workers accused of strike violence during the Cluses Affair. Sorel criticizes the trial as illustrative of the conservative, reformist politics produced by socialist participation in the French government. Despite these few references to actual strikes, an article Sorel published in 1900 devoted to a purely theoretical discussion of strikes, and *Reflections* itself, there appears to be no Sorelian text in which he provides a syndicalist analysis of the progress of an actual strike or strike violence.[45] Sorel's lack of interest in real strikes suggests that he ultimately views the idea of the strike as much more important to his revolutionary agenda than actual strike violence. This propensity to examine strikes abstractly also illuminates the ambiguity of his concept of violence: if the idea of the strike is more important than the real thing, it is understandable that Sorel would emphasize the moral ideas inspired by proletarian violence, rather than actual bloodshed.

Statistics and historical evidence concerning actual strike violence between 1900 and 1910 also help to explain why Sorel emphasizes the symbolism of proletarian violence. In *Strikes in France,* Edward Shorter and Charles Tilly argue that there was a sizable increase in the number and rate of strikes in France during this period because of the successful emergence of nationwide labor organizations, such as the avidly syndicalist Confédération Générale du Travail (CGT).[46] However, only approximately a fifth of these strikes ended successfully for the workers, with most culminating in failure or compromise. Although Shorter and Tilly claim that the increase in strikes was accompanied by a rise in violent disturbances, it remains the case that only 3.2 percent of the strikes between 1890 and 1914 were violent. Shorter and Tilly also challenge the conventional wisdom that government intervention in strikes favored employers. They argue that such intrusion typically decreased violence and, at the same time, benefited workers by helping them to secure at least some concessions from their employers.[47] The relative scarcity of strike violence, the strong likelihood of compromise or failure, and the intrusion of accommodationist gov-

dans l'affaire de Cluses. Il n'y a peut-être pas de fait plus curieux et plus caractéristique de notre temps." Georges Sorel, *Cahiers Georges Sorel,* no. 3 (1985), 109.

45. See Georges Sorel, "Les Grèves," *La Science sociale* 30 (October 1900), 311–333, and (November 1900), 417–436.

46. Edward Shorter and Charles Tilly, *Strikes in France* (London: Cambridge University Press, 1974), 46–51, 75. According to Shorter and Tilly, there were approximately 500 strikes between 1895 and 1900, 700 between 1900 and 1904, and 1,000 between 1905 and 1909. Sorel's syndicalist phase thus corresponds to a period when the number of strikes doubled in France. Shorter and Tilly have labeled this phase of strike activity (1880–1910) the "great mobilization of the working classes" because, for the first time in French history, workers formalized, nationalized, and politicized their labor organizations.

47. Ibid., 68–71, 378, 33.

ernment officials all suggest that proletarian violence was neither a very common nor a very effective syndicalist strategy. That conclusion is also supported by pragmatically minded intellectuals in the CGT who tended to frown upon the strategic use of violence in strikes out of fear of state repression.[48] When violence did occur during strikes, it tended to be spontaneous, often resulting from the frustration of a particularly long and unsuccessful action, the day-to-day misery experienced by many French workers deprived of wages, and the repression of workers by private policemen, scabs, or the government.[49] It was in this context of spontaneous, infrequent, and unsuccessful strike violence that Sorel turned his attention to the mobilizing force of symbolic bloodshed.

Although Sorel could not have known most of the details of this historical and statistical picture of strike violence in turn-of-the-century France, he did recognize one important dynamic: proletarian violence served to enhance the importance of individual skirmishes in the class war. Confirming Shorter and Tilly's recent analysis, Sorel observed that, in the course of a strike, actual or threatened proletarian violence often encouraged government intervention and, subsequently, employer concessions to their workers.[50] Although Sorel had no desire to endorse handouts that would pacify the working class, he appreciated that violence helped to exacerbate class antagonisms and placed workers in a position of strength vis-à-vis the bourgeoisie and the government. In this way, Sorel realized that the idea of proletarian violence was a more valuable weapon in the class war than actual bloodshed, a particularly powerful insight given the historical weakness of anarcho-syndicalist strike activity.

Sorel's critique of the French Revolution and his attempt to isolate a purely proletarian form of violence strongly influence the famous distinction he makes in *Reflections* between force and violence. Moreover, in distinguishing between what amounts to "good" and "bad" violence, Sorel illustrates his effort to grapple with the same theoretical dilemmas as Maistre and the French revolutionaries. Hostile to all forms of state violence and terror, Sorel maintains that there is a qualitative difference between bloodshed used to enforce or undermine structures of authority. Sorel labels the former "force," which he deems intrin-

---

48. The president of the syndicalist Fédération des Bourses de Travail from 1895 to 1901, Fernand Pelloutier, was an avid proponent of the general strike but loath to consider violence its principal vehicle. According to Jennings, Pelloutier, whom Pierre Monatte called "the father of revolutionary syndicalism," rejected worker violence because the state's military capacity was too overwhelming. What is more, he abandoned the anarchist "propaganda of the deed" because he did not want to "sacrifice innocent victims" in the revolutionary attempt to overthrow bourgeois society and the bourgeois state. Jennings, *Syndicalism in France*, 11–15.

49. Peter Stearns, *Revolutionary Syndicalism and French Labor: A Cause without Rebels* (New Brunswick, N.J.: Rutgers University Press, 1971), 68.

50. Sorel, *Reflections*, 77.

sically conservative in the sense that it serves to support a particular social, political, and economic order. Following Blaise Pascal, Sorel claims that justice is
a relative concept typically defined by the state.[51] This understanding of justice,
combined with his reading of Tocqueville, leads Sorel to reason that any use of
the state's mechanisms of violence will generate a self-defeating revolution. For
Sorel, state institutions are not neutral constructions suitable to any form of politics. Rather, he views them as the product of a particular set of time-bound,
class-based concepts such as capitalism and natural right, which are thoroughly
incompatible with anarcho-syndicalism. Sorel railed against the socialists of his
era because they held to the notion that socialism could be achieved only by
taking control—legally or not—of the bourgeois state.

If the function of force is conservation, the function of violence is liberation.
Technically speaking, violence—by which Sorel means proletarian violence—
plays no role in the founding of a new regime. It is exclusively a tool of rebellion: "we should say, therefore, that the object of force is to impose a certain
social order in which the minority governs, while violence tends to the destruction of that order."[52] True to his sociological orientation, Sorel claims that
violence is destructive of *social* order. Working-class violence corrodes the highly
structured, disciplined, and unequal relationship between the proletariat and the
bourgeoisie. Like stretching a rubber band to its limit, proletarian violence
achieves this goal by pushing class antagonism to its breaking point. Because violence entails rebellion, it can never be employed by the state—even a socialist
one—and can never be formal or legal. Furthermore, for Sorel, violence is moral
and, therefore, limited in scope and form. Any attempt to place proletarian violence in the service of the authority of the state risks Jacobinism. The effectiveness of violence rests largely, but not exclusively, on its capacity to undermine
the hegemony of bourgeois values, which permeate every aspect of the workers' social, political, and economic lives.

Although he reversed the meaning of the terms, Robespierre was, ironically,
the first in the French discourse on sacrificial violence to distinguish between
force and violence. In his pamphlet *Le Défenseur de la constitution,* Robespierre
inverts Sorel's distinction between force and violence, but precisely captures
Sorel's point.[53] With reference to English natural law, Robespierre discusses the
dubious arrest of three members of the French National Assembly:

51. Ibid., 37–41.
52. Ibid., 171. "Nous dirions donc que la force a pour objet d'imposer l'organisation l'un certain ordre social dans lequel une minorité gouverne, tandis que la violence tend à la destruction de cet ordre."
Sorel, *Réflexions,* 169.
53. Although Sorel was well schooled in the history of the French Revolution, I have been unable
to find any evidence that he was aware of Robespierre's distinction between force and violence.

Among the British, whom I am always very far from citing as a model, the law permits citizens to kill a police officer who infringes upon their liberty. This law is a consequence of natural right, which orders men to provide for their own protection, and to which it gives full rein, from the moment when the public officer, constituted to protect the rights of citizens, himself violates them . . . Following the spirit of this law, the three citizens illegally arrested by the men at arms would have had the right to fight off violence with force.

Chez les Anglais, que je suis très-loin de citer en tout pour modèles, la loi permet aux citoyens de tuer un officier de police qui attenterait à leur liberté. Cette loi est une conséquence du droit naturel qui ordonne à l'homme de pourvoir à sa propre conservation, et auquel elle rend son empire, dès le moment où l'officier public, constitue pour protéger les droits des citoyens, vient lui-même à les violer . . . Suivant l'esprit de cette loi, les trois citoyens arrêtés illégalement par des gens d'armes, auraient eu le droit de repousser la violence par la force.[54]

In mid-1792 Robespierre was understandably concerned with finding a justification for the legitimate use of violence against a quasi-royalist state, which he believed did not yet sufficiently embody the ideals of the Revolution. Deeming the "illegal" and thus illegitimate arrest of the three deputies to be "violence" and their resistance to be "force," Robespierre voiced the dilemma that all revolutionaries inevitably face: the justification of violent action taken on behalf of a notion of justice that is not yet legal. Unlike Sorel, however, he grounded his distinction between violence and force in a natural right to self-defense, a demonstration of his commitment to universal Enlightenment principles. Sorel rejects this bourgeois, metaphysical foundation for his concept of violence because he wants to avoid the Jacobin temptation to make the state a universal guardian of the right to self-defense.[55] One can even speculate that Sorel's inversion of the terms, making force illegitimate and violence legitimate, illustrates how much he wished to distance himself from the lure of state-sponsored revolution.

Sorel salvages revolutionary violence from the legacy of Jacobinism in order to articulate an anarchic idea of political foundation, which emphasizes processes, not outcomes, and ethics, not institutions. By equating force with terror, Sorel theoretically limits the role played by violence in the creation of a new regime. Proletarian violence rebelliously prepares for the founding moment by helping to destroy the bourgeois state. Sorel, however, never suggests that pro-

54. Maximilien Robespierre, *Œuvres complètes de Robespierre, le défenseur de la constitution,* vol. 4 (Paris: Librairie Félix Alcan, 1939), 62.
55. Sorel, *Reflections,* 37–41.

letarian violence should be used to create socialist economic or political institutions. As an anarchist, Sorel is committed to a paradoxical concept of political
foundation: a highly decentralized and moral community of producers unburdened by state structures. The only institutions that Sorel projects into the socialist future are worker syndicates, whose task is the cultivation of a particular
moral outlook, what Sorel calls the "morality of the producers." Sorel argues that
proletarian violence should play a creative and regenerative role in the achievement of this distinctive working-class morality. By allowing proletarian violence
to participate in the constitution of morality, yet forbidding it from taking part
in state formation, Sorel decisively departs from the visions of founding violence
rooted in Jacobin instrumentality and Maistrian eschatology. Sorelian violence
neither founds states through terror nor attenuates human guilt in anticipation
of millennial redemption. For Sorel, violence that serves the task of political
foundation—as the French revolutionaries understood it—becomes forceful
and immoral. Thus, Sorel ultimately agrees with Maistre that sacrificial violence
cannot found new political regimes, even if it can creatively and problematically
regenerate the morality from which new political forms ultimately spring.

Sorelian Sacrifice in Historical Perspective

Like the French revolutionaries and Maistre, Sorel turns to the distant past in
order to understand the connection between violence, moral regeneration, and
political foundation. Like them, he is concerned about moral decadence and interested in using violence as a remedy against it. For the revolutionaries, the idea
of moral renewal was a legacy of Enlightenment thinkers, such as Rousseau,
whose enthusiasm for the lessons of Greek and Roman antiquity profoundly
influenced the unfolding of the Revolution. Moral regeneration was also a
prominent theme in Maistre's work, but one that sprang from Catholic notions
of sin and redemption. The intellectual novelty of Sorel's interest in moral renewal can be partially attributed to his amalgamation of Marxist sociology and
Giambattista Vico's historicism. Sorel was seduced by Vico's concept of *ricorso,*
the idea that history alternates between periods of moral decadence and periods of regeneration.[56] Blended with class analysis, Vico's historicism leads Sorel
to consider how the syndicalist movement could act as an agent of moral renewal, ending the decadence of bourgeois life.

Digging though history, Sorel sought a form of violence that directly trans-

---

56. See Georges Sorel, "Etude sur Vico," *Le Devenir social,* 1896, 785–817, 906–941, 1013–46. For discussions of Sorel's reflections on Vico, see Jennings, *Georges Sorel,* 62–66; Stanley, *The Sociology of Virtue,*
190–192, 229–230; and Jules Monnerot, *Inquisitions* (Paris: Librairie José Corti, 1974), 13–22.

formed morality in ways that were consistent with anarcho-syndicalist principles. Sorel greatly admired the ancient Greek citizen-soldier who died in defense of the polis. Political self-sacrifice was a noble, heroic, and moral practice
that resulted from an ensemble of nonrational attitudes or feelings related to
civic duty. Although Sorel appreciated the communal spirit that accompanied
political self-sacrifice, its affinity to patriotism limited its efficacy. During his anarcho-syndicalist phase, Sorel had no interest in elevating love of state or nation
above that of class. Furthermore, because Sorel viewed dying for one's country
as a secular duty, he did not imagine that it would involve the same sacred, mythical power as religious sacrifice. Despite its being powerfully symbolic and unifying, political self-sacrifice did not offer Sorel a mechanism or process of moral
regeneration whose sublimity permitted sociopolitical change.

By contrast, early Christian martyrs displayed the requisite morals that Sorel
hoped would be cultivated within the syndicates. They also participated in a
form of violence long known for its remarkable, sublime powers of moral transformation. Finally, Christian martyrdom resonated with French culture, which
had a greater historical affinity to Christianity than to Greek political thought.
Sorel admired martyrdom's mythical, aesthetic, and redemptive qualities: the
brutality of the violence dramatically bonded together small, beleaguered groups
of Christians, making them more ardent in their belief in the Second Coming.
Moreover, the sublimity of that brutality—"sublimity" being Sorel's term for
the aesthetic and catalytic qualities of violence—could be transported through
time and space in the form of a myth, a narrative of images that animated the
Christian faithful. In this way, the affective impact of one martyr could radically
motivate and morally transform thousands of potential converts. This power of
the martyr particularly appealed to Sorel because it obviated the need for a violent experience. Christ himself illustrated that the myth of martyrdom was sufficient to build a vast religious movement. If a few martyrs could enable
Christians to overcome Roman persecution, Sorel imagined that such violence
could achieve something similar for anarcho-syndicalism.

Political Self-Sacrifice in Ancient Greece

In a significant amendment to the revolutionary cult of Roman antiquity, Sorel
first turns to the Greeks in order to cull a morality and form of violence suitable for the proletarian mission. In 1889 Sorel published *Le Procès de Socrate,* a
critique of Socratic rationalism and laudatory account of moral education in the
ancient Greek polis. Drawing an explicit contrast between ancient Athenians
and the nineteenth-century French, Sorel writes: "The Athenians of olden times

were quite superior to our envious, ignorant, and gluttonous bourgeoisie. The Jacobin type did not exist in early Athens. Citizens were not merchants, demanding a guarantee for their trade, protection of their industry, and soliciting government favors. They were soldiers whose existence was tied to the greatness of the city."[57] Extolling the virtues of citizen-soldiers, this passage juxtaposes the heroism and virility of Athenian citizens with the dependent, undisciplined French bourgeoisie. In the same work, Sorel approvingly cites a German historian of ancient Greece, Ernst Curtius, who describes ancient Greek culture in terms of "spiritual nourishment," "heroic feelings," and "a passion for lofty deeds." Curtius emphasizes the unity of Greek education, which "involved the whole man," as well as the importance of poetry and "sacred legends" for popular education.[58] Sorel is enamored of this type of education because it prepared Greek citizen-soldiers for a total commitment to the health of the polis. Inspired by Greek education and culture, Sorel celebrates the ancient civic virtue of self-sacrifice: "man discovers his own best qualities: courage, patience, disregard of death, devotion to glory, and the good of his fellows: in one word, his virtue."[59]

Sorel can appreciate the value of political self-sacrifice when he conceptualizes it in a heroic, martial fashion as opposed to a selfless, ascetic one. War is the context in which Sorel's citizen-soldier demonstrates his capacity for self-sacrifice. Recalling Maistre's association of war, bloodshed, and culture, Sorel embraces the idea that war generates superior citizens and elevated expressions of culture. "The whole of classical history," Sorel writes, "is dominated by the idea of war conceived heroically." He continues: "In their origin, the institutions of the Greek republics had as their basis the organization of armies of citizens; Greek art reached its apex in the citadels; philosophers conceived of no other possible form of education than that which fostered in youth the heroic tradition . . . In our own times, the wars of Liberty have been scarcely less fruitful in ideas than those of the ancient Greeks."[60]

According to Sorel, the crucible of war allowed the Hellenistic Greeks and, later, the French revolutionaries to forge their highest expressions of art, culture,

57. Stanley, *From Georges Sorel*, 62.

58. Ernst Curtius, *Histoire grecque*, vol. 2, trans. Auguste Bouché-Leclercq (Paris: E. Leroux, 1880–1883), 460. Quoted in Georges Sorel, *Le Procès de Socrate* (Paris: Félix Alcan, 1889), 7, 172.

59. Quoted in Stanley, *The Sociology of Virtue*, 35, 44. This quotation is from Pierre-Joseph Proudhon's *La Guerre et la paix* and is cited favorably by Sorel in his article "Essai sur la philosophie de Proudhon," *Revue philosophique de la France et de l'étranger,* January–June 1892, 622–639.

60. Sorel, *Reflections*, 166. "Les institutions des républiques grecques eurent, à l'origine, pour base l'organisation d'armées de citoyens; l'art grec atteignit son apogée dans les citadelles; les philosophes ne concevaient d'autre éducation que celle qui peut entretenir une tradition héroïque dans la jeunesse . . . De notre temps, les guerres de la Liberté n'ont guère été moins fécondes en idées que celles des anciens Grecs." Sorel, *Réflexions*, 163.

and morality. Here the issue is not blood sacrifice—the ability of the heroic soldier to take the lives of his enemies—but rather the willingness on the part of Greek and French revolutionary soldiers to sacrifice their own. What Sorel finds particularly noteworthy in his observations of military zeal is the extent to which soldiers act independently in the context of battle. He writes:"In the wars of Liberty each soldier considered himself as an *individual* having something important to do in the battle, instead of looking upon himself as simply one part of a military mechanism entrusted to the supreme direction of a master."[61] Apparently undisturbed by the fact that the French Revolutionary Army was a state institution, Sorel imagines revolutionary soldiers as heroic individuals committed to collective liberty in the context of a decentralized structure of authority. This emphasis on heroic, individual self-sacrifice—a decisive break with Peter Kropotkin's more communal, cooperative, and peaceful notion of mutual aid—is a distinguishing feature of Sorel's anarchism and helps to explain his revulsion toward indiscriminate, mass violence. In the heart of the ancient polis as well as within the French Revolutionary Army, Sorel finds a perfect example of secular self-sacrifice to animate the workers' syndicates.

Sorel's interest in secular, civic self-sacrifice, rooted in ancient Greece and exemplified by republican France, suggests a surprising affinity between Sorelian thought and republicanism. K. Steven Vincent argues that Sorel's connection to the French tradition of republican socialism has been underestimated. He maintains that Sorel's early works, such as *Contribution à l'étude profane de la Bible* and *Le Procès de Socrate,* celebrate the "heroic virtue of the Athenian *polis*" based upon "a strong family structure, a vital military life and the absence of a leisure class devoted to consumption and professional politics."[62] In adopting this trinity of civic ideals, Sorel drinks from the same well of republicanism as Machiavelli, Montesquieu, Rousseau, and, of course, the French revolutionaries. Moreover, Sorel's embracing of certain republican ideals illustrates an important, understated facet of his attitude toward the French Revolution. While Sorel loathes the institutional face of the Jacobins and their use of violence, he nonetheless conserves some of the moral aspects of their political project. Like the Jacobins, who believed that the resurrection of ancient civic virtues could stem the tide of Old Regime decadence, Sorel was convinced that similar virtues would be critical for the anarcho-syndicalist movement in its struggle to overcome modern bourgeois decadence.

---

61. "Pendant les guerres de la Liberté, chaque soldat se considérait comme étant un *personnage* ayant à faire quelque chose de très important dans la bataille, au lieu de se regarder comme étant seulement une pièce dans un mécanisme militaire confié à la direction souveraine d'un maître." Sorel, *Réflexions,* 243.

62. K. Steven Vincent, "Interpreting Georges Sorel: Defender of Virtue or Apostle of Violence?" *History of European Ideas* 12, no. 2 (1990), 246.

Although Sorel's recuperation of self-sacrificial morality from the Greek polis reflects only an early stage in his theoretical development of proletarian self-sacrifice, it also provides an important illustration of how the moral regeneration of the proletariat is limitedly violent. When Sorel uses examples and metaphors of war to describe this concept of political self-sacrifice, he studiously avoids the more excessive views of his predecessors. For instance, he offers no enthusiastic images of blood sacrifice, such as Brutus' filicide, which so captivated the Jacobin imagination. Unlike Maistre, whom he had read, Sorel displays no interest in the idea of redemption through bloodshed, nor does he embrace Maistre's apocalyptic descriptions of war's fertilizing of culture. Finally, Sorel—in his early intellectual and anarcho-syndicalist phases—lacks two proto-fascistic ideas of self-sacrifice and war. Before he abandoned anarcho-syndicalism around 1909, Sorel eschewed nationalist terminology. Sorel also never embraces any form of Ernst Jünger's post–World War I concept of *Fronterlebnis*. War may be the context in which Sorel develops a notion of political self-sacrifice, but his praise for war escalates into a celebration of neither nationalism nor the experience of violence.

From Greek Self-Sacrifice to Christian Martyrdom

Sorel's progress from a Greek notion of civic self-sacrifice to a Christian notion of martyrdom illustrates his rejection of the more aggressive and experiential form of sacrifice practiced during the French Revolution. Rather than perpetuating the bloody sacrificial tradition symbolized by the Roman republican patriot Brutus and realized by the French republicans during the Terror, Sorel turns instead toward the form of sacrifice modeled by Christ. Christ's martyrdom was violent, to be sure. But it was only a singular act of bloodshed with wildly disproportionate spiritual and political implications. During the Revolution, Christian martyrdom played a significant role when, for instance, Louis XVI suggested on the scaffold that he wished to die a martyr for his royal subjects. Similarly, the cult of revolutionary martyrs borrowed from the Christian sacrificial tradition in order to highlight the symbolic importance of those who sacrificed their lives for the Revolution. Ultimately, however, the Christological significance of the martyr made it a dangerously unstable symbol for the French republicans to claim as their own. As the example of Christ himself illustrates, the symbolic power of martyrdom is contingent upon the martyr's unique qualities. The self-sacrifice of theandric beings or kings greatly overshadows that of common soldiers or noteworthy revolutionary leaders. Although the revolutionaries attempted to overcome this deficit by lavishly commemorating revolutionary martyrs, their names and significance have not weathered time nearly as well as the "august" martyr, Louis XVI.

Writing more than a century after the Revolution, Sorel avidly sought to transplant certain aspects of Christian life, morality, and violence to the anarcho-syndicalist movement. He viewed Christian martyrdom in the same way that he perceived proletarian violence: both are predominantly notions of symbolic bloodshed. Sorel, of course, knew that the class war would take some lives, proletarian and bourgeois. Yet he strongly believed that Christian sacrifice would offer the proletariat a variety of collective benefits without either causing mass bloodshed or glorifying its experience. Sorel's adaptation of Christian sacrifice to anarcho-syndicalism thus illustrates a highly targeted revolutionary agenda designed to transform the deaths of a few workers into the mythos from which a new world order could emerge.

Sorel's views on martyrdom are complicated by his application of Vico's concept of *ricorso* to Christian history. In *La Ruine du monde antique,* Sorel praises the warrior mentality of the early Christians who constantly suffered persecution under the Romans. At the same time, however, Sorel castigates the church for allowing itself to become infected with the very decadence that made Rome susceptible to Christian influence in the first place. Sorel suggests that the social absorption of Christianity into Roman life decimated both the civic virtues of Roman republicanism and the potentially revitalizing spirit of an aggressive, disciplined group of Christian zealots. This example of mutual corruption shapes Sorel's fear that extensive, conciliatory contact between the proletariat and the bourgeoisie will have a similarly decadent effect. In his view, such corruption illustrates how quickly a period of moral regeneration can become decadent. Christian-Roman decadence also convinced Sorel that only certain forms of piety were suited to moral regeneration. As Vincent claims, "Sorel found the Augustinian strain of piety, with its emphasis on the helplessness of the human condition and the need for the Christian to rid himself of pride and to cultivate humility and a prayerful heart, a lamentable development. 'The ancient idea [of civic virtue] is completely obliterated by Saint Augustine.'"[63]

Sorel wanted workers in the anarcho-syndicalist movement to emulate the religious fervor of "primitive Christianity." He was impressed by the ability of the early Christians to combine a martial spirit, mythology of redemption, and a particular form of self-sacrificial violence. Sorel believed that these aspects of primitive Christianity permitted a small group of zealots to overwhelm the Ro-

---

63. Ibid., 248. Thomas Martin argues that Sorel's Jansenist upbringing contributed to his "reversion to Augustine's gloomy determinism and self-discipline." "Violent Myths: The Post-Western Irrationalism of Georges Sorel," *Democracy and Nature,* nos. 11–12 (September–October 1999), 52.

man Empire, a feat he greatly admired. The mobilizing force of Christian eschatology especially fascinated him:

> The Christian life of that time was dominated by the necessity of membership in the holy army, which was constantly exposed to the ambuscades set by the accomplices of Satan; this conception produced many heroic acts, engendered a courageous propaganda, and was the cause of considerable moral progress. The deliverance did not take place, but we know from innumerable testimonies of that time what great things the march toward deliverance can bring about.

> Tout cette vie chrétienne fut dominée par la nécessité de faire partie de l'armée sainte, constamment exposée aux embûches tendues par les suppôts de Satan; cette conception suscita beaucoup d'actes héroïques, engendra une courageuse propagande et produisit un sérieux progrès moral. La délivrance n'eut pas lieu; mais nous savons par d'innombrables témoignages de ce temps ce que peut produire de grande la marche à la délivrance.[64]

Here Sorel signals the didactic importance of Christian eschatology for the workers' movement. He particularly admires the process-oriented worldview of the early Christians, who managed to achieve significant "moral progress" thanks to the motivating power of two ideas, evil and deliverance. By highlighting the "march to deliverance," Sorel illustrates why the civic ideals of the Greek polis were insufficient to animate the proper spirit of self-sacrifice among the proletariat. The willingness to die for one's country may generate passionate, patriotic fervor, but it remains tethered to the immediacy of secular, terrestrial life. In contrast, "primitive Christianity" demonstrates the robust revolutionary power of a movement mythologically animated by an eternal struggle against evil and the (unfulfilled) desire for deliverance from that great conflict.

Sorel also considers sixteenth-century Calvinism instructive for the proletariat.[65] Just as he distinguishes between "primitive" Christianity and its mature, quiescent forms, he recognizes an important difference between Calvinism and what he calls "contemporary Protestantism." The latter form of Protestantism was ruined by Renaissance ideals just as Catholicism was corrupted by Roman decadence. Early Protestantism, however, displayed precisely those virtues that Sorel wished for the proletariat:

> Protestants organized themselves into a military force wherever possible; they made expeditions into Catholic countries, expelled the priests, introduced reformed wor-

64. Sorel, *Reflections,* 35; idem, *Réflexions,* 13–14.
65. Sorel, *Reflections,* 35.

ship, and promulgated proscriptive laws against papists . . . the Protestants, nourished on the reading of the Old Testament, wished to imitate the exploits of the conquerors of the Holy Land; they took the offensive, and wished to establish the kingdom of God by force. In each conquered locality, the Calvinists brought about a real catastrophic revolution, which changed everything from top to bottom.

Les protestants s'organisèrent militairement partout où cela leur était possible; ils faisaient des expéditions en pays catholiques, expulsant les prêtres, introduisant le culte réformé et promulguant des lois de proscription contre les papistes . . . Les protestants, nourris de la lecture de l'Ancien Testament, voulaient imiter les exploits des anciens conquérants de la Terre sainte; ils prenaient donc l'offensive et voulaient établir le royaume de Dieu par la force. Dans chaque localité conquise, les calvinistes réalisaient une véritable révolution catastrophique, changeant tout de fond en comble.[66]

Sorel admires the single-minded martial spirit of the early Protestants, which enabled them to undertake a "catastrophic revolution" in Catholic countries. According to Sorel, militant Calvinists uniquely embraced a "will-to-deliverance," a distinctly voluntaristic concept of redemption.[67] Rather than conceiving of deliverance as a final apocalypse, the Calvinists sought "to establish the kingdom of God by force." Sorel appreciates the Calvinist deliverance for its demonstration of warlike ardor and missionary zeal. The fact that the pursuit of such deliverance would ultimately be unlikely to bear redemptive fruit is of no consequence to him. Just as with the "primitive Christians," what matters above all is the *pursuit* of deliverance. It is for this reason that Sorel upholds the Wandering Jew as the symbol of the "highest aspirations of mankind."[68] Another process-oriented image of tireless struggle overshadowing ultimate goals, the Wandering Jew is an anti-Semitic, medieval, folkloric image of a Jew whose rejection of the Crucifixion condemns him to wander the earth until Christ's return. The primitive Christian, militant Calvinist, and Wandering Jew toil restlessly in the present for a redemptive future. That, Sorel believed, was the spirit that should animate proletarian violence and revolution.

Sorel's Viconian adaptation of Christian history to anarcho-syndicalism directly parallels his process-oriented view of Marxism. For him, the ideas of Christian deliverance and socialist revolution animate and shape the nature of their pursuit. The goal of anarcho-syndicalism is thus not the achievement of a successful revolution, but rather the totality of radical moral and material trans-

---

66. Sorel, *Réflexions,* 14–15.
67. Sorel, *Reflections,* 37.
68. Ibid.

formations required to attain such a revolutionary end. In *Reflections*, Sorel expands the analogy between Christianity and socialism by arguing that socialism is religious insofar as it consists of a set of irrefutable ideas. "It has been observed," writes Sorel, "that Christianity tends at the present day to be less a system of dogmas than a Christian life, that is, a moral reform penetrating to the bottom of the heart; consequently, a new analogy has been discovered between religion and the revolutionary socialism which aims at the training, preparation, and even reconstruction of the individual with a view to a gigantic task."[69] This claim underscores the didactic value of Christian moral renewal for the proletariat. At the heart of this "gigantic task" of "moral reform" rests a politico-religious concept of deliverance and a form of self-sacrificial violence, the leitmotifs of Sorel's vision for the anarcho-syndicalist movement. The last sentence in *Reflections* also highlights this point: "It is to violence that socialism owes those high ethical values by means of which it brings salvation to the modern world."[70] Not mere rhetoric, this phrase is a fervent reminder that Sorel's revolutionary socialism is a quasi-religious mixture of violent and redemptive ideas.

A core idea of *Reflections*, martyrdom is the violent practice used by the anarcho-syndicalists to bring "salvation to the modern world." For Sorel, acts of martyrdom must be limited because their importance rests in their ability to convey sacrificial ideas that further the socialist revolution. In his study of the impact of early Christian martyrdom on the institutionalization of the church, Sorel concludes that "the remarkable occurrences that took place during the scenes of martyrdom" are much more important than the "statistics of persecutions."[71] According to Sorel, the success of early Christian ideology depended upon rare but heroic instances of martyrdom. Indeed, he writes, "The martyrs did not need to be numerous to prove, through the ordeal, the absolute truth of the new religion and the absolute error of the old, thus to establish that there were two incompatible ways, and to make clear that the reign of evil would come to an end."[72] Sorel extols the quintessential Christian act of self-sacrifice as a violent mechanism of Manichaean differentiation between the forces of

---

69. "On observe aussi que, de notre temps, le christianisme tendrait à être moins une dogmatique qu'une vie chrétienne, c'est-à-dire une réforme morale qui veut aller jusqu'au fond du coeur; par suite, on a trouvé une nouvelle analogie entre la religion et le socialisme révolutionnaire qui se donne pour but l'apprentissage, la préparation et même la reconstruction de l'individu en vue d'une oeuvre gigantesque." Sorel, *Réflexions*, 32.

70. Sorel, *Reflections*, 249. "C'est à la violence que le socialisme doit les hautes valeurs morales par lesquelles il apporte le salut au monde moderne." Sorel, *Réflexions*, 255.

71. Sorel, *Reflections*, 184. "Des circonstances notables, qui se produisaient au cours des scènes de martyre, avaient beaucoup plus d'importance que la fréquence des supplices." Sorel, *Réflexions*, 182.

72. "Les martyrs n'avaient pas besoin d'être nombreux pour prouver, par l'épreuve, la vérité absolue de la nouvelle religion et l'erreur absolue de l'ancienne, pour établir ainsi qu'il y avait deux voies incompatibles entre elles, pour faire comprendre que le règne du mal aurait un terme." Sorel, *Réflexions*, 182.

good and evil. Sorel's use of religious language to describe the martyr's function illustrates the origination of the distinction between state force and proletarian violence. Early Christian martyrs successfully employed self-sacrificial violence in order to distinguish between the absolute goodness of Christianity and the evil of Roman paganism. Anarcho-syndicalists employ a similar form of bloodshed to intensify the separation of the "morality of the producers" from the decadence of the bourgeoisie. In this way, martyrdom converts violence into myth.

Sorel's observation that martyrdom helped in the emergence and development of a militant Christianity provides insight into the myth of the general strike, one of Sorel's most famous concepts. Jules Monnerot provides the most compelling analysis of this elusive concept with four essential insights.[73] First, Monnerot argues that Sorel's concept of the myth of the general strike is not an intellectual fabrication, which Sorel hoped to graft onto the anarcho-syndicalist movement. Rather, it is the product of Sorel's ethnographic observations of early twentieth-century political, economic, and social life. Although Sorel did not invent the notion of the general strike, Monnerot claims that the *myth* of the general strike is the outcome of *mythische Denken,* Monnerot's term for a mode of modern mythical thinking that Sorel attributes to his contemporaries' political views.[74] *Mythische Denken* is characterized above all by its emotive quality and resistance to rational, critical thought. Second, modern myths, like that of the general strike, are forms of affective communication that result from violent social trauma, such as war. Monnerot highlights Sorel's observation that both ancient and modern myths are born in blood. However, unlike ancient myths, which generate socially conservative rituals and support the status quo, modern myths are dynamic and creative. Their images, narrative structure, and affectivity inspire collective action on the part of individuals captivated by this thinking. Third, both Monnerot and Sorel describe the communication of myth in terms of contamination. Myth spreads epidemically because of the violent nature of its origin and content. Finally, Monnerot argues that modern myths are potentially revolutionary because they link human nonrational motivations to collective action, which together form the essential Sorelian components of

---

73. Two versions of this remarkable essay exist. For one without annotation, see Jules Monnerot, "Georges Sorel ou l'introduction aux mythes modernes," in *Science et conscience de la société* (Paris: Calmann-Lévy, 1971). For the version with notes, see Monnerot, "Georges Sorel," in *Inquisitions.*

74. Monnerot, "Georges Sorel," 18. Although the idea of workers' refusing to labor as a form of protest has its origins in the French Revolution, the modern concept of the general strike was born in the late 1880s and was first formally adopted by French workers at the Congrès Syndicale de Bordeaux in 1888. See Robert Brécy, *La Grève générale en France* (Paris: EDI, 1969), 26. There was always a vigorous debate among the various working-class organizations in France about the meaning of the general strike. For the anarchists, the idea typically involved violence and the expropriation of property. In contrast, socialists, especially reformist ones, tended to conceive of the general strike in pacifist and legal terms.

radical political movements. These insights help to explain how Sorel builds a myth of total labor stoppage into political eschatology. The myth of the general strike communicates the affective power of the self-sacrificial violence that gave birth to it and, in doing so, becomes a vital organizational and motivational ally of the working class in its revolutionary struggle.

In *Le Système historique de Renan,* a lengthy critical analysis of Renan's work, Sorel offers several additional insights regarding the connection between martyrdom and mythmaking. The text is structured according to the elaborate parallel that Sorel draws between the foundation of Christianity and socialism. The issue of violence emerges primarily in Sorel's analysis and critique of Renan's position on martyrdom. Renan maintains that even if there were few actual martyrs, and even if the details of those terrible acts were false or fabricated, "the frightful picture that they unfold before us is no less a reality."[75] Renan holds that those descriptions of martyrdom, true or not, had a significant impact on the foundation of the church: "The persecutions were a first-rate element in the formation of that great association of men who first made right triumph against the tyrannical claims of the state."[76] Although Renan describes Christians and Romans, Sorel could just as easily have written this sentence about parliamentary democrats and socialists. Moreover, the sacrificial logic is explicit: martyrdom fosters communal organization ("that great association of men") as well as the birth of a new morality, which Renan expresses as "right."

Renan's observations regarding early Christian martyrdom offered Sorel the basic elements from which he would later develop his concept of violence in *Reflections.* Sorel agrees with Renan that the spectacle of martyrdom engenders a "new aesthetic" that could have attracted converts to the church. Sorel and Renan also concur that the aesthetic of Christian persecutions possesses an erotic quality, which Sorel calls an "aphrodisiac" and likens to the impact of tauromachy.[77] Sorel even acknowledges that "the blood of the martyrs was the seed of Christianity."[78] Yet Sorel strongly disagrees with Renan's emphasis on the experience of violent self-sacrifice. Ultimately Sorel concludes that the aesthetics of violent martyrdom are best explained by "hysteria":

75. "L'effroyable tableau qu'ils déroulent devant nous n'en est pas moins une réalité." Georges Sorel, *Le Système historique de Renan* (Paris: G. Jacques, 1905), 304.

76. "Les persécutions ont été un élément de premier ordre dans la formation de cette grande association d'hommes qui la première fit triompher son droit contre les prétentions tyrannique de l'Etat." Ibid., 304–305.

77. Ibid., 305–306. Sorel's interest in tauromachy is shared by Georges Bataille as well as Michel Leiris, whose autobiographical book, *Manhood,* explores the psychosocial significance of sacrificial bullfights and virility. Michel Leiris, *Manhood,* trans. Richard Howard (Chicago: University of Chicago Press, 1984).

78. "Le sang des martyrs fut la semence de christianisme." Sorel, *Le Système historique de Renan,* 305–306.

In the final analysis, it is hysteria that would furnish us the explanation of the whole aesthetic of the martyr; hysteria of the victims renders them beautiful, giving them a sort of instantaneous idealization; the hysteria of the spectators saves them from the dangers of the erotic excitation that ordinarily accompanies bloody spectacles. There is therefore in this aesthetic a "delightful ambiguity."

C'est, en dernière analyse, l'hystérie qui nous fournirait l'explication de toute l'esthétique du martyr; l'hystérie des victimes les rend belles, leur donne une sorte d'idéalisation momentanée; l'hystérie des spectateurs les soustrait aux dangers de l'excitation érotique qui accompagne ordinairement les spectacles sanglants. Il y a donc dans cette esthétique une "charmante équivoque."[79]

Although Sorel does not use the word "sublime" in this passage, his critique of Renan's position on martyrdom moves in that conceptual direction. The "delightful ambiguity" of the Christian persecutions captures the paradoxical qualities of sublimity. In reflecting upon the function of the martyr, Renan places more weight on the experience of violence than does Sorel. For Sorel, hysteria—the psychological experience of sublimity—actually saves the spectator from the "erotic excitation that ordinarily accompanies bloody spectacles." Psychopathology thus guards Sorel's civic-minded, family-oriented, conservative, moral spirit from violent, erotic contamination.

Mass hysteria provides Sorel with an explanation of martyrdom's primary social function and, at the same time, with a reason to discount the importance of its violence. Hysteria contributes to what Sorel and Renan call "religious contagion," a description of how self-sacrificial violence fosters the spread of fanaticism. Calling this phenomenon "religious insanity," Sorel appears inclined to pathologize and thus dismiss its sociological importance.[80] However, what Sorel dismisses is not the impact of the idea of persecutions on the foundation of Christianity, but rather the real experience of that violence. In other words, Sorel rejects Renan's claim that the birth of Christianity required centuries of self-sacrificial deaths. Instead, he argues that Christianity was founded thanks to the contagious dissemination of mythic, sacrificial images of martyrdom. Sorel's concept of hysteria thus captures the psycho-aesthetic impact of the idea of violence as distinguished from the actual experience of it.

On the basis of his critical reading of Renan and his independent study of martyrdom, Sorel concludes that the concrete experience of violence—watching actual persecutions—produces sickness (*maladie*). Conversely, he also claims

79. Ibid., 307. Sorel's use of "delightful ambiguity" recalls Edmund Burke's description of the sublime as the delight inspired by terror.
80. Ibid., 308–309.

that "the spirit of martyrdom" possesses sublime, psychosocial properties from which the anarcho-syndicalists can benefit. Again turning to the early Christians for guidance, Sorel argues that they transformed sporadic tales of their own persecution into an elaborate saga of conflict between human beings and God, a theomachy. To assuage any doubt about the applicability of theomachy to the anarcho-syndicalist movement, Sorel writes: "This expression [*théomachie*] is borrowed from the second book of the Maccabees (7:19) and it offers a remarkable analogy to the *class struggle,* to which modern socialism has accustomed us."[81] Sorel deems the persecution of Christian martyrs to be valuable for the foundation of Christianity because it contributes to the myth that Christians are locked in a struggle with Satan until Christ's return. This Christian mythology is not only analogous to the myth of the general strike; it further highlights the limitations that Sorel imposes on proletarian violence. Sorel is disgusted by the reality that the blood of the martyrs has formed the seed of the church. That idea and the myth to which it gave rise, however, he considers invaluable.

The opposition of theomachy and tauromachy illuminates Sorel's theoretical distinction between symbolic and experiential sacrifice, a defining feature of his understanding of violence. In thinking about the revolutionary impact of bloodshed, Sorel rejects the bloody, erotic, experiential metaphor of the bullfight in favor of the symbolic, disciplined, eschatological battle with Satan. Tauromachy describes a battle between man and beast that ideally concludes with the sacrificial death of the bull. This decisive conclusion contrasts sharply with theomachy, which conveys the image of an open-ended struggle to conquer an undefeatable, divine being. It is the prolonged, mythic, bloodless, and, ultimately, symbolic nature of theomachy that appeals to Sorel. He contends in a variety of contexts, including his discussions of terror, war, strikes, and martyrdom, that repeated exposure to the experience of violence is inimical to moral well-being. Here Sorel describes the revolutionary potential of the martyr and illustrates his characteristic slippage between the idea and the experience of violence:

> In taking this point of view, one finds that the martyr assumes an entirely different significance than that attributed to him by Renan. One can break down the witnessing of the ordeal into three elements and say: the nobility of the victims' attitude demanded respect and proved that they were worthy of freedom;—the Spartan courage with which they died justified their belief in the triumph of the *Christian fatherland;*—their unwavering certitude made one presume the presence of the living Christ. That is the way that for men who remained more Roman than Marcus Aurelius, the spectacle of the martyr could become a serious reason to believe.

81. "Cette expression est empruntée au deuxième livre des Macchabées (VII, 19) et elle a une analogie remarquable avec celle de *lutte de classe* à laquelle nous a habitués le socialisme moderne." Ibid., 312–315.

En se plaçant à ce point de vue, on trouve que le martyre avait une toute autre portée que celle qui lui attribue Renan. On peut décomposer le témoignage de l'épreuve en trois éléments et dire: la noblesse de l'attitude des victimes imposait du respect et prouvait qu'elles étaient dignes de la liberté;—le courage spartiate avec lequel elles mouraient justifiait leur croyance au triomphe de la *patrie chrétienne;*—leur inébranlable fermeté faisait supposer la présence du Christ vivant. C'est ainsi que pour des hommes demeurés plus romains que Marc-Aurèle, le spectacle du martyre pouvait devenir une raison sérieuse de croire.[82]

Instead of focusing on the aesthetics of violence, Sorel highlights the symbolic and didactic qualities of martyrdom. Martyrdom displays heroism by offering its witnesses a sense of freedom and courage; it extols the value of a communal bond that is forged in this world and extends into the next; and it inspires faith among those least likely to believe. In sum, by drawing a visceral connection between individual suffering and redemption, martyrdom morally transforms those who witness it, an etymologically precise definition of the term.

By deemphasizing the importance of viewing actual self-sacrifices, Sorel disconnects moral and spiritual transformation from the experience of violence. So often misunderstood, Sorel's myth of the general strike communicates only images of violence and moral regeneration that neither originate in nor give rise to widespread sacrificial bloodshed. The myth of the general strike does require a few martyred workers, but this violence is simply the cost of an ongoing class struggle, not the intentional outcome of a militant proletarian strategy. What is more, this limited violence is sublime, an important characteristic that is captured and transported by the myth of the general strike. Because, for Sorel, founding political violence is literally and figuratively self-effacing, he can place no faith in its ability to establish institutions. The martyr dies; the immediate witnesses of the sacrifice are morally transformed; and the legendary, violent event is absorbed into a myth that preserves and perpetuates the sublime, morally regenerative power of the original sacrificial act. In contrast to the French revolutionaries' and Maistre's notions of moral regeneration, Sorel's is relatively bloodless.

Proletarian Martyrs: Sacrificial Politics without Sublation

Sorel's contention that proletarian violence remedies moral decadence rests upon his rejection of a major tenet of Western philosophy that morality is grounded in reason. Against this view, Sorel argues, "these [moral convictions] never depend on reasoning or any education of the individual will, but on a state

82. Ibid., 335–336.

of war in which men voluntarily participate and which finds expression in well-defined myths."[83] Morality, one of the principal fruits of religious conviction, is most ardent, or, as Sorel puts it, most sublime, in competitive, conflictive environments. In the political sphere, cooperation, bargaining, compromise, and party politics—the whole democratic parliamentary enterprise—exhibit nothing but decadence and are thus fetters on the moral development of the working class. Only class war enveloped in myth can morally regenerate the proletariat. Sorel believed that sublimity would ultimately resurface in this context of tumultuous moral formation, taking the form of literature, song, epic history, and, of course, violence. Recognizing the vital liaison between violence and sublimity, Sorel asks rhetorically: "Why is it that in certain countries acts of violence grouping themselves round the idea of the general strike produce a socialist ideology capable of inspiring sublimity, and why in others do they seem not to have that power?"[84]

Sorel's claim that morality cannot be grounded in reason reveals his ideological affinity to Maistre. Both thinkers argue that morality has a mysterious origin that reason cannot penetrate. For Maistre, this observation led him to assert the importance of the divine in the foundation of political institutions. Although Sorel embraces similar assumptions about morality's origins, he comes to radically different conclusions:

> Everyone senses, in a more or less precise manner, that one cannot found morality on the state, on the law, on economics, and, consequently, on any bourgeois institutions. Morality requires something mysterious or at least foreign to the institutions of our society; and it is that which one designates under the name of religion; but what do you do with this something? That is what they forgot to teach us.

> Tout le monde sent, d'une manière plus ou moins précise, qu'on ne peut fonder la morale sur l'Etat, sur le droit, sur l'économie et, par suite, sur aucune des institutions bourgeoises. La morale requiert quelque chose de mystérieux, ou tout au moins d'étranger aux institutions de notre société; et c'est cela qu'on veut désigner sous le nom de religion; mais où prendre ce quelque chose? C'est ce qu'on oublie de nous apprendre.[85]

83. Sorel, *Reflections*, 209. "Celles-ci [hautes convictions morales] ne dépendent point des raisonnements ou d'une éducation de la volonté individuelle; elles dépendent d'un état de guerre auquel les hommes acceptent de participer et qui se traduit en mythes précis." Sorel, *Réflexions*, 210.

84. Sorel, *Reflections*, 215. "Pourquoi les actes de violence peuvent-ils, dans certains pays, se grouper autour du tableau de la grève générale et produire ainsi une idéologie socialiste, riche en sublime; et ne semblent-ils pas le pouvoir dans d'autres?" Sorel, *Réflexions*, 216.

85. Georges Sorel, "La Crise morale et religieuse," *Le Mouvement socialiste*, no. 188 (July 15, 1907), 27.

Sounding Maistrian, Sorel describes the mystical origin of morality. On the basis of a similar supposition, Maistre concludes that morality is beyond human comprehension and thus cannot be tampered with. Those who try to alter God's creation, such as the French revolutionaries, risk terrible, divine punishments. In contrast, Sorel has a voluntaristic view of morality's mysterious origin. For him, morality's murky beginning does not prohibit meddling; rather, it offers a revolutionary opportunity. Inspired by historical examples, such as the early Christians, ancient Greeks, and even pre-Jacobin revolutionaries, Sorel surmises that it is possible to recreate the conditions under which new moral frameworks emerge. "It is easy to understand," he writes, "that a class can create its own moral concepts, which are in complete disagreement with the whole of the social structure. This possibility is one of the postulates of socialism founded on class struggle."[86] This task, however, cannot be accomplished rationally or scientifically. Instead, it must involve myth, violence, and, most important, sublimity, the constitutive elements identified by Sorel in historically successful moral transformations.

Sorel's fascination with sublimity feeds his belief that socialism involves a dramatic change in human consciousness. Similarly, Sorel is drawn toward historical events and social phenomena that are useful in either corroding decadent moral frameworks or establishing ones consistent with socialist principles. For example, Sorel favors workers' syndicates for the same reason that he admires monastic life: both are sublimations of martyrdom. Isolation, discipline, and a single-minded emphasis on a core set of principles foster autonomy, heroism, and an unwavering will to pursue a collective good. Similarly, in his discussions of class war and martyrdom, Sorel often refers to sublimity's capacity to transform human consciousness. In *Reflections,* for example, the chapter "The Ethics of Violence" is steeped in this Sorelian principle. Not only does proletarian violence illustrate the morals that Sorel holds in highest esteem; it surrounds that morality and the actions that it inspires with a sense of awe or sacredness. Sacrificial violence, however, cannot regenerate morality or consecrate political action without an accompanying myth. Thus, the myth of the general strike captures and organizes the gestalt of the class war, providing it with the redemptive meaning that Sorel considers essential to the anarcho-syndicalist movement.[87]

Although Sorel offers no lengthy discussion of the role played by violence in the transformation of consciousness, he does provide some clues to its effect

---

86. "Il est facile de comprendre qu'une classe puisse se créer des conceptions morales qui soient en complet désaccord avec tout l'ensemble de la structure sociale. Cette possibilité est un des postulats du socialisme fondé sur la lutte de classe." Ibid., 36.

87. Sorel, *Reflections,* 37.

on the individual. In another instance of Sorel's turning to psychology, Stanley argues that Sorel uses the work of Henri Bergson and Théodule Ribot to explain how sublimity helps to overcome the alienation caused by bourgeois utilitarianism:

> Sorel—again following Ribot—does not argue that pain is antithetical to pleasure. Especially in our moral life, "the sentiments in which pleasure and pain are united in deep combination exert considerable influence." It is when these two aspects of our being unite that we experience "what Ribot puts in the category of the *sublime,* which is not only an aesthetic sentiment, and which everyone agrees comes very close to morals" . . . It is in this sublime compassion that the social dimension of our psychology can be attained, but the social nature of the sublime inserts itself not only in compassion, but, Sorel adds, in the love between man and woman and in the love of the hero for the homeland, as well as in the laboring process.[88]

Stanley insightfully describes Sorel's understanding of the nexus between morality and sublimity. The sublime—part pleasure, part pain—is an "aesthetic sentiment" that is "close to morals" and builds a bridge between individual sentiments and "the social dimension of psychology." The social function of this individual sentiment provides Sorel with an "antidote" to bourgeois utilitarianism. In Sorel's view, the utilitarian calculus of maximizing pleasure and minimizing pain causes alienation because it separates human beings from the material world, leading them to reify other people as well as the objects of their labor. By collapsing the distinction between pleasure and pain and celebrating activities that foster that collapse, Sorel attempts to reestablish the social connectivity lost in bourgeois society. Thus, Sorel embraces sublimity because it encourages moral feelings that heighten social solidarity.

Although Stanley identifies only eroticism, patriotism, and production as the three social formations of sublimity, violence easily fits into this mold. Perhaps no violent social act inspires more "sublime compassion" than martyrdom because it gathers communities around a sacrificial death of immense positive, symbolic importance. The sublimity created by martyrdom serves to sacralize the moral beliefs at the core of the anarcho-syndicalist movement. For Sorel, what image could be more striking than that of a worker who dies heroically during a particularly vicious strike? He believed that such images would conjure a sense of sublimity among the proletariat: painful and joyful recognition of human sacrifice and immortality. This concrete violence, filtered and transported by the myth of the general strike, is revolutionary because it is sublime.

88. Stanley, *The Sociology of Virtue,* 147.

Moreover, it is an idea that anticipates the work of Georges Bataille, who uses the concept of violent sublimity to combat bourgeois utilitarianism, but with more radical consequences for individual psychology.

The sublime emerges wherever violent struggle exists on a grand, collective scale. Inevitably, such conflicts are morally significant because they involve competing ways of life and concepts of right. In his essay on Sorel, Monnerot recognizes that the sublime is one of Sorel's most important concepts because it captures a unique regenerative quality of violence: sacrifice that invokes the sublime is capable of renewing morality during periods of decadence.[89] It is for this reason that Sorel's *Reflections* places such importance on sublimity: "The notion of a proletarian general strike," writes Sorel, "awakens in the depths of the soul a sentiment of the sublime proportionate to the conditions of a gigantic struggle."[90] Furthermore, he claims, "In a country where the conception of the general strike exists, the blows exchanged between the workmen and the representatives of the middle classes have an entirely different import, their consequences are far reaching and they may beget heroism [the sublime]."[91] Thomas Ernest Hulme and Jack Roth mistranslate the French word *sublime* as "heroism." Although Sorel undoubtedly believed that violent class warfare conducted in the context of the myth of the general strike would engender heroism, it is specifically the generation of sublimity that allows such violence to be revolutionary. Thus, class violence without myth is unrevolutionary. And myth in the absence of self-sacrificial bloodshed lacks the sublimity to inspire new morals.

By making the generation of sublimity an essential condition of revolutionary struggle, Sorel further restricts his concept of violence. Violence creates sublimity under only two conditions: it must be accompanied by a myth that inspires heroism, glory, and distinctly martial values; and it must be self-sacrificial. For Sorel, martyrdom is sublime and constitutive of morality. Conversely, terror—a form of force—lacks this power. One is reminded of the French revolutionaries who were the first in this discourse on sacrificial violence to posit the causal connection between particular forms of violence and the construction of morality. Although this link between bloodshed and moral transformation initially helped the revolutionaries, their turning to state terror and the guillotine ultimately led Parisians to become repulsed by the conduct of the Revolution. Critical of the Revolution's political legacy and pervasive blood-

---

89. Monnerot, "Georges Sorel," 40–45.

90. Sorel, *Reflections*, 165. "La notion de grève générale prolétarienne . . . éveille au fond de l'âme un sentiment du sublime en rapport avec les conditions d'une lutte gigantesque." Sorel, *Réflexions*, 162.

91. Sorel, *Reflections*, 213. "Dans les pays où existe la notion de la grève générale, les coups échangés durant les grèves entre ouvriers et représentants de la bourgeoisie ont une tout autre portée; leurs conséquences sont lointaines et elles peuvent engendrer du sublime." Sorel, *Réflexions*, 214.

shed, Sorel ultimately comes to favor the real and symbolic violence of Christian sacrifice. Sorel claims that the proletariat will redeem the modern world, but not through an apocalyptic slaughter organized and executed by state institutions. Rather, Sorel envisions the birth of a new moral framework among a militant group of workers, well disciplined by their syndicates, and willing to sacrifice their lives for the idea of a world liberated from decadent, capitalist modes of production and power. Sorel recognizes that historically successful political and religious movements rest upon a mysterious bed of myth, sacrificial violence, and sublimity. To argue that the proletariat should take heed of that historical legacy is not so much revolutionary as historically pragmatic.

In wanting sacrificial violence to regenerate morality for the sake of revolutionary socialism, Sorel illustrates the limitations of his theory of sacrifice. Sorel's embrace of the Christian sacrificial tradition permits him to turn away from the mass violence and terror that gave the French Revolution its uniquely bloody imprint. His secularization of this tradition further allows him to dismiss the Christian fascination with blood that led Maistre to glorify endless cycles of violent redemption as a fulfillment of God's will. At the beginning of a century that would soon become characterized by scapegoating on a genocidal scale, Sorel resisted the temptation to lead the anarcho-syndicalist movement into a valley of death. He did not, however, fundamentally challenge the basic assumption held by Maistre and the revolutionaries that sacrificial violence affects human beings by altering their moral beliefs, transforming their perceptions of authority, and contributing to the establishment of political ideals. Sorel's concept of sublimity illustrates this point well because, while it occurs under rare violent and mythical circumstances, it nonetheless contributes to the mass acceptance of a new, presumably better, political system. It is true that Sorel removes sacrificial violence from its traditional role as the founding event of new political regimes. But because Sorel does not strip sacrifice of its capacity to generate political novelty through moral transformation, he ultimately fails to offer a theoretically viable solution for the problem originally encountered by the French revolutionaries.

Finally, thinking of Sorel as a pessimistic pragmatist offers an important insight into his concept of proletarian violence and its relationship to class war. Sorel's concept of violence is dialectical in nature, a relation that appears most obviously in his distinction between force and violence, the latter being both a reaction to the former and, in theory at least, capable of abstractly negating it. Yet Sorel never envisions the sublation of bourgeois force and proletarian violence. Such a conclusion was incompatible with his process-oriented view of Marxism, which emphasized struggle and transformation, not revolutionary finality. It conflicted with his hatred of the Terror and his rejection of Jacobin statism, both of which were linked to the willful attempt to use violence in order to end one regime and begin another. It violated his politico-religious view of socialism, which was motivated by the eschatological myth of the general strike. Finally, it clashed with his Viconian understanding of history, which warned that periods of regeneration, such as that prepared by the anarcho-syndicalist movement, always risked a decadent *ricorso*.

Sorel's fascination with theomachy, myth, and symbolic violence as well as his hostility to sublation all reflect an often-overlooked anti-utopianism in his thought. Throughout his intellectual career, Sorel resisted ideal political blueprints: he wanted neither to slip into Jacobinism nor to embrace Friedrich Engels' positivist reading of Marx. Had Sorel tried to articulate theoretically the synthetic outcome of the class struggle—a task that many Marxists undertook, much to Sorel's chagrin—the effort would have led him to make politically dangerous predictions about a future classless society. Rather than prophesying, Sorel conceived of an irresolvable class war characterized by certain kinds of violence and myth—all paradoxically part of an anti-utopian vision of an unpredictable future.

Although Sorel demonstrates his connection to the French discourse on sacrificial violence through his concept of martyrdom, concern with decadence, and desire for moral regeneration, his attempt to purge the French Left of Jacobinism is also a notable departure from this tradition of thought. Sorel admired men of action, conviction, and production; he spent his entire intellectual life searching for agents of moral and political redemption. Yet his socialist vision never resulted in any optimistic or certain belief that the redemptive moment would arrive. Fearful of the sunny utopianism that always threatened to transform turn-of-the-century French socialists into Jacobins, Sorel was reluctant to speculate about what the violent class struggle would ultimately produce. Instead, he believed that the potent combination of violence and myth remained dynamic and transformative so long as the workers' struggle continued. It is in this very limited respect that Sorel can be considered a theorist of violence without reserve. Although one could derive a concept of permanent revolution from his unwillingness to contemplate the sublation of class conflict, it is more likely that Sorel was interested in imagining a society capable of long-term self-defense against moral decadence. Sorel's theory of violence tries to capture the precise moment and conditions when the seeds of a new socialist morality germinate within the workers' syndicates. He recognizes that the maturation and institutionalization of that new moral outlook risks the onset of a new decadence. Hence, the class struggle, and the violence and mythology that support it, have no synthetic conclusion.

Sorel's hostility toward dialectical sublation also influences his view of the redemptive role of the anarcho-syndicalist movement. In *Reflections,* Sorel argues emphatically that the working class will bring salvation to the modern world. Central to this task is the proletariat's role in the constitution of the sublime. Like proletarian violence, Sorelian sublimity is a dialectical concept that lacks sublation. The sublime transforms morality by holding the individual experience of pleasure and pain in stasis, never letting one sentiment negate the other. Sublimity, engendered by martyrdom and communicated by myth, contributes to the moral regeneration of the working class. Returning to the religious origin of the term, Sorel articulates the sublime transformation of morality in terms of redemption. He argues that sublime phenomena are contaminating. Thus, the reconstitution of the sublime necessarily involves the communication of the sentiments that it invokes to the working class as well as to its dialectical counterpart, the bourgeoisie. Sorel also claims that the general strike—the mythopoeic context in which revolutionary syndicalist activity ideally takes place—is eschatological. Just as the idea of the Second Coming presupposes that the ever-increasing appeal of the "truth" of Christianity will culminate in total redemption, the myth of the general strike posits an ever-widening and all-encompassing class struggle whose redemptive qualities drive humanity continuously toward socialism. Many Christians argue that Christianity will achieve its full realization with the Second Coming; many Marxists make similar claims about socialism. Sorel, however, refused to embrace such synthetic, teleological moments, choosing instead to place his faith in spontaneous political action and the mythologies of those moments. Sorel's socialist deliverance is a politically dynamic, morally transformative, violent, and mythic process without end.

CHAPTER 4

From the Street to the Text

Depoliticizing Sacrifice in the Work of Georges Bataille

The French discourse on sacrificial violence began with the beheading of Louis XVI, whose execution injected ancient ideas about communal bloodshed into modern debates about political foundation. Because sacrificial violence appeared to play such a decisive role in the founding of the French Republic, it inspired several generations of French intellectuals, with wide-ranging political views, to contemplate its meaning in a revolutionary context. For different reasons, thinkers such as Joseph de Maistre and Georges Sorel rejected the achievements of the French Revolution, but articulated their sacrificial ideas in terms borrowed from the revolutionaries. Sacrifice appealed to Maistre and Sorel because they believed it capable of regenerating people's moral convictions. In Maistre's view, exposure to a violent, sublime experience, at once aesthetic and affective, was a powerful tool of social unification and control. Sorel admired how the sublime symbolism of self-sacrifice bonded together beleaguered communities of workers. Both men were captivated by the capacity of sacrificial spectacles to evoke irrational feelings and beliefs that transform morality and, thus, politics. Like the French revolutionaries, however, Maistre and Sorel were also betrayed by sacrificial violence. Ritual bloodshed meant to alter the political landscape either conservatively or progressively proved itself—in theory and in practice—to be unfit for the task.

The twentieth-century renegade surrealist Georges Bataille shares Maistre's and Sorel's fascination with sacrificial violence as well as their conviction that it could play an important role in the political realm. Mindful of the theological and political implications of the regicide, however, Bataille endeavors to rewrite the works of Maistre and Sorel. Although Bataille still hopes to find a role for sacrifice in modern life, he shifts its focus away from politics, morality, and the constitution of legitimate power. Instead, Bataille develops a theory of sacrifice that leads to the rupture of the historical relationship between sacrificial violence and political foundation. In seeking a revolutionary role for sacrifice, Bataille theoretically unmasks the great danger in using sacrificial violence to found new regimes: it generates authoritarian politics whose stability requires further bloody sacrifices. This realization breaks the continuity of the discourse on sacrificial violence by severing the historical relationship between violent revolutionary acts and political foundation.

Bataille holds a unique place in the French discourse on sacrificial violence. He so greatly transforms the concept of sacrifice shared by his predecessors that he can no longer foresee its playing a role in the constitution of politics. Like Maistre, Sorel, and the French revolutionaries, Bataille argues that sacrifice ameliorates the human condition. Thanks to his political activities during the 1930s as well as his novel understanding of sacrifice, however, Bataille becomes increasingly disillusioned with the political effects of sacrificial violence. At first, following Sorel, he seeks a role for sacrifice in the class struggle. Yet this effort occurs at precisely the time that fascism emerges in Europe. Fascism's overtly sacrificial motifs laid bare both the revolutionary possibility as well as the terrible risks of violent sacrifice in the service of founding politics. When Bataille turns his attention to fascism in an attempt to comprehend its significance for the working class, he discovers that fascism itself illustrates the frightful political outcome of vigilantly pursuing the French discourse's sacrificial logic. Any attempt to use sacrifice in order to constitute or reconstitute founding authority risks fascism.

Not wishing to abandon the possibility of a sacrificially liberating revolution, Bataille moves in two contradictory theoretical directions. On one hand, he begins to explore the ontological implications of sacrifice, a path that leads him nearly to abandon the politics of sacrifice. Rather than sacrificing others or oneself for the sake of political change, Bataille looks to erotic experience and literature as the loci of the sacrificial transformation of being. Bataille argues that erotic and textual self-loss will undo the bourgeois self and thus allow for the forging of a new, metapolitical community whose "foundation" remains permanently destabilized. Although this view of ecstatic sociability is more radical than anything Maistre, Sorel, or the French revolutionaries could have imagined, its achievement does not require actual sacrificial violence. Rather, according to Bataille, the final locations for the practice of sacrifice are the bedroom and the text.

On the other hand, Bataille's postwar writings challenge his apolitical sacrificial ontology by adopting a social scientific approach to the study of sacrificial violence. During this period, Bataille shifts his attention to the impact of unrecoverable sumptuary waste on international political economy. This theoretical reorientation leads Bataille to apply his distinctively radical prewar ideas to rather odd subjects, such as the Marshall Plan and nuclear war. By seeking to acquire useful knowledge about the functions of sacrifice, Bataille's postwar writings violate the spirit of his earlier theoretical aims. Although one can argue that sacrifice in eroticism and literature exceeds the limits of utilitarianism, foreign aid is undoubtedly useful. In short, after the war, Bataille puts sacrifice to work and betrays the theory of sacrifice, which he developed in the 1930s. Bataille may firmly repudiate the tradition of thought that began with the sacrifice of Louis XVI, but he also demonstrates his inability to sever his ties from it completely.

Any analysis of Bataille's work requires a cautious approach. As most Bataille scholars concede, interpreting Bataille is an exceedingly confounding endeavor. His work is contradictory and self-effacing. It appears in a variety of irreconcilable literary formats: pornographic, aphoristic, novelistic, poetic, and social scientific. Bataille also presents his readers with a labyrinthine tangle of terminology, symbolic images and metaphors as well as an experimental writing style designed to challenge and subvert the rules of discursive logic. Borrowing a favorite Platonic image, which he inverts, Bataille offers a body of work that can be compared to the sun. It is both illuminating and blinding. It is characterized by unpredictable bursts of theoretical energy intentionally destructive of rational thought and lacking in purpose and utility. Bataille must be admired for marshaling the service of reason in order to point out its limitations, a task whose impossibility he relished. But because Bataille's work is self-consciously self-subversive, even self-sacrificial, it stubbornly resists organization, categorization, reduction, and systemization—all the analytical frameworks typically employed for the sake of understanding. Bataille can be read and understood. But any interpretation of Bataille inevitably confronts the fact that he did not want to be used. Bataille hoped that his readers would experience the ontological effect of sacrifice: unrecoverable self-loss.

Bataille and the French Discourse on Sacrificial Violence

Bataille rejects the fundamental premise of the French discourse on sacrificial violence, namely that sacrifice fosters political foundation. Three related theoretical developments during the 1930s encouraged Bataille to make this break. First, Bataille reworks the concept of sacrifice from one that produces moral and political outcomes to one that is unrecoverable and unproductive. Bataillian sacrifice has an effect, but it is useless. During most of the 1930s, Bataille advocated a revolutionary agenda that depended upon this idea of sacrificial violence, but because he so significantly changed what sacrifice means, it could no longer facilitate the kinds of political outcomes imagined by the French revolutionaries, Maistre, and Sorel. Second, Bataille develops a sophisticated and novel understanding of the role of the sacred in the fascist movement. His attempt to use sacred categories in order to characterize the psychological structure of fascism ultimately leads him to view conventional politics as completely incompatible with his own revolutionary agenda. Although Bataille is intrigued by fascism's ability to mobilize the masses, he very quickly shifts his focus away from politics to purely intellectual collaborations and the formation of a secret society. These activities correspond to the third of Bataille's important theoretical developments during the 1930s: the creation of a sacrificial, metapolitical notion of community. This Bataillian community is so profoundly sacrificial that it exists in a permanent state of self-loss. Rather than emphasizing the importance of actual sacrificial violence, Bataille begins to characterize the sacrifices that make such a community possible in erotic and literary terms. Although Bataille's postwar writings partially contradict his theoretical innovations of the 1930s, it is both significant and ironic that Bataille transforms the form of violence that inaugurated the French Republic into a largely apolitical and unproductive practice.

Bataille's reflections on sacrifice are initially inspired by the same event that animated those of his predecessors: the regicide of Louis XVI. He returns to the Place de la Concorde, formerly the Place de la Révolution, the Parisian square bloodied by the beheading of Louis XVI. For Bataille, the sacrificial execution of Louis XVI signifies the demise of both royal and divine sovereignty, a view consistent with that of the French revolutionaries. But whereas the revolutionaries cut off one head only to establish their own, Bataille interprets the headless royal body as a sign of a depleted authority that also challenges any future establishment of legitimate, elevated power. Reflecting on the significance of the regicide in his journal *Acéphale*, Bataille writes: "As a result of the Revolution, divine authority ceases to found power: authority no longer belongs to God but to the time whose free exuberance puts kings to death, to the time incarnated today in the explosive tumult of the people."[1] This statement recalls the words spoken by Louis Pierre Manuel to the members of the Club des Ja-

---

1. "L'autorité divine, du fait de la Révolution, cesse de fonder le pouvoir: l'autorité n'appartient plus à Dieu mais au temps dont l'exubérance libre met les rois à mort, au temps incarné aujourd'hui dans le tumulte explosif des peuples." Georges Bataille, "Propositions sur la mort de Dieu," *Acéphale* 21 (January 1937). Quoted in Georges Bataille et al., *Acéphale* (Paris: Editions Jean-Michel Place, 1995), 20. Bataille's reflections on the regicide appear in the first issue of *Acéphale*, whose publication date was the anniversary of the king's execution.

cobins.[2] Both Bataille and Manuel claim that revolutionary sacrificial violence helps to replace the king's divine authority with that of the people. While it might appear that Bataille is tapping into the republican tradition in order to lend an air of legitimacy to the revolutionary fervor of his left-wing compatriots, the "explosive tumult of the people" is actually far removed from Jacobin calls for popular sovereignty or justice.[3] Bataille locates revolutionary authority in a moment of "free exuberance" that violently sweeps away the king but never actually allows for a renewed accretion of his power. For Bataille, the sacrifice of the king is a permanent destabilization of political power, which the people come to possess but cannot reestablish.

The sacrificial death of the king entails an anarchic political foundation, but one that extends beyond Sorel's anarchism. In Bataille's view, the regicide makes it impossible for the Place de la Concorde to commemorate any authority other than the one that is permanently empty. Rising in place of the king is the acephalic figure whom André Masson drew for the cover of the journal *Acéphale,* a potent symbol of this subversive notion of authority that refuses to recuperate what it has lost.[4] In 1836, in defiance of this emptiness, Louis-Philippe placed the Obelisk of Luxor in the center of the Place de la Concorde. Bataille, however, rejects the symbolism of Louis-Philippe's gesture: "The Place de la Concorde is the space where the death of God must be announced and shouted precisely because the obelisk is its calmest negation."[5] Louis-Philippe's obelisk cannot replace the statue of Louis XV, which occupied the square until the rev-

2. With reference to Brutus' bust, which had just been brought into the Club des Jacobins, Manuel said: "It is here that the fall of kings was prepared, the fall of Louis the last. Here must repose the image of the one who first wanted to purge the earth of kings. Sirs, here is Brutus, who will remind you of all the moments that, to be a citizen, one must always be ready to sacrifice everything, up to one's children, to the happiness of one's country." ("C'est ici que s'est préparée la chute des rois, la chute de Louis le dernier. Ici doit reposer l'image de celui qui le premier voulut purger la terre des rois. Messieurs, voici Brutus, qui vous rappellera à tous les instants que, pour être citoyen, il faut toujours être prêt à sacrifier tout, jusqu'à ses enfants, au bonheur de son pays.") P. J. B. Buchez and P. C. Roux, *Histoire parlementaire de la Révolution française ou journal des assemblées nationales depuis 1789 jusqu'en 1815,* vol. 17 (Paris: Librairie Paulin, 1835), 182.

3. Denis Hollier claims that Bataille had long contemplated a plan to celebrate the execution of the king with a Mardi Gras–like carnival. Hollier also unearthed a letter from Bataille to Jean Paulhan dated January 6, 1939, in which Bataille suggests a link between carnivals and the foundation of democracy. Hollier, "January 21st," *Stanford French Review* 12 (spring 1988), 31–32. In the letter to Paulhan, Bataille adds that such founding carnivals were prevented by "police prohibition" during the French Revolution. Georges Bataille, "Letter from Georges Bataille to Jean Paulhan," in *The College of Sociology,* ed. Dennis Hollier, trans. Betsy Wing (Minneapolis: University of Minnesota Press, 1988), 196.

4. Masson's figure is a standing, headless, naked male body with outstretched arms. In place of his nipples, there are five-pointed stars. Instead of a normal abdomen, he has visible entrails. A skull has replaced his genitals. In his left hand, he holds a ceremonial dagger; in his right, a flaming grenade.

5. Georges Bataille, "The Obelisk," in *Visions of Excess,* ed. Allan Stoekl, trans. Allan Stoekl, Carl R. Lovitt, and Donald M. Leslie Jr. (Minneapolis: University of Minnesota Press, 1985), 215.

olutionaries tore it down. The regicide dissipated not just monarchical authority, but the possibility of founding *any* authority. Bataille summons Nietzsche's
madman to announce the impossibility of the obelisk's representing of a unified
and hierarchical authority, both head and heaven. The king was sacrificed, and
with him God as well, a murder that had originally prompted Nietzsche's madman to declare: "Do we not feel the breath of empty space?"[6] For Bataille, the
obelisk betrays the vital emptiness of the Place de la Concorde. Nothing can be
established there, not even Sorel's anarcho-syndicalism, which fills the "empty
space" with the sovereignty of the working class. "The obelisk," Benjamin Noys
observes, "is the 'calmest negation' of the death of God because it arrests the disorientation caused by the loss of a transcendental signifier with its 'sovereign
permanence.'"[7]

   Because the obelisk is like an authoritative pile driven into a foundational
swamp filled with sacrificial blood, it cannot return to the French what they, in
a fit of revolutionary fervor, destroyed. In the Place de la Concorde, spatially
speaking, an empty notion of authority surrounds a traditionally elevated one.
As Denis Hollier writes, "Bataille's Place de la Concorde . . . is the place where
loss is incarnate—embodied in a man who identifies himself by his lack. The
headless man, Acephalus, rises up where the guillotine let in the freezing gales
of empty space."[8] Hollier's observation reveals Bataille's agreement with Maistre:
the regicide was a profoundly evil act, which Maistre lamented and Bataille celebrated. Rather than auguring the return of God, as Maistre had hoped, the regicide killed him, leaving in his place an absence so complete that it forbids the
accumulation of transcendental power. Negativity or destruction without rec-
ompense: such is the fruit of the regicide and the basis for Bataille's concept of
sacrificial violence. The regicide does not make way for the obelisk, which represents none other than the next generation's sovereign intentions. Rather, the
regicide calls into question any future claim to authority, leaving the Place de la
Concorde to represent not a place of peace, but rather one of permanent disorientation and subversion. Somewhere under the obelisk remain the impres-
sion of the guillotine and the blood of the king.

   Informing Bataille's novel interpretation of the regicide, antipathy toward
morality, and subversion of power—indeed, his attitude toward politics *in toto*—
is a trenchant rejection of idealism. He rejects all traditions of thought that value
the ideal or elevated over the material or base. One of his most eloquent critiques of idealism appears in an early essay in which Bataille argues that the big

---

   6. Quoted in Denis Hollier, *Against Architecture: The Writings of Georges Bataille,* trans. Betsy Wing
(Cambridge: MIT Press, 1992), 138.
   7. Benjamin Noys, *Georges Bataille: A Critical Introduction* (London: Pluto, 2000), 78.
   8. Hollier, *Against Architecture,* xxii.

toe is "the most *human* part of the body."[9] Using the big toe as a metaphor for seductive baseness, Bataille explains that human beings reject aspects of their uniqueness when they celebrate all that is noble and pure in the hope of masking all that is low and impure:

> Although within the body blood flows in equal quantities from high to low and from low to high, there is a bias in favor of that which elevates itself, and human life is erroneously seen as an elevation . . . Human life entails, in fact, the rage of seeing oneself as a back and forth movement from refuse to the ideal, and from the ideal to refuse—a rage that is easily directed against an organ as *base* as the foot.[10]

Bataille uses the image of the big toe to criticize the metaphysics of elevation. Humans err in their belief that humanity is uniquely an ideal achievement. Idealism is reason's attempt to hide the truth about being human from human beings. This error led human beings to demonize the very part of their bodies that Bataille argues is the most human, an exercise in self-loathing. Without the "grotesque" big toe, humans could not stand erect, nor could they differentiate themselves from beasts. This observation recalls Maistre's claim that the greatest human achievements are mired in the worst. Bataille's celebration of the big toe is a reminder that what it means to be human is inescapably deformed, dirty, base, immoral, material, and incapable of rational thought. At the same time, however, Bataille does not seek to elevate the big toe to a higher status. Its value consists paradoxically in its abjectness. Like the regicide, the big toe symbolizes a permanent destabilization of the boundaries established by idealistic thought.

When the former royal executioner Sanson guillotined the king, neither monarchists nor republicans imagined that the sacrifice would be a permanently destabilizing loss. Both the Roman and Christian sacrificial traditions instructed otherwise. During the Revolution, the examples of Brutus and Jesus illustrated that different forms of sacrificial violence could be used to destroy as well as create authority. In the minds of the revolutionaries, and then later in the writings of Maistre and Sorel, the concept of sacrificial violence became inextricably linked to the formation of both political and spiritual communities bound together by traditionally elevated notions of power. Sacrifice accomplished this remarkable task by skillfully manipulating the sacred categories that structure people's perceptions of authority. Impurity and purity, sin and redemption, moral decadence and regeneration—these are the dueling sacred polarities altered by sacrificial bloodshed in the French discourse. Sacrifice negotiates be-

---

9. Georges Bataille, "The Big Toe," in Stoekl, *Visions of Excess,* 20. This article originally appeared in 1929 in *Documents,* an art journal in whose founding Bataille participated.

10. Ibid., 20.

tween these terms by fostering different forms of exchange. Kill the king, the revolutionaries believed, and the republic would be purified. Embracing a similar logic, Maistre claimed that the Terror would punitively cleanse the French of their secular hubris. More than a hundred years later, Sorel argued that proletarian martyrs would regenerate working-class morality, saving—in the religious sense of the word—French society from bourgeois decadence. In all three cases, the sacrificial death of one human being generated new social bonds by neutralizing and reconfiguring the sacred bases of the old ones. Sacrificial loss thus came to be associated with the creation of new morality, new authority, and new political regimes.

Sacrificial Innovation in the Work of Bataille

Bataille's interpretation of the regicide as a sacrifice that cannot recover what it has lost presents a radical challenge to the Roman and Christian sacrificial traditions as well as to their incorporation into the French discourse on sacrificial violence. Unrecoverable sacrificial loss is a violent operation that only wastes. In producing nothing useful, sacrifice subverts all idealistic distinctions. Stripped of idealism, Brutus' filicide and Jesus' crucifixion can no longer participate in the task of foundation because sacrifice loses its ability to produce popular authority or redemption. In order for authority to be legitimate or for redemption to cleanse bodies or souls, the sacrificial operation must be capable of establishing stable, hierarchical boundaries between sacred polarities. Cathartic, expiatory, and redemptive exchange permits this delimitation to take place because violent loss is balanced against some kind of psychological, spiritual, or moral gain. However, regicide that does not recover something from the violent destruction of the king—that does not make sacred *in a particular way*—is useless. In this way, Bataillian sacrifice permits no establishment, no obelisk, no higher source of power or authority, because it is a total loss without sacred exchange. It has no capacity to establish order, as, for instance, between sacrilegious and divine bloodshed, or between force and violence. It can neither recover, nor make useful, the pure sacred authority of the king. Only if conceived in ideal and compensatory terms can the collective taking of a life delineate between high and low, pure and impure. If the desire to practice the art of politics were compared to the myth of Icarus, a favorite of Bataille's, then sacrifice would correspond to the sun's blinding, wasted energy, which melted Icarus' wings, reminding all human beings of the fragility of their activities and their existence. Bataillian sacrifice challenges human beings to confront and test the limits of their being, without ever allowing for the reestablishment of order. It is a violent and ecstatic state of permanent alternation between purity and impurity.

With no finality, no conservation, and no reserve, Bataille's concept of sacrifice reflects not just a critique of idealism but also, more specifically, of Hegelian dialectics. Bataille attended Alexandre Kojève's lectures on Hegel during which Kojève famously declared history to be over. Bataille's confrontation with Hegelian philosophy left him feeling "suffocated, crushed, shattered, killed ten times over."[11] If history was over, what was left to do? In a letter to Kojève, Bataille wondered what it meant to act freely in such a condition: "If action ("doing") is—as Hegel says—negativity, the question arises as to whether the negativity of one who has 'nothing more to do' disappears or remains in a state of 'unemployed negativity.' Personally, I can only decide in one way, being myself precisely this 'unemployed negativity' (I would not be able to define myself more precisely)."[12]

If history has indeed ended as a result of a long dialectical process of negativity that preserved what it sublated, then, Bataille argues, negativity itself is no longer subject to restriction. Bataille uses the term "unemployed negativity" to describe himself at the end of history: a human being whose destructive capacities have neither use nor meaning. Yet the fulfillment of Hegel's philosophical and dialectical account of history renders an altogether different kind of negativity. By placing negativity in a dialectical movement, Hegel subsumes it (and violence) within philosophy, giving it order, reason, and purpose. Unemployed negativity frees violence from philosophical (and Hegelian) restriction. It also gives birth to a new type of unrecognized consciousness, which is quite literally nothing.[13] In a posthistorical world, where the dialectic is finished with its "work" and negativity is unemployable, violence destroys without conservation. Unrecoverable loss thus becomes the leitmotif of all sacrificial violence in the modern age.

In developing an anti-idealist and antidialectical concept of sacrifice, Bataille brings to its culmination a philosophical trend that began with Maistre, who was the first in the discourse to theorize sacrificial violence without sublation.

11. Quoted in Noys, *Georges Bataille*, 7.

12. Georges Bataille, "Letter to X, Lecturer on Hegel . . . ," in Hollier, *The College of Sociology*, 90.

13. Stoekl writes: "Absolute knowing reaches its end—and this is the solution this letter [Bataille to Kojève] puts forward—but this end is possible only because there is, rigorously, nothing; paradoxically, we cannot even speak of Bataille, since the person of Bataille is an objectification . . . The recognition at the summit—at the end of history, at the moment of absolute knowing—is overturned, and becomes the full recognition of empty negativity ('full' because this recognition does not deceive itself with art or with religion—which would only call this negativity 'sin,' and so forth)." Stoekl's reading of Bataille's critique of Hegel clarifies the idea of a consciousness that is nothing at the end of history. Since negativity has no use, it cannot be sublimated into art or religion, which objectify it, making it servile. Allan Stoekl, "Hegel's Return," *Stanford French Review* 12 (spring 1988), 122.

Maistre pessimistically imagines a guilty world convulsed by an inconclusive alternation between crime and sacrificial punishment. This ceaseless movement between sin and redemption continues, however, until Christ's return, which Maistre describes as the "death of death." In this final moment, the soul is liberated from the sinful body, an absolute idealism prophesied by Christian eschatology; one final sacrifice ends salutary sacrificial violence.

Sorel pushes Maistre's antisublating sacrificial dialectic one step further. The anarcho-syndicalist movement, gripped by the myth of the general strike and passionately inspired by its own martyrs, does not participate in Marx's historical and material dialectic, which culminates in a classless society. Instead, Sorel's anti-utopian pessimism leads him to conceive of the anarcho-syndicalist revolution from a superstructural standpoint. Dialectical conflict caused by material conditions exists, but its significance for Sorel rests uniquely in the moral regeneration of the proletariat, which is ultimately an ideal transformation. The creation of a superior, proletarian moral position is not, however, achieved through a revolutionary moment of sublation. Sorel leaves the class struggle permanently fixed in the convulsive moment of sacrificial conflict and moral regeneration, a dialectical antagonism that cannot propel history forward without risking renewed moral decadence. Thus, martyrdom contributes to the moral regeneration of the working class only so long as the conflict that necessitates self-sacrifice continues unabated. Unlike Maistre, Sorel offers no resolution to this perpetual struggle, illustrating a further hemming in of sacrificial sublation.

In Bataille's work, sacrificial violence is entirely relieved of its dialectical and ideal burdens, freeing his concept of sacrifice from philosophical and religious rationalism. Consequently, the ends to which the French revolutionaries, Maistre, and Sorel committed sacrificial violence become unfeasible. Before Bataille, one of the hallmarks of the discourse was its emphasis on moral regeneration. Maistre, Sorel, and the French revolutionaries all believed that, in giving meaning to a particular kind of death, sacrifice transformed individuals morally. That moral change, in turn, facilitated the foundation of a new political regime based on a new concept of authority. While Bataille agrees that sacrifice entails a consecratory process, he also strips the sacrificial operation of useful purpose and dialectical finality, rendering it unassimilable to any rational purpose conceived religiously, historically, or philosophically. A form of violence that produces nothing useful, sacrifice is too destabilizing to generate moral content, which, by definition, resists ambiguity in distinguishing between right and wrong.

Because sacrifice resists rational or moral purpose, Bataille provides it with a radically different charge. During most of the 1930s, Bataille views sacrifice as a form of collective violence, but one that no longer operates within the domain of people's beliefs, serving to structure and bound them in politically

meaningful ways. Instead, Bataille conceptualizes the effects of sacrificial violence ontologically because he identifies reification, not moral decadence, as the
fundamental modern problem. In his view, capitalism, utilitarianism, and parlia-
mentarianism have reduced human beings to servile things. The spirit of Bataille's diagnosis of the human condition is not, prima facie, dissimilar from that
of either Maistre or Sorel. They, too, argue that the morally regenerative properties of sacrificial violence will serve to heal human beings of their reification.
But because Bataille includes morality itself among those phenomena that contribute to the decadence of the modern age, he rejects his predecessors' concern
with a return to moral and spiritual wholeness. Bataille criticizes the goal of human wholeness as a religious and philosophical fantasy that serves only to enslave human beings to the ideal dictates of reason and morality. Furthermore,
even if wholeness were desirable, sacrificial violence, as Bataille conceives of it,
no longer possesses a regenerative capacity. Rather, sacrifice is a violent operation that exposes human beings to death, loss, rupture, and fragmentation—
elements of accursedness that Bataille treats as essential components of humanity.
Rather than allowing human beings to flee from their base humanity into realms
of idealism and purity, such as religion, philosophy, or politics, Bataille suggests that sacrifice offers them a visceral reminder that their humanity is thoroughly intertwined with what humans reject as radically other, namely, death
or not-being. Thus, the antidote to reification in the modern age consists
not in regenerative morality or reconstructed wholeness, but rather in a confrontation with what Bataille calls the accursed share (la part maudite).[14] For
Bataille, unity and wholeness are antithetical to being human, which avoids reification only when it confronts its own absence, an experience achieved through
sacrifice.

Although Bataille radically rejects many of the previous definitions of sacrificial violence in the French discourse, he retains its most important feature: communality. Even in Bataille's hands, sacrificial violence illustrates the paradox of a
community built around violent destruction. Maistre characterized sacrificial loss
conservatively: death reinvigorated preexisting, divinely sanctioned, social and
political norms. The French revolutionaries and Sorel viewed sacrifice more creatively as the collective taking of a life for the sake of a new sociopolitical order.
Because Bataille defines sacrifice as violent, unrecoverable loss, it contributes to
a concept of community fundamentally opposed to those envisioned by Maistre,
Sorel, and the revolutionaries. Republicanism, monarchism, and anarcho-syndicalism all presuppose the possibility of authority, even if they posit radically dif-

---

14. For his postwar reflections on sacrifice, sovereignty, and the human condition, see Georges Bataille,
The Accursed Share, 3 vols., trans. Robert Hurley (New York: Zone, 1991).

ferent embodiments of it. Bataille's concept of sacrifice gives rise to a community in which the act of foundation never coheres. What binds the community together is the shared experience of unrecoverable violent loss. Sacrifice cultivates community by fostering a nondiscursive communication between human beings whose sundered individuality permits the formation of an ecstatic bond. This bond gives rise to a metapolitical community in which sovereignty has neither basis nor dominion. In Bataille's view, sacrifice cannot participate in the construction of republicanism, monarchism, or anarcho-syndicalism because, like the obelisk, those ideas of community betray their sacrificial origin by positing the possibility of a renewed erection of authority. Bataille's concept of sacrifice invites reflection on what community would be if it were never to recover what was violently destroyed to create it. This is a fundamentally antipolitical notion of community insofar as it subverts all the concepts that have historically made politics possible. Although Maistre, Sorel, and the French revolutionaries agree on little politically, all posit a theory of sacrificial violence that requires replacement or recovery of that which sacrifice destroys.

"Unemployed Expenditure," Human Potlatch, and the Class Struggle

For Bataille, the 1930s were a highly productive period that encompassed both his most passionate engagements in the politics of the day and the beginning of a decisive theoretical retreat from them. This trajectory can be explained, in part, by the fact that the 1930s proved extraordinarily challenging for French intellectuals of all stripes. With the emergence of fascism in German and Italy as well as the consolidation of authoritarian communism in Russia, parliamentary regimes such as France's had much to contend with, both inside and outside their borders. Faced with these significant political threats from the right and the left, the French Third Republic did not fare well. It suffered from corruption, most notably the Stavisky Affair of 1933. It virtually crumbled when fascists marched in Paris in 1934, leading Bataille, who was then a member of the group Contre-Attaque, to participate in a massive left-wing counterdemonstration in defense of the Third Republic. Ironically for Bataille, who harbored no love for parliamentary democracy, this would be his only significant political activity. The successive embarrassments and visible weaknesses of the Third Republic generated a political atmosphere that, according to Denis Hollier, led many French intellectuals to look admiringly at the installation of strong governments around them.[15] Fragile democracy at home and charismatic author-

15. Hollier, *The College of Sociology,* ix.

itarianism abroad also led many intellectuals, including Bataille, to begin to reflect upon concepts of community that might heal the gaping social wounds
that seemed to be ripping Europe apart.[16]

Early in the 1930s, Bataille joined Boris Souvarine's anti-Stalinist Cercle
Communiste Démocratique, a group of intellectuals dedicated to a reevaluation
of Marxist revolutionary thought in light of what they presciently considered
to be the failure of Soviet communism. This collective political endeavor exhibited certain Sorelian tendencies, most notably a revisionist Marxism, an interest in Trotskyism, an anarchist streak, a concern for proletarian communal
formation, and an enthusiasm for proletarian violence. Bataille and his colleagues also supplemented their reading of Sorel with more recent theoretical
developments. In lieu of the economic explanations of revolution inherited
from Marx or the moral ones borrowed from Sorel, Cercle members looked for
"new social forces behind the economic mechanism revealed by Marx, and
above all, the integration of the discoveries of psychoanalysis into political sociology."[17] According to Robert Stuart Short, the Cercle was divided into two
camps: "those who considered revolution as a moral ideal, an absolute, like Pierre
Kahn, and those who saw it as an irrational explosion."[18] Demonstrating an early
split with Sorel, Bataille placed his allegiance with the "irrational explosion"
camp, which he articulated in two important articles, "The Notion of Expenditure" and "The Psychological Structure of Fascism," both published in the
Cercle's journal La Critique sociale. Bataille abandoned the idea that revolution
involved morality, an illustration not only of his rejection of Sorel's claim that
revolutionary violence must be moral, but also of his general hostility toward
idealism.

Attempting to place ethnographic research on sacrifice in the service of proletarian revolution, Bataille lays out the foundation of his theory of sacrifice in
his essay "The Notion of Expenditure."[19] In Marxist fashion, Bataille argues that
modern society has been structured by its obsession with productive activity and
use of the principle of utility as the measure of all things. Whereas Marx, and

16. Jean-Michel Heimonet confirms Hollier's assessment: "Influenced, as we shall see, in an ambiguous manner by these vast movements of social cohesion, the personalities about whom we are talking
[Bataille, Jules Monnerot, and Roger Caillois] shared among them, in addition to a knowledge (nourished by readings of Hegel, Nietzsche, and Freud), they were all three disciples of Durkheim and even
more of Mauss), the ardent will to create a *community*, to form a social aggregate in which the members,
like initiates, communicated, unacquainted with the cynical laws of interest and beyond even the simple
bonds of blood, by the thread of a pure bond of magical sympathy." Jean-Michel Heimonet, *Politiques de
l'écriture* (Paris: Jean-Michel Place, 1989), 17.

17. Robert Stuart Short, "Contre-Attaque," in *Entretiens sur le surréalisme* (Paris: Mouton, 1968), 148.

18. Ibid., 149.

19. Georges Bataille, "La Notion de dépense," *La Critique sociale*, no. 7 (January 1933), reprinted in
Réimpression de La Critique sociale, ed. Boris Souvarine (Paris: Editions de la Différence, 1983).

Sorel to an even greater extent, stress the role of economic production in human self-realization, Bataille considers the making and acquisition of things, as well as the reproduction of human life, to be extremely narrow formulations of human activity. They exclude what Bataille calls "the principle of *unproductive expenditure*," a form of exchange based on waste as opposed to acquisition. Thanks to his reading of Marcel Mauss, Bataille became acquainted with potlatch, a form of sacrifice practiced by certain North American indigenous peoples that, in Mauss's view, fosters social obligation, organization, and unity. Bataille was particularly attuned to the radical social implications of this collective, violent, antagonistic destruction of goods or wealth.[20] In Mauss's view, unproductive expenditure promotes social relationships and collectivistic morality without resulting in either an accumulation of wealth or a balancing of accounts. Potlatch thus illustrates a kind of social contract, but a violent one based on waste. Mauss believed that potlatch would be instructive for curbing the bourgeois individualism that results from modern capitalism because potlatch offers an alternative collectivist ethic. Bataille, however, argues that an amoral application of unproductive expenditure is better suited to challenge the bourgeoisie.

Bataille rejects Mauss's interpretation of potlatch as a conservative form of ritual destruction that reforges preexisting social norms and bonds. In his reformulation of potlatch, Bataille hypothesizes "that potlatch is the means by which the established order is periodically disrupted, and the anguishing confrontation with death symbolized in the destruction of goods ritually dramatized."[21] Unlike Mauss, Bataille has no interest in conserving any aspect of the status quo. He views potlatch as merely a particular example of a more general sacrificial operation, distinguished by its ability to make unrecoverable loss sacred. Whereas Mauss takes a moral interest in potlatch because it exchanges sacrificial loss for social obligation, Bataille argues that it makes violent loss sacred, ambiguous, and destabilizing. Furthermore, Bataille expands the domain of unproductive expenditure beyond the economic realm: "Luxury, mourning, war, cults, the construction of sumptuary monuments, games, spectacles, arts, perverse sexual activity (i.e., deflected from genital finality)—all these represent activities which, at least in primitive circumstances, have no end beyond themselves."[22] For Bataille, unproductive expenditure involves real and symbolic sacrificial

20. Michèle Richman claims that Bataille's and Mauss's positions concerning potlatch should not be misconstrued as equivalent. Mauss considered potlatch to be an aberrant form of gift exchange, a "war of wealth," which conflicted with his belief that gift giving could serve as an anti-individualistic but nonetheless harmonious tool of social organization. *Reading Georges Bataille: Beyond the Gift* (Baltimore: Johns Hopkins University Press, 1982), 8–19.

21. Ibid., 19. Bataille's rereading of Mauss is well documented in Richman's *Reading Georges Bataille*.

22. Georges Bataille, "The Notion of Expenditure," in Stoekl, *Visions of Excess*, 118.

waste. Because modern societies have banished all but the most benign of those activities, modern human beings are left without any significant or meaningful ways to partake of sumptuary loss. Bataille relishes unproductive expenditure because it directly challenges modern France's ethic of accumulation and utilitarianism and thus forms the basis of a sacrificial economy at odds with the social, economic, and political foundations of modern society.

By fusing the notion of class conflict with his concept of sacrifice, Bataille reveals a new basis for proletarian revolutionary fervor. He views the history of modern society as a regressive withering away of unproductive expenditure, whose disappearance has provoked class conflict, strengthened reification, and heightened the revolutionary activities of the proletariat. Trapped by a system of exchange based on an ethic of accumulation, the proletariat has been alienated from and enslaved by the bourgeoisie, who have achieved their status through only production and miserliness. Unrecoverable sacrificial loss thus offers the proletariat both a means to combat its servile condition and a practice essential to the ontological reconstitution of humanity. Such a sweeping view of the role of sacrifice in the proletariat's revolutionary struggle reveals a Sorelian influence. But whereas Sorel considered the bourgeoisie insufficiently capitalistic, Bataille views them as too concerned with production and accumulation and thus as the enemies of a sacrificial economy based on waste. Echoing Sorel's lament of the bourgeoisie's loss of sublimity, Bataille writes: "Today the great and free forms of unproductive social expenditure have disappeared."[23] Unlike Sorel, however, Bataille's point is that the proletariat overcomes its servile status by sacrificially destroying its masters and their chosen forms of exchange.[24]

The concept of unproductive expenditure not only helps Bataille to diagnose the pathologies of the modern condition; it also points to violent sacrifice as a uniquely salutary mechanism of revolutionary change. "Class struggle," writes Bataille, "becomes the grandest form of social expenditure when it is taken up again and developed, this time on the part of the workers, and on such a scale that it threatens the very existence of the masters." "Social expenditure" anticipates the return of unproductive loss to the modern world. Bataillian class conflict is thus a kind of human potlatch, which is not to be confused with symbolic forms of sacrifice:

---

23. Ibid., 124.

24. In addition to reflecting upon the significance of sacrificing particular victims, such as the bourgeoisie, Bataille was interested in different forms of self-sacrifice. Because Bataille viewed self-sacrificial violence in terms of automutilation, however, it has few of martyrdom's overt political implications and is thus beyond the scope of this discussion. Georges Bataille, "Sacrificial Mutilation and the Severed Ear of Vincent Van Gogh," in Stoekl, *Visions of Excess,* 61–72.

As for the masters and the exploiters, whose function is to create the contemptu-
ous forms that exclude human nature—causing this nature to exist at the limits of
the earth, in other words in mud—a simple law of reciprocity requires that they
be condemned to fear, to the *great night* when their beautiful phrases will be
drowned out by death screams in riots. That is the bloody hope which, each day,
is one with the existence of the people, and which sums up the insubordinate content of the class struggle.

   Class struggle has only one possible end: the loss of those who have worked to
lose "human nature."[25]

Using language absent from Sorel's reflections on violence, Bataille describes
revolutionary potlatch, the violent destruction of the bourgeoisie by the proletariat. This revolutionary vision assumes that the proletariat, who are the servile
yet subversive excrement of the capitalist system, will themselves become agents
of this sacrifice. The class that was once a waste product reconfigures its humanity by violently, sacrificially, and unproductively destroying the bourgeoisie.
A task that Bataille considers bloody, chaotic, and expedient, the sacrifice of the
bourgeoisie again allows unproductive expenditure to play a role in social unification. Although Bataille recognizes that unproductive expenditure can be
symbolic, he offers no evidence to suggest that social expenditure is a Sorelian
escape from the experience of bloodshed. Instead, Bataille argues that social expenditure entails the violent return of the expelled, whereby the proletariat re-
claims its humanity, or its "human nature," through sacrifice.

   Two surprising elements emerge from Bataille's application of unproductive
expenditure to class conflict. The first is his claim that the bourgeoisie works
to "lose" proletarian human nature, which the proletariat recuperates through
social expenditure. The second is the complete absence of a language of purity
and impurity to describe this process. Both ethnographic evidence and Bataille's
reliance on Marxist thought during the early 1930s contribute to his retention
of an essentialist idea of human nature. Bataille nostalgically maintains that ancient societies with well-established sacrificial practices were better able than
modern societies to provide their inhabitants with outlets of sumptuary loss
conducive to human nature. What is more, Bataille agrees with both Marx and
Nietzsche that modern society is stripping human beings of capacities essential
to a healthy state of being. Thus, a return to unproductive sacrificial loss allows
human beings, and the proletariat in particular, to experience the accursed share
(*la part maudite*) of their nature, which has been reduced to servility. Although
that experience appears to require a reversal of the demonization that has rele-
gated the proletariat to the status of capitalist waste, Bataillian sacrifice offers no

25. Bataille, "The Notion of Expenditure," 126, 127–128.

such outcome. Bataille's *great night* is not a form of purification, through which the sacrifice of the bourgeoisie results in the proletariat's return to daylight. Quite the contrary; Bataille's sacrificial revolution also plunges its proletarian agents into the *great night,* which, by preventing their moral renewal, results in their ontological transformation.

Through social expenditure—the practice of unproductive sacrifice—the proletariat plummets into an abyss where, paradoxically, it recovers its humanity by liberating itself from all sources of reification, such as politics traditionally understood. Ontologically transformed by an all-consuming human potlatch, the proletariat becomes the avant-garde of a new metapolitics. Bataille describes the result of this sacrifice in terms of consumption: "And if I consume in this excessive manner, I reveal to my peers what I am intimately: communication is the means by which separate individuals communicate. All is transparent, open, infinite, among those who consume intimately."[26] The revolutionary practice of unemployable sacrificial loss exposes a nondiscursive, noncontractual communication between individuals who, through participation in the experience of sacrificial violence, challenge their individuality. This experience of self-loss and ecstatic connectedness is the useless ontological effect of sacrificial violence. Writing about Bataille's novel interpretation of potlatch, Allan Stoekl points out: "Potlatch can no longer be used for reactionary ends: now all human beings are free to lose themselves in it."[27] Because unproductive expenditure destabilizes bourgeois ontology by reclaiming *la part maudite,* it also ruptures the organizations, structure, institutions, and ideas that are founded upon that conception of humanity. The possibility of community, however, is not altogether lost. As Bataille claims, communication between sundered beings emerges when they lose themselves in a sacrificial experience, thus permitting a communality unfettered by rational discourse or sociopolitical ideals. The social unity that results from unproductive sacrificial violence is thus rooted in the emptiness created when human beings confront what is beyond the scope of their humanity. The empty, headless space left by the regicide of Louis XVI is identical with the self-subversion initiated by participation in social expenditure. Both sacrificer and sacrificed are lost.

From a Critical Analysis of Fascism to a Critique of Politics

Bataille's essay "The Psychological Structure of Fascism" both expands upon and departs from his earlier development of unproductive expenditure.[28] Unpro-

---

26. Richman, *Reading Georges Bataille,* 21.
27. Allan Stoekl, "Introduction," in *Visions of Excess,* xvii.
28. Georges Bataille, "La Structure psychologique du fascisme," originally published in *La Critique so-*

ductive expenditure appeals to Bataille because its rupture of exchange—economic, contractual, spiritual, and sacrificial—generates an ontologically fragmenting affectivity. Although it has been conceptualized in different ways, sacrificial affectivity has been the hallmark of the French discourse on sacrificial violence. One of Bataille's unique contributions to the discourse is to characterize the affective power of sacrifice in ontological as opposed to moral terms. In his essay on fascism, Bataille develops a terminology that explains the ontology of sacrifice as well as its political importance. Like his predecessors, Bataille recognizes that political power is not a purely rational construction. This insight informs his desire to elucidate the attraction of fascism by revealing the complexity of the sacred concepts from which fascist power is constructed. Bataille's analysis of fascism's sacred power also contributes to his discussion of unproductive expenditure, which itself entails only a narrow view of the role of the sacred in political life. Most important, Bataille's fascism essay reveals that his sacrificial view of proletarian revolution is in tension with his critical understanding of fascist power. Seeking to prevent the proletarian revolution from taking a fascist turn, Bataille argues that any attempt to use sacrifice for the sake of political foundation risks fascism, the logical culmination of sacrificial founding violence used to constitute authority. By claiming that unproductive sacrificial loss ruptures political authority, Bataille's discussion of fascism begins his repudiation of the French discourse on sacrificial violence.

In his essay on unproductive expenditure, Bataille offers no vocabulary for the internal dynamics of transformative sacrificial processes. How does the unrecoverable sacrifice of a person or thing affect the participants? What role does such sacrifice play in the realm of politics? Seeking to answer these questions in his essay on fascism, Bataille significantly broadens his analysis of sacrifice from a study of the act itself to an inquiry into the sacred concepts upon which it depends. He introduces the concepts of homogeneity and heterogeneity in order to describe two opposing modes of existence, each of which highlights different roles of the sacred in modern life. Homogeneity, which is similar to the profane, describes societies structured by production, rationality, specialization, organization, conservation, predictability, and preservation. For Bataille, these terms characterize modern Western bourgeois society, which excludes anything that does not conform to its homogeneous structure. "Above all," writes Michèle Richman, "homogeneity is identified as *commensurability* among elements and a *consciousness* of the process whereby 'human relations can be maintained by a reduction to fixed rules based on the identity of person and well-defined

ciale in November 1933 and March 1934, is reprinted in Souvarine, _Réimpression de La Critique sociale,_ 159, 205.

situations: in principle, violence is excluded from the course of an existence so defined.'"[29] The hallmark of the homogeneous society is the contract, which forms the basis of all social bonds because, as Jean-Michel Heimonet observes, "the contract establishes a general equivalence among men, things, and men and things."[30] Heterogeneity, which is more closely associated with sacredness, is a bipolar category that encompasses everything that is unproductive, irrational, incommensurable, unstructured, unpredictable, and wasteful. While homogeneity excludes violence, heterogeneity is the chief domain of violence. Bataille offers five descriptions of heterogeneous elements: (1) taboo and mana; (2) everything resulting from unproductive expenditure, including excrement, eroticism, and violence; (3) ambiguous phenomena that are simultaneously attractive and repulsive; (4) excess, delirium, and madness; and (5) any reality that is affectively forceful or shocking.[31]

The bipolarity of heterogeneity captures two related but opposing, shifting, and unstable characteristics of sacred things: purity and impurity.[32] Pure sacred and impure sacred, which Bataille labels "right" and "left" respectively, challenge Mauss's and Durkheim's rigid theoretical views on sacred objects, which they consider (negatively) as the source of all prohibitions.[33] Mauss and Durkheim qualify the sacred as dangerous and repulsive. In contrast, building upon Maistre's observation that the pure authority of the king requires the impure violence of the executioner, Bataille captures the ambiguity of the sacred by qualifying it as a form of energy that fluctuates between two oppositely charged poles.[34] Bataille also counterintuitively describes both heterogeneous sacred polarities as sovereign in an effort to convey the double significance of the sacred. When qualified with the word "imperative," the term "sovereign" describes sacred

29. Richman, *Reading Georges Bataille,* 40.

30. Jean-Michel Heimonet, "From Bataille to Derrida: *Différence* and Heterology," *Stanford French Review* 12 (spring 1988), 138.

31. Georges Bataille, "The Psychological Structure of Fascism," in Stoekl, *Visions of Excess,* 142–143.

32. For a discussion of Bataille's and Durkheim's concepts of the sacred, see Richman, *Reading Georges Bataille,* 43–49.

33. See Emile Durkheim, *The Elementary Forms of Religious Life,* trans. Joseph Ward Swain (New York: Free Press, 1965), 52–57. Durkheim held steadfastly to the sacred/profane dualism, an allegiance that prevented him from sharing Bataille's insight that sacred things could be ambiguously pure (right) and impure (left). Describing Bataille's modification of Durkheim, Stoekl writes: "Above all, Bataille considers society and the sacred that motivates it not as a simple coherent unit, but as *double,* split between a 'right-hand' sacred of conservation and renewal, and a 'left-hand' one of expenditure and destruction." Allan Stoekl, *Agonies of the Intellectual* (Lincoln: University of Nebraska Press, 1992), 19. See also Richman, *Reading Georges Bataille,* 45–49; and Hollier, *The College of Sociology,* xxiii–xxv.

34. Heimonet confirms this observation: "In fact, an essential characteristic of heterogeneous reality is its ambiguity, the fact that it can change sign, pole, or valence and provoke impartially attraction and repulsion." "From Bataille to Derrida," 139.

things, such as kings, who are noble, pure, elevated, and singular.[35] In contrast, Bataille uses words like "base," "abject," and "accursed" to characterize subversive sovereignty, sacred power that is ignoble, impure, mired, or chthonian. The executioner, who also participates in the formation of monarchical power (imperative sovereignty), exhibits subversive heterogeneity that is radically impure, and as a result is placed completely outside the social hierarchy defined by the king. Thus, Bataille's theoretical elaboration on Maistre's original distinction reveals that both the king and his executioner are sovereign, but in consequence of opposite sacred qualities and with different ontological effects.

Bataille's dualistic concept of heterogeneity serves as the basis for his novel understanding of sovereignty. Because heterogeneity is its primary animating force, sovereignty has two forms, the imperative and the subversive. Imperative sovereignty describes ruling power whose legitimacy is constructed on a hierarchical, elevated, and amplified basis. In his postwar writings on sovereignty, Bataille describes its imperative form as belonging to kings, priests, chieftains, and "*all men* who possess and have never entirely lost the value that is attributed to gods and 'dignitaries.'"[36] Although imperative sovereignty is the preeminent source of state power and is typically associated with mastery and supremacy, Bataille argues that it is actually servile because it is useful. In contrast, subversive or revolutionary sovereignty derives its power from the abject and useless. Bataille writes: "Life *beyond utility* is the domain of sovereignty."[37] Subversive sovereignty is experienced as unproductive loss and dissolution; instead of authoritatively establishing limits (laws), this revolutionary form of power comes into being when limits are transgressed. For this reason, sacrifice plays an essential role in the invocation of an impure heterogeneous sovereignty. When useless, sacrifice also gives rise to an acephalic community, which has no trace of imperative sovereignty and, therefore, no leader or authority. No headless community can form, however, if its members seek to conserve some aspect of the sacrifice. Bataille rejects sovereignty that relies upon purity and hierarchy in order to establish dominion.

Bataille uses the concepts of homogeneity and heterogeneity to describe the affective qualities of political power embodied by leaders, institutions, symbols, and the like. All traditional forms of political power combine homogeneous and heterogeneous elements, albeit in different ways. Consider three extremes: liberalism, monarchism, and fascism. The liberal state is the most homogeneous.

35. Heimonet observes that kingly sovereignty "escapes the norm, [and] the common measure"; instead of being rejected as radically other, it is "placed at the peak of the social hierarchy." Ibid.

36. Bataille, *The Accursed Share*, vol. 3, 197.

37. Ibid., 198.

As Stoekl interprets Bataille's fascism essay, however, homogeneous forces never completely exclude heterogeneous ones, even in liberal states: "The imperative, or sovereign, form of heterogeneity goes to aid the homogeneous forces: it guarantees the stability of a society, which can give itself meaning only through the sadistic exclusion of impure heterogeneity."[38] Stoekl's reading of Bataille suggests a quasi-Weberian interpretation of liberal states: parliamentary regimes remain stable thanks to legal-rational authority, which they achieve, in part, through the force of the law, namely violence. The homogeneous state maintains, through the army and police, a store of imperative heterogeneity, which guards the boundaries of the state's homogeneous authority through violent exclusion. Monarchies and fascist regimes operate differently. As Stoekl points out, "The king or the fascist leader (as imperative heterogeneity) is in a way excluded from the homogeneous activities of society, but he dominates that society and embodies it."[39] In the case of the king, the imperative sovereignty of the monarchy, which itself relies on the equally imperative heterogeneity of Christianity, cooperates with and co-opts the subversive (impure) heterogeneity of the executioner in order to police the boundaries of the royal body. For the fascist leader, as Bataille's essay reveals, the mixture of homogeneity and heterogeneity becomes increasingly potent and complex. His analysis, which focuses particularly on fascism's appropriation of religion and the military, reveals a fascination with the important role of imperative heterogeneity in the fascist movement. Although Bataille recognizes, even admires, the revolutionary potential of this mixture of pure and impure sacred fascist power, he remains convinced that only communities organized on the basis of subversive heterogeneity can be truly liberating.

The fluidity of the categories used by Bataille to describe the psychological structure of fascism demonstrates the importance of the sacrificial mechanism, which inserts an element of agency into what otherwise appears as an unchangeable world of sacred polarities. The crucifixion of Christ clearly demonstrates this mechanism when it transforms the impure, bleeding, and agonized body of Christ into the pure, transcendental figure of the *corpus mysticum*. Bataille, like his predecessors in the discourse, recognizes that sacrificial violence makes things sacred. Unlike them, however, Bataille also realizes the theoretical importance of the capacity of sacrifice to negotiate between different forms of the sacred. For Bataille, the imperative heterogeneity of the army is not the same kind of sacred power as the subversive heterogeneity of the proletariat. Indeed, in his discussion of the army, Bataille characterizes it as imperatively heteroge-

---

38. Stoekl, *Visions of Excess*, xvii.
39. Ibid.

neous: hierarchy and discipline in the service of death. Because the army amal-
gamates purity and violence, it possesses an ambiguous attractive power, which
Bataille describes in the following way: "This process is the intermediary
through which disgusting slaughter is radically transformed into its opposite,
glory—namely, into a pure and intense attraction."[40] Although armies are not
engaged in sacrificial acts per se, the military demonstrates that violence can be
transformed into a positive, glorious accessory of political power. Similarly, religion has a dual characterization that contributes to its own form of attraction.
Bataille writes: "The supreme being of theologians and philosophers represents
the most profound introjection of the structure characteristic of *homogeneity* into
heterogeneous existence: in his theological aspect, God preeminently fulfills the
sovereign form."[41] Religion is attractive because it elevates the abject through
sacrificial symbolism, such as Christ's sacrifice. Religion confers order, status,
and purity on death, which is originally and profoundly impure.

In describing the affective power of fascism, Bataille focuses on the army and
religion because of their long, combined historical complicity in the foundation and exercise of political power. Bataille perceives both institutions as possessing violent and/or sacrificial mechanisms that provide for the purification
of impure heterogeneity. In their ability to convert subversive heterogeneity into
pure or imperative heterogeneity—to transform abject sacred into pure sacred—
the army and the church support the augmentation and stabilization of authoritarian political power. Like the French revolutionaries, Maistre, and Sorel,
Bataille appreciates that the effectiveness of political power—its authority—is
intimately linked to the affectivity of violence. Bataille's analysis of the emergence of fascism also suggests that he is particularly attuned to the affective impact of fascism's use of *both* martial and religious violence. "Fascist power,"
Bataille writes, "is characterized by a foundation that is both religious and military, in which these two habitually distinct elements cannot be separated."[42]
Bataille discovers that fascism taps into the same sacred well of affectivity as other
regimes, but in ways that vastly increase mass enthusiasm.

Although Bataille admires fascism's ability to convert impure heterogeneity
into a pure sweetener of its authority, he rejects the desirability of a revolution
based on imperative heterogeneity. Like other forms of Western politics, fascism
is politically unfeasible without imperative heterogeneity, the pure sacred product of armies or churches. Sword and scepter participate in the establishment of
authority by conferring legitimacy upon the exercise of power, which is elevated and concentrated in the leader or *Führer*. With or without these institu-

40. Bataille, "The Notion of Expenditure," 150.
41. Bataille, "The Psychological Structure of Fascism," 153.
42. Ibid.

tional props, Western forms of authority, be they traditional, legal-rational, or charismatic, rely on the pure sacred qualities of imperative heterogeneity. Furthermore, in the Western political tradition, this uplifting of power to the status of right always occurs at the expense or with the complicity of subversive (impure) heterogeneity. What makes fascism unique, according to Bataille, is that it is the most authoritative of all political regimes. Bataille compares the "total power" of the fascist chief with that of a king, who "manifests . . . the fundamental tendency and principle of all authority: the reduction to a personal entity, the individualization of power."[43] Fascism requires supreme authority, which is concentrated like royal power in its chief. It is this kind of authority that Bataille hopes to destroy by marshaling the impure heterogeneity of unproductive sacrificial violence.

There is little question that Bataille's attitude toward fascism is equivocal. He may not like the authority generated by fascism's imperative heterogeneity, but he cannot help but admire its awesome power to captivate the masses. A handful of Bataille's statements during the 1930s, such as "we intend to make use of the weapons created by fascism," are probably sufficient to warrant labeling Bataille a "left-fascist," the term Richard Wolin uses to describe "an avowed endorsement of fascist methods for left-wing political ends."[44] Rather than defending Bataille against those who accuse him of fascist sympathies, a task that has been accomplished by others, I want to point out one important instance in which Bataille's critics have misconstrued his position on fascism.[45] In *The Philosophical Discourse of Modernity*, Jürgen Habermas argues that, even though Bataille wants to distinguish his political vision from fascism, he fails. Habermas quotes the following sentence from the end of Bataille's fascism essay as evidence that Bataille's "dream" for the working class is a fascist "aestheticized, poetic politics purified of all moral elements": "The example of fascism, which today calls into question even the existence of the labor movement, suffices to demonstrate what we might expect from a favorable recourse to renewed affective forces."[46] Though perhaps reflecting a problem of translation from French to German to English, this sentence, as it appears in Habermas' text, is

43. Ibid., 148.

44. Richard Wolin, "Left Fascism: Georges Bataille and the German Ideology," *Constellations* 2, no. 3 (1996), 419.

45. For those who defend Bataille from the fascist label, see Michel Surya, *Georges Bataille, la mort à l'oeuvre* (Paris: Gallimard, 1992), 266–277, 353–362; and especially Denis Hollier, "On Equivocation," *October* 55 (winter 1990), 3–22. For critiques of Bataille's fascist ideas, see Jürgen Habermas, *The Philosophical Discourse of Modernity*, trans. Frederick Lawrence (Cambridge: MIT Press, 1987); Wolin, "Left Fascism," 397–428; Martin Jay, "The Reassertion of Sovereignty in a Time of Crisis," in *Force Fields* (New York: Routledge, 1993), 49–60; and Anthony Stephens, "Georges Bataille's Diagnosis of Fascism and Some Second Opinions," *Thesis Eleven*, no. 24 (1989), 71–89.

46. Habermas, *The Philosophical Discourse*, 220–221.

misleading because of "we" and "favorable." I translate the sentence as follows: "The fact of fascism, which has just called into question the very existence of the workers' movement, suffices to demonstrate what is possible to expect from an opportune recourse to renewed emotional forces."[47] In contrast to Habermas, I read Bataille's sentence as a warning to the workers' movement that any immediate recourse to "renewed emotional forces" may lead toward fascism, not toward liberation. This interpretation is supported by the last line of Bataille's essay, which appears just two sentences below the one quoted by Habermas and calls for the "emancipation of human lives" through "deep subversion" (subversive heterogeneity), not through "radical imperative forms" (fascism).[48] By misconstruing at least one of the ways in which Bataille tries to distinguish subversive from imperative heterogeneous politics, Habermas misses an important indication of Bataille's critical stance toward fascism and his skepticism of traditional political solutions to the problems of the human condition.[49]

Bataille's analysis of homogeneity and heterogeneity reveals why he rejects sacrificial violence's long historical association with the foundation of political regimes. Viewed productively, sacrificial violence uses death to facilitate a sacred

47. "Le fait de fascisme, qui vient de mettre en cause l'existence même du mouvement ouvrier, suffit à montrer ce qu'il est possible d'attendre d'un recours opportun à des forces affectives renouvelées." Bataille, "La Structure psychologique du fascisme," in Souvarine, *Réimpression de La Critique sociale,* 211.

48. Habermas' quotation of the final sentence of Bataille's essay is also misleading: "A systematic knowledge of the social movements of attraction and repulsion [that is, of emotional ambivalences released by the heterogeneous] proves itself a weapon at the moment when fascism stands opposed not so much to communism as to radically imperative forms . . . of subversion." Habermas, *The Philosophical Discourse,* 221. Habermas makes it sound as if fascism stands opposed to the radical imperative forms, which themselves are subversive. The original text and the Stoekl translation, however, convey a different meaning: "Un système de connaissances portant sur les mouvements sociaux d'attraction et de répulsion se présente de la façon la plus dépouillée comme une arme. Au moment où une vaste convulsion oppose, non pas exactement le fascisme au communisme, mais des formes impératives radicales à la profonde subversion qui continue à poursuivre l'émancipation des vies humaines." Bataille, "La Structure psychologique du fascisme," in Souvarine, *Réimpression de La Critique sociale,* 211. "An organized understanding of the movements in society, of attraction and repulsion, starkly presents itself as a weapon—at this moment when a vast convulsion opposes, not so much fascism to communism, but radical imperative forces to the deep subversion that continues to pursue the emancipation of human lives." Bataille, "The Psychological Structure of Fascism," 159. In contrast to Habermas' quotation, Stoekl's translation captures Bataille's attempt to distinguish "radical imperative forces" from "deep subversion." Deep subversion refers to the subversive heterogeneous forces that Bataille believes will animate a workers' revolution and prevent the reconstitution of the forms of authority that characterize and corrupt the modern age.

49. Wolin's interpretation of Bataille's fascism essay displays even greater carelessness than Habermas'. Referring to "The Psychological Structure of Fascism," Wolin writes: "Bataille concludes his endorsement of fascist politics with the following encomium: '*Heterogeneous* fascist action belongs to the entire set of higher forms. It makes an appeal to sentiments traditionally defined as *exalted* and *noble* and tends to constitute authority as an unconditional principle, situation above any utilitarian judgment.'" Wolin, "Left Fascism," 414. Wolin errs in suggesting that this idea of authority appeals to Bataille, who consistently criticizes all that is exalted and noble.

exchange: regicide—a subversively heterogeneous act—permitted the king's former subjects to transfer some of the king's imperative sovereignty to themselves. French popular sovereignty, as Tocqueville so astutely observed, was kingly authority in a different guise. In rejecting the productive use of sacrifice, Bataille forbids sacrificial violence from playing a role in the formation of authoritative forms of political power. In his own reading of Bataille's fascism essay, Hollier captures the importance of Bataille's position:

> The fascist political structure brings to light the unconscious basis of all political systems to the extent that they are based on representation (which has monocephalic tendencies). The heterogeneous, as here constituted by power, has no other function than to guarantee the homogeneity of the entity it commands. By contrast, the *Lumpen*—which, unlike an organized proletariat, represents nothing— would be a heterogeneity that, turned loose, would bring on the disintegration of all the structures guaranteeing the homogeneity of the social edifice.[50]

Hollier extends Bataille's critique of fascism to politics in general. Just as sacrifice that produces nothing useful cannot participate in the establishment of authority, the *Lumpenproletariat,* who represent nothing useful, subvert representation, the basis for all political power.[51] Hollier uses the *Lumpenproletariat* to make this point, arguing that Bataille views them as the abject part of the proletariat and thus the most subversive. If all political regimes use heterogeneous forces in order to ensure stable representation, then Bataille's resistance to this use of imperative negativity is a "movement toward disputing any form of ideological closure."[52] Productive sacrifice seeks such closure by augmenting authority and stabilizing representation. In contrast, unproductive sacrifice neither founds nor legitimates these political ideas. For Bataille, true revolutionary movements free heterogeneity of all purpose, and thus render it subversive of representation and political power.

50. Hollier, *Against Architecture,* 125–126.

51. Heimonet adds that Bataille's rejection of representation extends to art as well: "In a text entitled *The Sacred* [*Le Sacré*], after stressing the vacuity of the homogeneous world, from which he [Bataille] says the fundamental values of 'the beautiful' and 'the good' have been disqualified, he continues: 'It becomes clear thereafter that art, being no longer able to express anything whatsoever from outside itself that might be incontestably sacred . . . could no longer survive if it did not have the power of attaining the *sacred moment* by its own resources.' To say that art for its survival can no longer count on any but its own powers is to say, on the one hand, that, in a world deprived of all values, of all powerful referents, this art can no longer be mimetic—and, on the other hand, that it is placed, without having any choice, outside reality, society, and history, to appear as the last and most deceiving place of refuge for what Bataille calls an 'unemployed negativity' ('*négativité sans emploi*')." Heimonet, "From Bataille to Derrida," 144. In other words, art is deceptively useless. It seeking to represent, art objectifies, an end that Bataille considers intolerable. However, in a world shorn of stable values, representation becomes impossible even for art.

52. Marina Galletti, "A Failed *Collège?*" *Stanford French Review* 12 (spring 1988), 71.

In his critique of fascism, Bataille discovers that a liberating, authority-based politics is oxymoronic and thus impossible. He attempts to move beyond this dead end by revisiting the dilemma of the French revolutionaries: how to found a new regime on the ashes of a monarchy: "It seems therefore that revolutionary movements that develop in a democracy are hopeless, at least so long as the memory of the earlier struggles against the royal authority has been attenuated and no longer necessarily sets *heterogeneous* reactions in opposition to imperative forms."[53] Bataille declares the proletarian revolution in France to be hopeless because the French have forgotten the significance of the regicide. With the memory of the revolutionary struggle ("*heterogeneous* reactions in opposition to imperative forms") against monarchism gone, it is impossible to fight against monarchism's modern incarnation, fascism. It is in this respect that Bataille considers the democratic struggle against the rise of fascism to be a Tocqueville-esque unfolding of "the fate of the Revolution." For Bataille, revolution involves not the erection of imperative heterogeneous forms, which leads to authoritarian politics, but rather the success of a subversive impure heterogeneity. To accomplish this goal, Bataille looks beyond the political struggles of the day. "It remains possible to envision," he claims, "at least as a yet imprecise representation, forms of attraction that differ from those already in existence, as different from present or even past communism as fascism is from dynastic claims." Bataille describes what would be required to develop such "forms of attraction" in terms that anticipate the work of the rest of his career: "A system of knowledge that permits the anticipation of the affective social relations that traverse the superstructure and perhaps even, to a certain extent, do away with it, must be developed from one of these possibilities [forms of attraction]."[54] In typically cryptic prose, Bataille declares the need to explore the possibility of a community that has jettisoned the historical baggage burdening both communism and fascism. This task requires an epistemology capable of revealing the contours of a radically subversive concept of social relations, which, Bataille believes, will finally liberate human beings from all political bondage.

From Morality to Virility: Sacrifice and Metapolitics

By the middle of the 1930s, Bataille shifted his theoretical orientation toward ontological characterizations of sacrifice and antifoundational notions of community. This transition was particularly apparent in 1935, when Bataille, André

53. Bataille, "The Psychological Structure of Fascism," 159.
54. Ibid.

Breton, and Roger Caillois organized a left-wing antifascist group named Con-tre-Attaque. As its name implies, Contre-Attaque advocated a forceful response to French fascism, a position that was consistent with Bataille's critical analysis of fascism in 1933. Contre-Attaque declared itself an antinationalist organiza-tion engaged in a struggle for the creation of a "human community." It also pro-fessed anticapitalist and antireformist political positions that were quite common for the period.[55] What distinguished Contre-Attaque and, at the same time, made it politically suspect was the willingness of several of its members, most notably Bataille, to embrace a *"Lebenspolitik,"* or political activity as an expres-sion of virile life force. Bataille wanted working-class revolutionary activity to contain the same self-sundering effervescence that characterized his concept of unproductive expenditure. In contrast to the revolutionary republican fraternity, who wished to possess the king's power, Bataille pushed Contre-Attaque to em-brace a paradoxically depleted male virility, which would arouse the social af-fectivity of the proletariat. Virility, a concept that enjoyed a wide currency in France during the 1930s, represents Bataille's attempt to ontologize, rather than moralize, the experience of sacrificial violence.[56] For Bataille, virility possessed ontological value because it described an a priori state of being eroded by the reifying processes of modernity. In seeking to mobilize sacrificial violence for the sake of a renewed virility, Contre-Attaque sought to change the world through personal, not political, transformation.

Contre-Attaque addressed what Bataille called "the horror of human impo-tence."[57] In seeking to "confront this horror directly," Bataille turns to "violent drives" that would augment and liberate the power of the masses. Sounding al-most Sorelian, Bataille writes: "What drives the crowds into the street is the emotion directly aroused by striking events in the atmosphere of a storm, it is the contagious emotion that, house to house, from suburb to suburb, suddenly turns a hesitating man into a frenzied being."[58] Although Bataille does not use the term "striking" to mean cessation of work, "striking events" captures the residue of Sorel's myth of the general strike as well as a more cataclysmic no-tion of violence that would have been unfamiliar and repugnant to Sorel. Bataille's emphasis on virility and "drives" also touches on familiar Sorelian themes. However, Bataille offers no mediating myth to explain the emotional commitment of the proletariat, nor a notion of virility that has any traditional

---

55. See Surya, *Georges Bataille,* 269.

56. Bataille's interest in virility was certainly stimulated by his friendship with Michel Leiris, whose autobiographical book, *Manhood,* written in the early 1930s and published in 1939, delves into the mul-tifaceted significance of the concept. Michel Leiris, *Manhood,* trans. Richard Howard (Chicago: Univer-sity of Chicago Press, 1984).

57. Georges Bataille, "Popular Front in the Streets," in Stoekl, *Visions,* 161.

58. Ibid., 162.

moral content. The transformation of the "hesitating man" into a "frenzied be-ing" is a decisive departure from Sorel's politics, which never relied on ecstatic images of revolutionary fervor.[59]

Although virility is commonly defined as an accumulation of male forces, es-pecially sexual potency, Bataille views it through the lens of unproductive ex-penditure. The result is a concept of male power that relies on an ontology of waste, not accumulation. For Bataille, the male erection has no purpose other than to waste itself, an image captured by Troppman, the main character in Bataille's novel *Le Bleu du ciel (Blue of Noon)*, written in 1935 but not published until 1957. Susan Rubin Suleiman remarks that Troppman is symbolically cas-trated, a reflection of Bataille's characterization of the impotence felt by an-tifascist French intellectuals in the 1930s. For instance, when Troppman is unable to make love to a beautiful woman named Dirty, she euphemistically taunts him: "If only you could lose your head."[60] Suleiman argues that this slippage between castration and decapitation indicates *increased* virility from a uniquely Bataillian perspective:

> Decapitation is a symbolic castration, if Freud is to be believed; but Troppman is already symbolically castrated, so his decapitation would be redundant. (Troppman, incidentally, was the name of a mass murderer beheaded in Paris in 1870.) Unless, of course, "losing his head" *restored* his potency, according to that characteristically Bataillian equation which states that a violent loss of control is the precondition of *jouissance,* a radical letting go.[61]

It is precisely this "violent loss of control," anticipated by unproductive ex-penditure, celebrated in *Blue of Noon,* and captured in Bataille's Contre-Attaque writings, that characterizes Bataille's concept of virility. Virility is paradoxically a form of orgiastic powerlessness or *jouissance,* a sort of antiauthoritarian au-thority. This state of being forms an exact parallel to Bataille's notion of sub-

59. Sorel always maintained that proletarian success depended upon a conservative moral outlook with respect to work, family, and sexuality. Surya points out that Contre-Attaque supported the idea of a "moral" revolution, but one that was hardly traditional: "It is thus that Contre-Attaque inscribed in its program nothing less, pell-mell, than the emancipation of children from parent's educational tutelage (bourgeois and capitalist), the free expression of sexual drives (including those considered 'neurotic'. . .), the free play of passions, the free man eligible for all the pleasures that are his due, etc." ("C'est ainsi que Contre-Attaque inscrit à son programme rien moins, pêle-mêle, que l'affranchissement des enfants de la tutelle éducative parentale [bourgeoise et capitaliste], la libre expression des pulsions sexuelles [y com-pris celles considérées comme 'névrotiques . . .]', le libre jeu des passions, l'homme libre candidat à toutes les jouissances qui lui sont dues, etc.") Surya, *Georges Bataille,* 270–271. In this respect, virility and solar energy are similar: both express power by wasting it.

60. Quoted in Susan Robin Suleiman, "Bataille in the Street: The Search for Virility in the 1930s," in *Bataille: Writing the Sacred,* ed. Carolyn Bailey Gill (New York: Routledge, 1995), 31.

61. Ibid.

versive or acephalic sovereignty.[62] In disposing of itself effervescently, virility permits ontological self-sacrifice in the service of a revolution that wastes unproductively all that it opposes. The revolutionary role of sovereign virility is thus metapolitical because it promises a self-wounding masculinity that turns the proletariat inward and upon itself. Sovereign virility also thwarts traditional notions of political foundation, which require idealism and elevated authority.

Contre-Attaque's revolutionary politics of virility illustrate Bataille's prewar, apolitical thought. An element of Bataille's ambivalence toward politics can be attributed to the failure of workers' organizations in France and throughout Europe to stand up to the fascist threat during the 1930s. As Henri Dubief remembers, Contre-Attaque tried to foment antifascist revolution by bypassing workers' organizations: "It was a question less of organizing a defended retreat from fascism than of overcoming it by the mobilization of the popular masses, delivered from the structures of sclerotic workers' organizations."[63] Bataille's political ambivalence also surfaced as a result of his fundamental distaste for conventional political activities, a position he emphatically maintains in his Contre-Attaque–inspired essay "Popular Front in the Street" (1936). Above all, it is revolutionary activity animated by virility that pushes Bataille away from all recognizable politics. In its place, Bataille offers only images of undifferentiated mass action energized by irrational, erotic, virile exuberance. "The Popular Front," he writes, "is above all now a movement, an agitation, a crucible in which formerly separated political forces meld with an often tumultuous effervescence."[64] The ultimate goal of Bataille's Popular Front is for the masses to become consciously aware of their own virility and to destroy everything and everyone complicit in their servility. Insofar as the enslavement of the proletariat is a direct consequence of the modern condition, Bataille envisions a revolution that seeks to end both men and politics, traditionally understood: "And for us having the debate means having it in the street, it means having it where emotion can seize men and push them to the limit, without meeting the eternal obstacles that result from the defense of the old political positions."[65]

Bataille announced his final retreat from politics in June 1936, when, in the

62. Scholars disagree about the meaning of Bataille's insertion of self-annihilating virility into politics. Jean-Michel Besnier argues that, at the time of Contre-Attaque, Bataille sought to guide the working class toward a state of ecstatic effervescence rather than political action traditionally understood. Jean-Michel Besnier, "Georges Bataille in the 1930s: A Politics of the Impossible," *Yale French Studies,* no. 78 (1990), 177–179. In Besnier's view, Bataillian virility so fundamentally changes human beings that they are no longer suitable for politics. Suleiman, however, disagrees with Besnier about Bataille's political intentions while he was a member of Contre-Attaque. She claims that he foresaw "'a takeover of political power,' including the use of authority and discipline." Suleiman, "Bataille in the Street," 37.

63. Quoted in Besnier, "Georges Bataille in the 1930s," 178.

64. Bataille, "Popular Front in the Streets," 165.

65. Ibid., 163.

first issue of his journal *Acéphale,* he wrote: "It is time to abandon the world of the civilized and its light."[66] Within a year, Bataille embarked on two collaborations, each illustrating what this abandonment would mean. The first was the formation of the Collège de Sociologie, a gathering of a wide range of intellectuals determined to explore the sociological implications of the sacred in modern life. According to Richman, the Collège distinguished itself from the Durkheimian school, which "refus[ed] to recognize that collective [sacred] phenomena, though marginalized in the West, could nonetheless provide insight into the affective basis of modern social structures."[67] Instead of emphasizing the "rational foundations of modern society," as the Durkheimian school did, the Collège "deem[ed] all communal activities, in the sense of inducing communion or unity, as sacred."[68] Concerning politics, the Collège self-consciously proclaimed in its "Declaration": "The College of Sociology is not a political organism."[69] However, it remained concerned with the impact of current political events on the decline of virility: "The College of Sociology regards the general absence of intense reaction in the face of war as a sign of man's *devirilization.* It does not hesitate to see the cause of this in the relaxation of society's current ties, which are practically nonexistent as a result of the development of bourgeois individualism."[70] Disgusted by quotidian politics and concerned with resuscitating virility, the Collège—and Bataille in particular—attended to the formation of alternative communities, a direction signaled by Bataille when, in his review of Jules Monnerot's critique of Durkheim, he wrote: "The possibility of intentional communities is, for each of us, a decisive one."[71]

Bataille's idea of an intentional community challenges liberal notions of social unity and political activity. The members of the Collège rejected the idea that community could be molded from the reasoned articulation of human interests. Instead, they concluded that men were united by what repelled them.[72] This paradox is significant because it illustrates Bataille's reliance on the dynamic properties of sublimity, a violent attraction and repulsion that animated the prac-

66. "Il est temps d'abandonner le monde des civilisés et sa lumière." Georges Bataille, "La Conjuration sacrée," *Acéphale* 1, no. 1 (June 24, 1936), 2. Quoted in Bataille et al., *Acéphale.*

67. Michèle Richman, "Introduction to the *Collège de Sociologie:* Poststructuralism before Its Time?" *Stanford French Review* 12 (spring 1988), 82.

68. Ibid., 87. Richman adds: "Sacred sociology thus rejects the Durkheimian prejudice that the significance of collective experience is recognized and transmitted through participation in a transcendent consciousness identified as reason, logos, or spirit."

69. Georges Bataille, Roger Caillois, and Michel Leiris, "Declaration of the College of Sociology on the International Crisis," in Hollier, *The College of Sociology,* 45.

70. Ibid.

71. Quoted in Richman, *Reading Georges Bataille,* 45. It is noteworthy that Bataille founded the College of Sociology with Jules Monnerot and Roger Caillois.

72. Hollier, *The College of Sociology,* xix.

tices of the French revolutionaries as well as the theories of Maistre and Sorel. Liberal communities build social unity upon the utmost marginalization of sublime phenomena, which are generally inconsistent with the liberal emphasis on individual liberty and equal rights. For Bataille and the other members of the Collège, it was individual self-abnegation achieved through violent, sacred, sublime activities, such as sacrifice, that allowed for the formation of community. Thus, the Bataillian community is neither a rational nor a lingual construction per se. Rather than a social contract that balances individual loss with social gain, Bataille's intentional community requires permanently sundered selves—a community of ecstatic loss.

Although it may seem counterintuitive to locate eroticism among the attractively repellent activities that "produce" Bataillian community, Bataille argued in the late 1930s that eroticism—especially perverse, decadent, and nonproductive sexuality—offered a pathway to collective freedom unencumbered by servility. Disappointed by the failure of proletarian politics, Bataille shifted the locus of revolutionary activity away from the street to the bedroom and affirmed this displacement of political activity by virile eroticism with the claim: "The world of lovers is no less *true* than the political world."[73] Bataille's "world of lovers" is a metaphor for the bonding effect of a male sacrificial virility that no longer exerts itself through direct action. As Suleiman observes, "virility has become less a matter of action than of 'total existence,' the opposite of 'acting, depicting, or measuring.'"[74] The world of lovers generates virility unfettered by utility. According to Bataille, chance, risk, and intense passion conspire to bring men into the bedroom with their female lovers. There, men are willful, creative, and free—all the experiences denied to them by the political world. Together, but not equally, the lovers experience an ecstatic state of unproductive sacrificial loss. This highly erotic encounter dangerously pushes its participants to the limit of their individual selves while offering them an intensely human experience, because, without genital finality, it is useless. Unlike the political world, the world of lovers permits virile men to reach "human existence": "The whole of existence is consumed by it [the lovers' world], and politics cannot do this. It is characterized not by traits of the fragmentary, empty world of practical action but by those belonging to *human existence* before it has become reduced to servility."[75] In looking to erotic sacrifice for the generation of virility and "human existence," Bataille abandons political activity. The world of lovers illustrates the important connection between unproductive sacrificial loss, virility, and communality rooted in a limit-experience. Bataille, however, offers only the male

---

73. Georges Bataille, "The Sorcerer's Apprentice," in ibid., 20.
74. Suleiman, "Bataille in the Street," 39.
75. Bataille, "The Sorcerer's Apprentice," 20.

lover the possibility of achieving an ecstatic state through the mediation of his female partner. From the perspective of the female lover, there is a double sacrifice at work: her body for male virility and, ultimately, her self. Clearly no feminist, Bataille transforms women into objects so that men may lose themselves as subjects and generate a form of unproductive male power characterized by self-loss. Rather than dying at the hands of men, Bataille's women facilitate men's near-death, orgasmic, limit-experience, tellingly called in French *la petite mort*.

The sacrifice that takes place in the lovers' world may have no political context or content, but it does participate in the formation of community. "Love," writes Bataille, "expresses a need for sacrifice: Each unity must lose itself in some other that exceeds it."[76] Loving is a dialectical activity in which two individuals lose themselves in a self-abnegating and thus unifying experience. Consistent, however, with Bataille's critique of Hegel, loving offers no sublation because it is meant to be useless, that is, nonprocreative. Bataille's emphasis on the sacrificial interruption of the lovers' dialectical completion also represents a broader criticism of Hegel, who discounts the importance of lovers in his own dialectic of recognition.[77] Loving mirrors sacrifice because it involves the achievement of collective unity at the expense or loss of individual existence. Although the conjugal union also involves a dialectical movement that results in the formation of a kind of community, Bataille considers this type of union to be "joyless" because it is based on self-interest, reproduction, and law. In contrast to marriage, which, according to Bataille, denies individuals the ability to depart from their restricted existences, the world of lovers offers a pathway toward community rooted in sacrificed being:

> I propose to assume as a law that human beings are never united with each other except through tears or wounds, an idea that has a certain logical force in its favor. When elements arrange themselves to create the whole, this is easily produced when each of them loses, through a tear in its integrity, a portion of its particular being for the benefit of the communal being. Initiations, sacrifices, and festivals represent just such moments of loss and communication between individuals.[78]

This passage captures the important interconnectedness of sacrifice, ontology, and community in Bataille's thought. Human beings are not united by self-interest or altruism; they are not bound together by fear, faith, or contract. Com-

---

76. Georges Bataille, "The College of Sociology," in Hollier, *The College of Sociology,* 337.

77. See G. W. F. Hegel, *Phenomenology of Spirit,* trans. A. V. Miller (Oxford: Oxford University Press, 1977), 106; and Merold Westphal, *History and Truth in Hegel's Phenomenology* (New Jersey: Humanities Press International, 1990), 132.

78. Bataille, "The College of Sociology," 338.

munity begins only when useless, violent, and wasteful activities force humans to confront death, calling the integrity of their selves into question. This confrontation with nonbeing is liberating because it generates a nonservile ontology. Indeed, in this state of being, one is not even a slave to one's self. Bataille writes: "The sacrificial tear opening the festival is a liberating tear. The individual who participates in the loss is vaguely aware that this loss engenders the community sustaining him."[79] Community and liberty thus paradoxically arise during frenzied, violent moments of self-disintegration, when communication between individuals is nondiscursive and ecstatic.

The group Acéphale, Bataille's final collaboration of the 1930s, attempted to use sacrificial practices in order to conjure a Bataillian community into existence. Unlike the Cercle or Contre-Attaque, Acéphale was a secret society whose members expressed no interest in engaging in politics or organizing a mass movement. Instead, Acéphale met and conducted sacrificial rites in the Saint-Nom-la-Bretèche forest outside Paris. In an effort to practice what the Collège had been content merely to debate, Acéphale sought to reconstitute the sacred in everyday life. Its goal, according to Stoekl, was "to stimulate the rebirth of the kind of social values Bataille had espoused in the *Critique sociale* essays: expenditure, risk, loss, sexuality, death."[80] In creating Acéphale, Bataille wished to bypass politics, which had proved to be only an impediment to the formation of his sacrificial community. The members of Acéphale ominously contemplated conducting a real human sacrifice, but no one was willing to play the role of executioner. The failure of these sorcerer's apprentices—the term used by Bataille to describe Acéphale's "work"—illustrates the exhaustion of Bataille's concept of sacrifice.

There is a direct connection between Bataille's reading of the regicide of Louis XVI and Acéphale's conjuring of a sacrificial community. The sacrifice of the king and of politics prepares for the possibility of a community formed by a tragic but joyful disposition toward death. Death is vital to communal formation because, as Richman remarks, "it reveals to all persons both their finitude and extension into unbounded ecstasy."[81] In notes titled "Joy in the Face of Death," Bataille ruminates on the regicide's principal mystery, which inaugurated the discourse on sacrificial violence: "Human hearts never beat as hard for anything else as they do for death." Maistre marvels at soldiers' enthusiasm on the battlefield. Sorel reflects on the attractive, contagious, and sublime qualities of martyrdom. Bataille responds similarly to the importance of the experience of sublime violence: "It seems that a sort of strange, intense communication

79. Ibid., 339.
80. Stoekl, *Visions of Excess,* xix.
81. Richman, "Introduction to the *Collège de Sociologie,*" 86.

is established among men each time the violence of death is near them." Bataille, like Maistre and Sorel, believes that the individual experience of death promotes a kind of ecstatic communication that possesses important social effects. Unlike them, however, Bataille points to a fundamental disruption of being as the impulse to communicate:

> The grave, decisive change that results from death is such a blow to spirits that, far from the usual world, they are cast, transported and breathless, somewhere between heaven and earth, as if they suddenly perceived the dizzying, ceaseless motion possessing them. This motion then appears to be partly dreadful and hostile, but *external* to the one threatened by death or the one dying; it is all that is left, depriving the one who watches the dying as much as the one who dies. Thus it is that, when death is present, what remains of life only lives on outside, beyond and *beside itself*.[82]

Ecstatic experience—life that "lives on outside, beyond and *beside itself*"—is the basis for the kind of communication that renders Bataillian community possible. This experience is instantiated sacrificially, allowing the sacrificer to participate in the unrecoverable loss of the sacrificed. The cumulative effect of such a confrontation with death is ontological destabilization, which Bataille characterizes as a permanently wounded self. For Bataille, the regicide involves such a total loss that it augurs the formation of a community in which all political concepts, including man himself, have been sundered, leaving nothing behind save unemployed negativity itself.

While participating in Acéphale, Bataille held that sacrifice's tearing of being would join humans together through communication that invoked a unique communality: "Those who look at death and rejoice are already no longer the individuals destined for the body's rotten decay, because simply entering into the arena with death already projected them outside themselves, into the heart of the glorious community of their fellows where every misery is scoffed at . . . The community is necessary to them in order to become aware of the glory bound up in the instant that will see them torn from being."[83] Here Bataille presents his alternative to the Hegelian notion of community rooted in the rational achievement of mutual recognition. At the end of history, when man is nothing but unemployed negativity, reason and recognition no longer produce social unity. Those who attempt to join together on these bases unwittingly enslave themselves. Indeed, communal formation or foundation and the setting of rules or laws are anathema to what Bataille has in mind. Heimonet explains: "In

---

82. Georges Bataille, "Joy in the Face of Death," in Hollier, *The College of Sociology*, 326–327.
83. Ibid., 328.

a lecture in 1948, Bataille will return to the question of community—only to affirm that 'the basis of any possible community' is 'the absence of community' . . . which means that the reality of the community is the only demand of the activating desire which wants it and which is bound to a 'will to exist' that is rightly insatiable and hence unrealizable in the order of presence."[84] Heimonet's description of a Bataillian community suggests an impossible social entity because it is perpetually sundered by members who are themselves unemployed negativity. Bataille's is a community of shared self-loss that partakes of the same communication and intimacy as the lovers in their self-abnegating erotic embrace. This sacrificial community celebrates ecstatic violence that restores a lost totality to human beings. It is thus the expression of a sacred bond that occurs as the result of a violent communication between human beings who have confronted the terrifying experience of nonbeing.

A community that requires the annihilation of the bourgeois subject and, ultimately, the fragmentation of being itself has no limits. Born sacrificially, Bataille's concept of community retains none of the conventions that have historically shaped politics, such as language, reason, authority, or individual subjectivity. Without these elements, the contractual bond that stands as the basis of liberal politics becomes meaningless. Instead, sacrifice fosters communication that takes place outside the subject in the form of an experience that is beyond reason and knowledge. In his wartime writings, Bataille uses the term "inner experience" to characterize this ecstatic form of being, communication, and sociability. Indeed, Bataille devotes a trilogy of works—*Inner Experience, Guilty,* and *On Nietzsche*—to the exploration of what he recognizes as a quasi-mystical, impossible experience.[85] Some scholars, including Noys and Hollier, have argued that inner experience is not so much a retreat from politics as a radical attempt to critique the detrimental impact of politics on the human condition. Others, such as Jean-Luc Nancy, Maurice Blanchot, and Alphonso Lingis, have attempted to expand upon Bataille's esoteric concept of community in their own works, titled *The Inoperative Community, The Unavowable Community,* and *The Community of Those Who Have Nothing in Common,* respectively. Yet insofar as these authors have sought to put Bataille's ideas to use, they have violated Bataille's own ethic of uselessness.

Unable to find a location for the revolutionary practice of sacrifice in the street, bedroom, or forest, Bataille pushed his revision of the French discourse

84. Heimonet, "From Bataille to Derrida," 143.

85. In his essay "The Practice of Joy before Death," Bataille acknowledges the mystical quality of his thought: "While it is appropriate to use the word *mysticism* when speaking of 'joy before death' and its practice, this implies no more than an affective resemblance between this practice and those of the religions of Asia or Europe." "The Practice of Joy before Death," in Stoekl, *Visions of Excess,* 236.

on sacrificial violence in two altogether different theoretical directions.[86] The first, which continued Bataille's apolitical sacrificial motifs of the 1930s, involved locating sacrifice in text. With this approach, writing itself became a sacrificial practice through which author and reader unproductively lost themselves. Second, after the end of World War II, Bataille surprisingly undertook a social scientific study of sacrifice, an enterprise that led him to write a three-volume work titled *The Accursed Share*. Although Bataille's postwar writings on sacrifice remain faithful to the prewar themes of unproductive expenditure, base materialism, and revolution, they also evince a certain political pragmatism, as if Bataille—for the first time in his life—felt compelled to demonstrate that his theory of sacrifice was useful and, thus, applicable to current events.[87]

On the eve of World War II, Bataille remained characteristically equivocal on the issue of the practice of sacrifice. In the final article of the last issue of *Acéphale,* Bataille claimed that writing constituted an initiation into the practice of joy before death, but that it was insufficient: "The texts that follow cannot alone constitute an initiation into the *exercise* of a mysticism of 'joy before death.'"[88] Although Bataille declares language and text an insufficient "*exercise*" of the practice of joy before death, his willingness to consider words on a page a complement to the actual experience of sacrificial violence indicates one important direction of his postwar work. A medievalist librarian by training and a prolific writer, Bataille had always depended upon the text to communicate his ideas. With the failure of Acéphale, text itself assumed the heavy burden of conveying sacrificial loss.

Bataille's realization that literature offers an important "sacrificial space" took shape during his participation in the Collège, when, Richman argues, Bataille came to understand that there were important limitations to the practice of sacrifice in modern society: "Sovereign communication would be stimulated by its proximity to death and manifested through laughter or eroticism. However, with the realization that the modern equivalent to a sacrificial space is literary, that writing had become tantamount to a *tauromachie,* Bataille had to consider the relevance of the criteria of the general economy to language, writing, and literature."[89]

Although Richman acknowledges that "sovereign communication" cannot

---

86. There is a parallel between Bataille's and the Marquis de Sade's location of violence in the text. See Carolyn J. Dean, *The Self and Its Pleasures* (Ithaca: Cornell University Press, 1992).

87. This change in theoretical orientation is captured in the first sentence of the preface to *The Accursed Share:* "For some years, being obliged on occasion to answer the question 'What are you working on?' I was embarrassed to have to say, 'A book on political economy.'" Bataille, *The Accursed Share,* vol. 1, 9.

88. Bataille, "The Practice of Joy before Death," 236.

89. Richman, "Introduction to the *Collège de Sociologie,*" 92.

be captured rationally or discursively, she argues that Bataille himself concluded that literature captures this very moment. When "writing . . . become[s] tantamount to a *tauromachie,*" the moment of violent sacrificial loss appears as a discursive event.[90] In an essay written in the 1950s, Bataille concedes: "Only sacred, poetic words, limited to the level of impotent beauty, have retained the power to manifest full sovereignty. Sacrifice, consequently, is a *sovereign, autonomous* manner of being only to the extent that it is uninformed by *meaningful* discourse."[91] Although Bataille's point is that the sacrificial experience of loss can be conveyed only by meaningless discourse—discourse that sacrifices itself—his location of sacrifice in and through literature reflects a dramatic change from the prewar years. By situating sacrifice in text, Bataille's writing evokes a performative contradiction: it symbolically represents unproductive sacrificial loss in spite of the fact that it is a rational, discursive, meaningful, purposive creation. This characterization of sacrifice as an interaction between reader and text illustrates one effect of Bataille's abandonment of politics. Sacrifice and literature—violent loss, done to or by the text—is only indirectly relevant to collective action for the sake of fundamental political change. Just as the violence of a bullfight described discursively is not the same as the actual experience of it, sacrifice in the work of Georges Bataille is analogous to neither the regicide of Louis XVI nor the Terror.

Just as textual sacrifice betrays unproductive expenditure, Bataille's postwar social science engages in a similar violation. Reasoned, social scientific, and systematic, *The Accursed Share* broadly seeks to challenge utilitarianism and to overturn the ethical grounds of modern capitalism. Bataille critically describes capitalism as a "restricted economy" because it is a closed system of accumulation and growth. In juxtaposition to this narrow formulation of economic activity, Bataille introduces the notion of a "general economy," which encompasses rational accumulation as well as irrational waste and destruction. Signaling the substance of his ethical revolt against capitalism, Bataille writes: "If a part of wealth (subject to a rough estimate) is doomed to destruction or at least unproductive use without any possible profit, it is logical, even *inescapable,* to sur-

90. The association of tauromachy with sacrifice and virility, and the placement of these themes in text, can also be found in the work of Bataille's friend Michel Leiris. For example, in *Manhood,* Leiris writes: "When I go to a bullfight, I tend to identify myself either with the bull at the moment the sword plunges into its body, or with the matador who risks being killed (perhaps emasculated?) by a thrust of the horn at the very moment when he most clearly affirms his virility." *Manhood,* 42. Leiris attempts to capture with words an experience that Bataille hoped would be instantiated textually. It is also noteworthy that Georges Sorel's fascination with tauromachy helped him to formulate a critique of the experience of such sacrificial violence.

91. Georges Bataille, "Hegel, Death and Sacrifice," *Yale French Studies,* no. 78 (1990), 25.

render commodities without return."[92] Thus, *The Accursed Share* takes its name from that part of wealth or surplus in the general economy that humans wastefully sacrifice without the expectation of any meaningful, productive return.

It is true that *The Accursed Share* revisits eroticism and sovereignty, topics that led Bataille away from politics in the 1930s. After the war, however, Bataille treated these concepts politically. For instance, in the epilogue of *The History of Eroticism,* Bataille speculates that human beings will be driven to a "catastrophic war" unless they find outlets, such as eroticism, for their excess energy. Similarly, in "Sovereignty," Bataille argues that "sovereignty is no longer alive except in the perspectives of communism."[93] In the case of both eroticism and sovereignty, Bataille is expressly looking for instances of unproductive expenditure or sacrifice, which may save human beings from their dangerously compulsive, modern need to engage in economic accumulation without loss.

What sets *The Accursed Share* apart from Bataille's prewar work is also what implicates Bataille in his own critique of the French discourse on sacrificial violence. Like his predecessors, Bataille ultimately puts sacrifice to work, a theoretically problematic endeavor that finds its strangest outlet in his consideration of the Marshall Plan. At the conclusion of World War II, Bataille was fearful that competition and excessive economic production in the United States and the Soviet Union would precipitate a devastating third world war. This Cold War pessimism was alleviated only by the appearance of the Marshall Plan, which Bataille interpreted as a form of unproductive expenditure. Here he describes the Marshall Plan in terms of the general economy: "*Mankind will move peacefully toward a general resolution of its problems only if this threat causes the U.S. to assign a large share of the excess—deliberately and without return—to raising the global standard of living, economic activity thus giving the surplus energy produced an outlet other than war.*"[94]

By associating the Marshall Plan with unproductive expenditure, Bataille falls into the same theoretical trap as Sorel, Maistre, and the French revolutionaries. Bataille's argument for economic sacrifice may be less pernicious than the French revolutionaries' conviction that human sacrifice would help them to found a republic, but they nonetheless share an expectation that sacrifice will produce specific, ideal, and peaceful political outcomes. The belief that sacrifice will generate an ideal politics of any sort directly contradicts Bataille's fascism essay, where he argues that any attempt to use sacrifice for the sake of traditional (elevated) sovereignty risks a violent, authoritarian politics. That es-

92. Bataille, *The Accursed Share,* vol. 1, 25.
93. Ibid., vol. 2, 187–188, 261.
94. Ibid., vol. 1, 187.

say illustrates, above all, that one cannot use fascist techniques to achieve antifascist ends without complicity in fascism's imperiousness. Similarly, the Marshall Plan may have provided humanity with an outlet for surplus energy, but it also "wasted" wealth productively, served utilitarian-minded liberals, and elevated American international interests, none of which was even remotely akin to the apolitical intentional communities originally desired by Bataille.

His postwar work notwithstanding, Bataille fundamentally rejects the basic premise of the discourse on sacrificial violence that sacrifice founds new political regimes. By the end of the 1930s, Bataille declares politics an impossible task, rendering irrelevant the issue of foundation. If a wholly unproductive sacrifice were to create anything, it would be metapolitical communities without conventional notions of authority and identity. As Bataille pushes the concept of sacrifice to its limit, shifting its locus from the street to the bedroom and text, he reveals the difficulty experienced by Maistre, Sorel, and the French revolutionaries in assigning a political role to sacrifice. They put sacrificial violence to work in the establishment of politically significant fictions such as citizenship, authority, morality, and representation. In each case, there was an expectation that the sacrificial crime would lay the groundwork for a new era of justice. Following the Marquis de Sade, Bataille comes to appreciate the political absurdity of founding sacrifice: "*An already old and corrupt nation, courageously shaking off the yoke of its monarchical government in order to adopt a republican one, can only maintain itself though many crimes; for it is already a crime, and if it wants to move from crime to virtue, in other words from a violent state to a peaceful one, it would fall into an inertia, of which its certain ruin would soon be the result.*"[95]

Sade observes that the regicidal crime, which inaugurated the French Republic as well as the French discourse on sacrificial violence, is a sacrifice destined to repeat itself because it strips away the possibility of distinguishing right from wrong. In other words, violent political foundation undermines its own possibility. Sade's admonishment applies to the Terror, when the French revolutionaries tragically repeated the regicide thousands of times. It anticipates Maistre, who imagines a world in which the unending sacrifice of the innocent redeems the sins of the guilty. It foresees the work of Sorel, whose myth of the general strike depends upon the working class's martyred repetition of Jesus' crucifixion. And, finally, it highlights the absurdity of Bataille's postwar search for unproductive expenditure in quotidian politics. In each of these cases, sacrifice works to produce virtue and redemption. Sade's argument is straightforward: violent sacrifice never founds politics without also giving rise to an endless

---

95. Georges Bataille, "The Sacred Conspiracy," in Stoekl, *Visions of Excess,* 178. This epigraph appears just above Kierkegaard's.

repetition of the original crime. Bataille ultimately develops this insight into a notion of violent waste, which he hopes will demolish the modern fictions that leave human beings powerless and servile. Bataille's sacrificial community does not repair, restore, or regenerate. It is incapable of establishing, founding, and inaugurating. It "begins" with the violation of the limits that make politics possible, and, tragically, it must exist in a permanent state of violation.

Conclusion

The French discourse on sacrificial violence began when the French revolutionaries recovered ancient Christian and Roman ideas about sacrifice and
applied them to the task of founding one of the first modern republics. The
revolutionaries never generated a theory of sacrifice per se, but their violent language and practices inaugurated a postrevolutionary French debate about the
foundational role of sacrificial violence. From the revolutionaries, the principal
interlocutors in this debate—Maistre, Sorel, and Bataille—learned that violent
sacrifice facilitates the processes of conferring moral legitimacy to political
power and setting boundaries for political identity. As Nietzsche understood,
because sacrifice affects collective moral perceptions, it also helps to structure
political power and identity. With the capacity to render evil good or good evil,
the sacrificial process is able to reconfigure the feelings that accompany and reinforce the legitimacy of communal values. It is in this way that sacrificial violence participated in the transformation of French subjects into republican
citizens. To Maistre, Sorel, and Bataille, the revolutionaries also demonstrated an
overarching confidence that extraordinary scapegoats and revolutionary martyrs
would "seal the decree, which declares France a republic."[1] Inspired by the ancient belief that political foundation requires blood, this sacrificial hubris, together with capacity of sacrifice to reorient the sacred qualities of political power
and identity, proved theoretically irresistible to a variety of postrevolutionary
French intellectuals interested in challenging the Republic. Despite the fact that
Maistre, Sorel, and Bataille are often critical of this hubris, each of them ulti-

---

1. "Sire . . . résignez-vous à ce dernier sacrifice par lequel vous ressemblerez davantage au Dieu qui
va vous en récompenser." Henri Sanson, *Sept générations d'exécuteurs* 1688–1857, 6 vols. (Paris: Dupray de
la Mahérie, 1862), vol. 3, 477.

mately succumbs to the same temptation to place sacrifice in the role of dramatically and violently transforming the modern political condition.

In contrast to contemporary Anglo-American political theory, modern French thought has evidenced a greater inclination to excavate the distant past for ideas and practices that might serve to redeem the present. While it is undeniable that this theoretical approach is tinged with romanticism and nostalgia, it has also generated a wealth of insights concerning the formation of political communities. When, for instance, Maistre claims that executioners are the terror and bond of human associations, he is voicing the fact that humans use violence to create and maintain *all* forms of political power. In his view, humans can escape this grim reality only by accepting the binding, redemptive power generated by the sacrifice of a Christian god. For Sorel, it is capitalism that drives the unprecedented human dislocation, suffering, and death of the nineteenth and twentieth centuries. Modern redemption can be achieved only through proletarian martyrs who inspire a myth of the general strike and, ultimately, a moral renewal that leads to the realization of socialism. Like Maistre, Sorel appreciates the important role played by violent images and narratives in the construction of modern political communities.

By rejecting the French revolutionary, Maistrian, and Sorelian inclinations to invert values through sacrifice, Bataille nearly overturns the discourse on sacrificial violence's redemptive, communal impulse. Placing republicanism over monarchism, Christianity over secularism, and socialism over capitalism does not, according to Bataille, fundamentally address the modern slavishness caused by reifying ideologies, such as idealism and utilitarianism. Thus, Bataille attempts to dismantle the hierarchical binaries that underlie the French discourse of sacrificial violence. Not only does Bataille argue against giving moral preference to purity, elevation, mind, and light; he also maintains that their binary opposites—pollution, baseness, body, and darkness—are of great value for human existence. By stripping away the Western metaphysical preference for the good or the just, Bataille overthrows the concept of the individual as well as its supporting notions of political authority and community. All that remains of politics in Bataillian thought is a metapolitical community paradoxically held together by collective fragmentation and loss. It is only in the post–World War II period, when Bataille comes to accept that humans can ameliorate their existing political condition through sacrifice, that his critique of the French discourse on sacrificial violence collapses. Like his predecessors, Bataille tries to put sacrifice to work in the creation of a new, redemptive political future.

Maistre's, Sorel's, and Bataille's retrievals of ancient sacrificial ideas have overshadowed the skepticism with which they greeted the French Revolution. It is worth recalling that Maistre considered the French Revolution—and the Reign of Terror in particular—to be an act of fundamental evil. With the exception of symbolic Catholic sacrifice, such as the Eucharist, Maistre levied nothing but criticism upon sacrificial practices, which he viewed as primitive attempts to achieve salvation. Maistre's critique of the Revolution also illuminates a significant risk of the Enlightenment: armed with the ideology that humans are capable of rationally and intentionally altering their political world, the revolutionaries quite logically believed that they could create a republic by deploying the same forms of violence that appeared to have founded past political regimes. Maistre attempted to combat the arrogant positivism of this reasoning with the rigid mysticism of his own. In the final analysis, however, Maistre's theoretical strategy amounts to demonizing revolutionary sacrifices and celebrating Christian ones, a retort to the French Revolution that offers little political comfort.

Sorel's skepticism of revolutionary sacrifice emerges from several fronts. It is, first and foremost, a reflection of his commitment to anarchism, which led him to reject state authority and violence. It also emerges from his process-oriented view of Marxism, a revolutionary attitude that places greater value in moral and political transformation than in institutional finality. For Sorel, anarcho-syndicalists needed to control neither the state nor its violence in order to move down the path toward socialism. Instead, Sorel argued that the proletariat should model their struggle against capitalism on the eternal battle between Christians and Satan, a moral war, fueled by martyrs, that has profoundly transformed the material conditions of millions of human beings. Though akin to the formation of a cult of revolutionary martyrs during the Revolution, Sorel's proletarian martyrs are neither numerous nor instruments of state control. Instead, they serve as reminders that Sorel rejected the sacrifice of scapegoats as well as the experience of violence. For religious and psychological reasons, Sorel held that the revolutionary power of the myth of self-sacrifice far outweighed the moral impact of any other form or experience of bloodshed. Thus, like Maistre's, Sorel's fundamental distrust of the instrumentality of violence led him to embrace its symbolic forms. By jettisoning Maistre's blood-soaked theodicy, however, Sorel's theory of sacrifice becomes the least violent in the French discourse. Though Sorel does not completely abandon the ancient belief that political foundation requires violence, or that sacrifice alters moral perceptions, his amalgam of anarchism, process-oriented Marxism, and Christianity powerfully challenges the view that political beginnings in the modern age necessitate the spectacular blood sacrifices of the French Revolution.

Bataille's critique of French revolutionary sacrifice evinces the skeptical spirit of Maistre's and Sorel's, but radically revises their theoretical approaches. Unlike his predecessors, Bataille argues that sacrifice returns nothing to the sacrificer. His central insight is that the sacrificial process entails unrecoverable and unproductive loss: regicide leaves nothing but an empty, bloody space depleted of authority. Conversely, when sacrifice is used to found religion or politics, the metaphysical expectation that ritual death will benefit the sacrificers becomes a pillar of support for violent, elevated, reifying authority. Ever distrustful of the ideologies that transform human beings into the servants of some "higher" cause, Bataille turns against French revolutionary sacrifice because it carries the seeds of fascism.

While sacrifice that produces authority may be politically dangerous, Bataille's unproductive sacrifice retains a vital revolutionary objective: the attenuation of ontological harm caused by bourgeois homogeneity. Rejecting Sorel's revolutionary prudishness, Bataille argues that violent and sumptuary losses are essential aspects of human existence and binding elements of communality. Rejecting Maistre's theological surrender of human autonomy to God, Bataille links unproductive sacrificial loss to the achievement of a particular kind of human sovereignty that paradoxically entails powerless power, depleted virility, and headless authority—an obvious collapse of the French discourse's traditional, hierarchical binaries. Finally, rejecting twentieth-century, neoliberal, contractual justifications of social inequality and political servitude, Bataille holds out the possibility that metapolitical communities will form around renewed practices of unproductive expenditure. Thus Bataille rereads the event that inaugurated the French discourse on sacrificial violence: rather than having founded a modern republic, the regicide of Louis XVI initiated the twilight of Western politics by illustrating that humans are united by that which repulses them. Such is the accursed nature of Bataille's atheological, sacrificial "politics."

Despite the important threads of skepticism that run through the works of Maistre, Sorel, and Bataille, these intellectuals ultimately cannot resist the theoretical power and practical possibilities of the sacrificial process. Surrendering their aversion to political foundation through sacrifice, each of them places a version of sacrificial violence in the service of modern political change and redemption. Maistre, Sorel, and Bataille wish to build "better" forms of sacrificial violence into their own political theories. In this way, they tragically and ironically repeat in the realm of theory the same error unintentionally committed by the French revolutionaries when they attempted to save the Republic through terror. Even Bataille, who clearly recognizes Maistre's and Sorel's theoretical failures, allows his post–World War II work to fall into the same trap. As a result of these theoretical self-betrayals, the discourse on sacrificial violence ironically appears to champion the violent, sacrificial politics that it seeks to challenge. How ironic is it that Maistre's, Sorel's, and Bataille's theories are so often labeled dangerous and violent when their work collectively criticizes founding political sacrifice in the modern world?

The desire to reclaim the ancient crime is by no means unique to French history and political theory. Contemporary national and international conflicts, especially in the Middle East, powerfully demonstrate the political appeal of sacrifice. More motivated by Mohammed than by Christ, many of the actors in these disputes shed sacrificial blood for reasons that are hardly foreign to the Western theoretical tradition or unfamiliar to students of Maistre, Sorel, and Bataille. Indeed, the theoretical assumptions that guide Palestinian martyrs or Al Qaeda terrorists are intimately related to the sacrificial concepts that have captivated modern French theory. After all, it was during the French Revolution that the first terrorists were inspired by Roman Republican sacrifices to decapitate enemy compatriots in order to legitimate a modern republic. French revolutionary terrorists were also motivated by Christian history to form a cult of martyrs around which to gather the new republican community. When Palestinian nationalists undertake martyrdom operations against Israelis for the sake of statehood, and use Islam to justify such sacrifices, they effectively illustrate the same forms of founding violence that have captured the Western imagination for millennia. Similarly, when Al Qaeda transnationalists attacked New York in order to hasten the restoration of the caliphate, their sacrificial logic was no less obscure than that contained in *La Marseillaise:*

> Aux armes citoyens!
> Formez vos bataillons,
> Marchons, marchons!
> Qu'un sang impur
> Abreuve nos sillons.
>
> To arms, citizens!
> Form your battalions,
> March on, march on!
> May their impure blood
> Water our fields.

The French national anthem reflects the sacrificial acts of the French revolutionaries. Maistre's, Sorel's, and Bataille's theoretical adaptations of sacrifice to modern political conditions further illustrate the sublime attraction of sacrificial ideas to those who seek to remake politics. So long as modern political actors believe that they can create new forms of political authority and identity, and so long as these concepts incorporate pure and impure sacred qualities, sacrifice will remain a popular expression of modern political violence.

Insofar as it is part of the debate in Western political thought concerned with violence and political beginnings, the French discourse on sacrificial violence is particularly relevant to modern terrorism. Unlike liberalism, which holds that violence plays no role in the creation of legitimate political communities, the discourse on sacrificial violence views the formation of community through the lens of communal bloodshed. To borrow once again from Ernest Renan, who eloquently captures this position: "A nation is therefore a large-scale solidarity, constituted by the feeling of the sacrifices that one has made in the past and of those that one is prepared to make in the future."[2] Renan observes that nations are bound together by the decidedly illiberal "feeling" of past sacrifices and preparation for future ones. Expanding upon this observation, Maistre, Sorel, and Bataille explore theoretically how sacrifice delineates communal power and identity through sacred violence. Their central point is subversive of the dominant political order as well as of mainstream political theory: prior to the social contract is the sacrificial crime. Although it may be repugnant, this perspective will aid scholars who seek to understand the political implications of terrorism, which so often uses sacrificial violence in order to create and destroy nation-states.

No obvious political label can be attached to those who engage in the politics of sacrifice. The French revolutionaries' authoritarian republicanism, Maistre's reactionary Catholicism, Sorel's anarcho-syndicalism, and Bataille's renegade surrealism illustrate the broad appeal of this form of bloodshed. The reasons for this surprising agreement about the adaptability of sacrifice to modern politics are captured by the French discourse on sacrificial violence. As the quintessential form of communal violence, sacrifice offers those who wish to reconfigure the political future a spectacular link to a distant, mythologized past. In a world increasingly bereft of sacred places and sublime acts, political sacrifice enthralls oppressed and frightened peoples, providing them with a violent outlet for expressing agency and generating collective meaning. The logic of sacrifice, which today remains the central organizing principle of the world's major religions, appeals to those bent on translating religious devotion into political obedience. Catharsis, expiation, and redemption—the sacred terms of exchange that make up the logic of sacrifice—have great political value, for they describe the moral and spiritual benefits achieved by communities whose members engage in violent sacrificial acts. Finally and lamentably, sacrifice remains part of the modern political condition because, as Machiavelli observed long ago, political authority requires an element of sacredness. Without gods to establish the right

2. Ernest Renan, "What Is a Nation?" in *Nation and Narration,* ed. Homi Bhabha (New York: Routledge, 1990), 19.

to rule and the legitimacy of laws, modern political actors must find alternative sources of the sacred. Inspired by the legendary association between violence and political foundation, many will turn to sacrifice, callously unaware that any regime founded by sacrificial violence will perpetually renew itself through repetition of the original crime.

Index